PAINTED BY W. GUSH. ENGRAVED BY T.B. WELCH, PHILA.

REV. JOSHUA SOULE D.D.

Bishop of the Methodist Episcopal Church South.

LIFE AND TIMES

OF

WILLIAM M'KENDREE,

BISHOP OF THE METHODIST EPISCOPAL CHURCH.

BY ROBERT PAINE, D.D.,
BISHOP OF THE METHODIST EPISCOPAL CHURCH, SOUTH.

IN TWO VOLUMES.
VOL. II.

Nashville, Tenn.:
PUBLISHING HOUSE OF THE METHODIST
EPISCOPAL CHURCH, SOUTH.
1874.

STEREOTYPED AT THE SOUTHERN METHODIST PUBLISHING HOUSE,
NASHVILLE, TENNESSEE.

TO THE

REV. A. L. P. GREEN, D.D.

No traveling preacher now living was more intimate with Bishop McKendree in the latter part of his life, or endeavored more constantly and tenderly to render his declining years serene and cheerful, than yourself; and, as a memorial of your reverential regard for him, as well as the fraternal friendship between yourself and the author, during forty years, he respectfully asks permission to dedicate to you this second volume of the Life and Times of Bishop McKendree.

CONTENTS.

CHAPTER I.

CHAPTER II.

CHAPTER III.

CHAPTER IV.

CHAPTER V.

CHAPTER VI.

CHAPTER VII.

CHAPTER VIII.

CHAPTER IX.

CHAPTER X.

APPENDIX.

LIFE AND TIMES

OF

BISHOP M'KENDREE.

CHAPTER I.

Tennessee Conference in 1823—Bishops McKendree and George present—Vertigo—McKendree's purpose to cross the mountains in the winter abandoned—The promise to take him to Baltimore in the spring—Starts in March, 1824—Companions in travel—Difficulties on the route—Crosses the Cumberland Mountains—Winton's—Wilkerson's—Crosses the Alleghany Mountains—The night at the hut—Crosses the Yadkin in a canoe—Wilkesboro—Salem—Guilford Battle-ground—The effect of that battle in 1791—Person county—Crosses Roanoke River—At Taylor's—Boydtown—Adams's—Crossing Meherrin River—Calls on the families of his friends on his route—R. C. Boothe's—In Petersburg, Virginia—Richmond—Alexandria—Georgetown—At Judge McLean's—McKinney's—Mr. Calhoun's letter—Dr. Bascom Chaplain to Congress—In Baltimore—W. Wilkins—Dr. Samuel Baker—Impression made by the tour.

On the 26th of November, 1823, the Tennessee Annual Conference began its session in Huntsville, Alabama. Bishops McKendree and George attended. The health of the former was very infirm from a complication of chronic diseases, and his strength was nearly exhausted from travel and exposure, having recently attended the Missouri and Kentucky Conferences; yet he would undertake to preside when invited to do so. On one occasion, and during the pendency of some rather perplexing business, he became a little excited and confused from vertigo. It was the first, and, indeed, the only time, the writer ever saw him so in the chair. His old and faithful friend, Thomas Logan Douglass, observed his embarrassment, and modestly assisted to relieve him upon the question of order under consideration. After the session of the day had closed, the same friend visited him privately, and told him he had noticed he was suffering from vertigo; and when he should find himself in that condition, he ought not to consent to take the chair. The Bishop took the suggestion very kindly, thanked him, but seemed dejected at the apprehension of becoming useless in the Church. What old and laborious minister, who has come to the "sear and yellow leaf of life," cannot sympathize with him in these feelings?

After the close of the Conference, Brother Douglass and the writer waited upon the Bishop to ascertain his contemplated movements before the ensuing General Conference. He replied that he must be in Baltimore by the 1st of May, and that to be certain of it, he must start forthwith to cross the mountains. We reminded him it was then about the 1st of December, the roads were already bad, the weather cold, and the distance so great that, before he could make it, he would be caught in the snow-storms of the mountains, and be compelled to take refuge in some cabin, where he would find himself without acquaintances or comforts; that, in view of his feeble health, we could not consent to see him start on such a journey, especially without a traveling companion. We therefore advised him to remain with us until the spring should open, and promised that if he would do so, we—being delegates to the General Conference—would go with him to Baltimore. After hesitating awhile, he yielded to our remonstrances, with the proviso we should start whenever he should require, and travel at such stages as he could bear.

The winter of 1823-4 he spent in Middle Tennessee, alternating between his brother James's, in Sumner county, Nashville, and his brother-in-law, Nathanael Moore's, near Columbia, preaching whenever he could, meeting the classes occasionally, and corresponding with old friends.

Early in March, 1824, notice was given us that we must be ready to comply with our promise in a few days, as he would start on his journey to Baltimore. The winter had been a very cold and wet one; the spring opened slowly, and the roads were horribly muddy. We found him quite feeble, and scarcely able to sit up. But go he must, and start he would. For a week or two during the past winter, the writer had been engaged, at his dictation, in preparing an address to the General Conference, explaining his views as to the constitutionality and expediency of the questions which had agitated the General Conference, and vindicating his own course in the premises. He also dictated a valedictory address to the Conference, both of which documents were to be presented if, by any means, he should be prevented from attending it. During the process of composing these addresses, his accustomed caution and fine taste in the selection of the simplest and most expressive words, were very strikingly exhibited. These documents constituted our recreation, whenever a leisure hour occurred, throughout that whole tour, from the 10th of March to the 1st of May. They were transcribed, or rather written almost anew, about three times, amended, revised, and corrected with the greatest possible care. Every word was weighed, every sentence criticised to a degree which gave a new apprehension of the labor of composing.

Our company consisted of the Bishop, in his barouche, drawn by two small but excellent horses; Mr. and Mrs. Douglass, on horseback—neither of them weighing less than two hundred pounds—their faithful servant Aaron, leading a pack-horse, and the writer, on horseback. Sometimes he would ride my horse a little, especially when the road became difficult, or endangered an upset; but usually, he kept his seat in the carriage while I drove.

We passed up the Cumberland River, spending a night with his old co-laborer and friend, the father-in-law of Brother Douglass, the Rev. John McGee; thence recrossing the river at the mouth of Caney Fork, we struck out along a very rugged road—the old trail of the emigrants to the western country—for the Cumberland Mountains. We found the roads exceedingly broken and rough. To add to our troubles, torrents of rain poured upon us. The unbridged streams were swollen so as to endanger our safety; and houses were few, and comforts scanty. Our stages were short—sometimes we were compelled to halt and tie up for a day. Occasionally the Bishop was so wearied and painful, he would get out and lie down to rest on the side of the road.

Descending the mountain, we crossed the beautiful Clinch River; spent a delightful Sabbath at Kingston; preached to large congregations; visited some of the Bishop's old friends, the Wintons and others; proceeded through Knoxville to Strawberry Plains, resting a day and night with his valued former fellow-laborer, the Rev. Thomas Wilkerson,*

---

*Thomas Wilkerson was received on trial in 1793. After traveling ten years in the Virginia Conference, he located, and removed to the West. Here he resumed his labors, and was very useful late in life. He married an excellent lady, and their house was a delightful resting-place for the travel-worn and weary old Bishop. Mr. Wilkerson had traveled extensively in the West as well as in the East, and was universally esteemed for his talents and piety. His simplicity of manners, his dignity, amiability, and remarkably good sense, gave him great influence among all classes, and particularly among the most intelligent. After his reädmission into the itinerancy, his name continued upon the Minutes down to 1850. I have often thought that, in his intellectual, moral, and social characteristics, he strikingly resembled Bishop Roberts. Bishop McKendree had known him many years, and loved him highly, regarding him as singularly prudent and reliable in every thing.

of precious memory, and near Jonesboro encountered the Alleghany Mountains. Our tour across this mountain was, if possible, more disagreeable than over the Cumberland; but at last it was accomplished; and, just at nightfall, near the foot of the mountain, we found quarters at a miserable little hut. It was our only chance. It was getting dark; no other house for several miles, and the Bishop was sick and in great pain. Indeed, he was almost utterly exhausted. We carried him into the house, and laid him half dead upon a miserable bed, in a dirty room, which served as a parlor, bed-room, dining-room, and kitchen. After supper, of which none of our company partook but the Bishop's driver and our colored companion, there is a distinct recollection that somebody—not the colored man—fed, washed off, and plentifully greased the legs of three jaded horses. Then returning to the hut, through a drenching rain, he found that he must share with the Bishop a very narrow bed, or seek sleep upon his blanket on the floor.

Next morning was the blessed Sunday! It had rained all night, and every little mountain brook now brawled and foamed as it dashed headlong toward the valley. Now, what was to be done? To stay there, even on Sunday, was out of the question, unless it was sinful not to do so. The Bishop had neither eaten nor slept—he was feverish, nervous, and profoundly silent, lying on his wretched bed, with closed eyes. Brother Douglass and the writer held a consultation. We learned that the Yadkin

River was nine miles ahead: it was a fearful mountain torrent when swelled by rain—if not crossed immediately, it would detain us several days, as there was no ferry-boat; and finally, that there was no white man's house this side the river where we could stay. We agreed it was necessary to go at once, and, after every thing was ready, the Bishop was aroused and politely asked to take his seat in the carriage. He remonstrated, but, as we could not stay, he submitted, and we hurried off.

On arriving at the Yadkin, it was found to be unfordable, and rapidly rising, with every prospect of overflowing its banks before night. We soon ascertained, from a group of negroes assembled to see the river, that the ferry-boat had been carried off by the flood, that there was no lodging-place for us on this side, and that we must cross soon or retrace our steps to our late miserable stopping-place. "There!" said the Bishop, "what have you gained in breaking the Sabbath?" We replied, that it was a work of mercy to get him to a place where he could eat and rest; and besides, we were going to Wilkesboro, to have preaching at night. We made a bed for him with the cushions of the carriage and our blankets, under the shade, and he was soon fast asleep. But how to cross the river was the question. Ascertaining that there was a large canoe, dug out of the body of a huge tree, lying a mile or two above, we presently got it floated down, and quickly carried all the baggage and equipments across, with Mrs. Douglass to keep "watch and ward" over them. Then the horses swam over by the side of our craft, and finally the carriage was placed astride it and carried over. This was a difficult and hazardous affair, but it was quickly and safely done. As the canoe left the bank and started with its bow up the stream, to make the landing on the other side, all the carriage-wheels, impelled by the force of the rapid current, began to revolve, and the spectators, who watched our movements with great interest, at once shouted, "Steam-boat! steam-boat!" This aroused our sleeping friend, and he saw with alarm his carriage whirling across the torrent. He looked around, and horses, baggage, and friends had all gone. Soon, however, he was hailed from the other shore, and informed that all was safe. In a short time he was across, and moving rapidly. Wilkesboro was soon reached, and delightful quarters obtained. The Bishop had a clean and comfortable bed, enjoyed a sweet, sound night's sleep, and next morning was ready to resume his wearisome journey. He and Mr. Douglass were both now in the bounds of their former field of labor, and many old acquaintances greeted them with a hearty welcome. The latter preached at night to a large audience. It was one of his best sermons—clear, evangelical, eloquent, and powerfully impressive. The Church was edified, and penitents came forward for prayer.

The Bishop and his party left Wilkesboro, North Carolina, on the 29th of March, and stayed that night at the village of Jonesville, where he found an old friend (Parks) likely to die. Of course he visited and prayed with him. The next night was spent in Huntsville, and on the 31st we came on to Salem, the seat of the famous Moravian Female School. The town seemed orderly and prosperous, and the whole is owned by a German colony. In the afternoon we were conducted by the Superintendent to "the Sisters' House," where were 115 young ladies, students of the school; thence to the church, and heard the grand old German organ; thence to the cemetery, the Potter's House, and garden—all neatly and beautifully arranged. There were no idlers nor drunkards there. Every thing moved like clock-work.

On the 1st of April we rode from Salem to Mendenhall's—another old friend of both the Bishop and Mr. Douglass. The next day we passed over the old Guilford Court-house battle-ground, on which a battle was fought between Lord Cornwallis and General Greene, March 15, 1781. It was one of the hardest battles of the Revolution, and the loss in killed and wounded was about equal on both sides. Lord Cornwallis claimed a victory, of which Mr. Fox remarked, when it was reported in the British Parliament, "Another such victory will ruin our army in America." Indeed, this battle was the turning-point in that struggle, as it frustrated the plan of the British commander, diverted his course, and induced him to retreat next day, with our men in hot pursuit. And then the skill and courage of a part of our army, on that occasion, awakened stronger confidence on our side, and resulted in a more vigorous prosecution of the war; so that seven months afterward, (on the 19th of October, 1781,) Lord Cornwallis surrendered, at Yorktown, the whole army, and peace and independence followed. As we rode over this field, the Bishop pointed out where the lines were posted during the engagement, and some trees which were said to have lost their tops by the artillery. From his familiarity with the topography of the place and the incidents of the day, it is more than likely that he was in that battle with the Virginia troops; but here, as elsewhere, he became reticent when it was attempted to draw him out upon this subject; for, although he was not only in the rebel army, but was certainly an officer in the battle of Yorktown, yet he always avoided conversation upon war-topics with young preachers, and generally even with his old comrades and friends.

We had now arrived in a section of the country where Mr. Douglass and myself were born, and where we intended to rest awhile among our relations; so, leaving my company at Mendenhall's, with a promise to meet again and pursue our journey together, the writer departed. Passing through Greensboro, (where he had the pleasure of meeting again with the families of Judge Dick and Dr. R. P. Williamson,) he went into Person county, and spent over a week with his relations there. In the meantime the Bishop arrived, and in a few days we left, and resumed our way. Soon we passed my father's former residence, then my grandfather's—places endeared by earliest and fondest reminiscences—and on the next day, the 10th of April, crossed the Roanoke River, and stayed among the Taylors (Allen, Howell, and Edmund) several days. These were Methodists of the old and genuine stamp, and old friends of McKendree and Asbury. The Bishop visited Boydtown—subsequently the seat of Randolph Macon College, which has lately been transferred to Ashland, to prove an honor and a blessing to the State and the Church.

On the 12th of April, we went thirty-five miles, to the elegant and hospitable residence of Brother Adams. In crossing the Meherrin River, we found it very high and rising rapidly, the long bridge without banisters, one side considerably lower than the other, and a torrent of water rushing over more than half of the bridge. The Bishop was startled, and thought it hazardous to attempt to drive over; but, giving him the reins, I alighted, coaxed the frightened horses upon the bridge, and wading, led them safely over. In a brief time afterward the entire bridge was covered with the swollen stream, and, I believe, washed away.

As we proceeded by easy stages through Virginia, it was very impressive to hear the Bishop call the names and give the history of almost every family whose residence we passed. He would frequently say, "Robert, I must stop awhile here; I knew the old folks, and must look after the children." Sometimes the interviews were deeply affecting—they would embrace him, and once or twice an old, gray-headed sister would, almost involuntarily, try to kiss him. Tears, smiles, and prayers followed, and after prayer we would hurry away.

In the afternoon of April 13th, we drove to Robert C. Boothe's, and tarried there until next morning. It was a fine specimen of a Virginia Methodist family, and the Bishop was truly at home. Thence we went to Petersburg, where he was admitted on trial, in 1787. Brother Archer's was his pleasant lodging-place, as it had often been before. The stationed preacher, G. W. Charlton, was considered a very promising young preacher. On Sunday, at eleven o'clock, the Bishop preached to a large audience of old acquaintances, and their children, many of whom he had baptized in their infancy. The sermon over, they crowded around him, fervently welcoming him back again in his old age and feebleness. After Sunday, he proceeded to Richmond, and remained there until the 19th. He preached, on Sunday, at Shochoe Hill, one of his characteristic sermons, to a very large, attentive, and weeping audience.

From Richmond we passed on to Alexandria, staying a night at Brother Ware's, another at Fredericksburg, and the third at Dumfries. Passing in sight of Mount Vernon, the conversation naturally turned to General Washington, whom he greatly admired and loved. We stopped to lunch at the old, forsaken parish church, and, driving out a flock of goats, entered it. The usual inscriptions (the Ten Commandments, Creed, and Lord's Prayer) were over the pulpit, and upon a pew was the name of "George Washington," in gilt letters, and next to it "Robert Treat Paine." It seemed a pity that such a house should be given to the goats. The residence of Brother Hoffman furnished the Bishop a kind and comfortable home in Alexandria for a day or two. Here I formed the acquaintance of that eloquent and good minister, William Ryland, and was deeply impressed with his piety and talents.

Several days were spent at Brother Foxhall's, in Georgetown, and at the house of Judge McLean, the Postmaster-general. Mr. Monroe was then in the last term of his presidency, and J. C. Calhoun was Secretary of War, while Thomas L. McKinney was in the Indian Department. Several official letters now before the writer, addressed to the Bishop, attest the deep interest felt by these officers of the General Government in the civilization and Christianization of the Indians — one of them, dated April 26, informing the Bishop that "an additional allowance of $300 had been agreed on in favor of the school of Upper Sandusky." Another letter from Mr. Calhoun, addressed to Gen. Crowell, Agent for the Creek Indians, says, "The President takes a deep interest in the success of every effort the object of which is to improve the condition of the Indians, and desires that every aid should be furnished by the Indian Agents in advancing so important an object," etc. While these communications evince the estimate placed by the President and Mr. Calhoun upon the Indian Missions, they also show their high regard for the venerable Bishop to whom, in a great degree, they attributed the establishment and success of these missions, and through whose influence these allowances were made.

We had the pleasure of seeing our mutual friend,

Dr. Bascom, here. Through Mr. Clay he had been, unexpectedly to himself, elected a Chaplain to Congress, and, as it was in session, he was here in his official character. Unfortunately, his first sermon, although eloquent and able, was too long to suit the taste of his audience, who preferred short sermons and long dinners; so that, while the most intellectual and piously-disposed part were delighted with his preaching, a good many were disinclined to hear him again. On visiting him, he was found in bed, suffering from a very painful affection. He was, however, devoting every hour which he could employ to the study of the Hebrew language, under the tuition of an able Hebraist.

On the 28th of April we reached Baltimore, and were domiciled in the family of William Wilkins, Esq. It was a delightful family. In view of the Bishop's need of medical attention, his physician and devoted friend, Dr. Samuel Baker, claimed and took him to his house. Here I surrendered my precious charge, after nearly two months' constant intercourse, on a tour of more than a thousand miles of slow and toilsome travel. But they were months of inestimable value to me. From many days' conversation with that wise and holy man, I learned and enjoyed much. The origin, nature, and proper administration of Methodism; the character and labors of its early ministers; the importance of adhering closely to all its essential peculiarities; the duties of its officers, and especially of its pastors, and the indispensableness of zeal, holiness, and promptness, were topics upon which he delighted to dwell. And now, after the lapse of forty-five years, I must avow that my sentiments upon these subjects are still *McKendreean;* and, I presume, will remain so through the remainder of my life. Most devoutly do I thank God for having, in his providence, given me the inestimable privilege of so intimate an association with a man so wise and pure.

CHAPTER II.

General Conference of 1824—Messrs. Reece and Hannah—Committees—Petitions—Report on Episcopacy—Winans on the report and the constitution—"The constitutional test"—Bishops' veto—Amendment to the constitution proposed by the Bishops and others—J. Soule's views—Question carried—The suspended resolutions question—Left as unfinished business—Quorum broken—Bishop Roberts and Freeborn Garrettson—Soule and Hedding elected Bishops—Ordained—Sketches—Bishop McKendree's address—He is gratified.

On Saturday, May 1, 1824, the Delegated General Conference began its fourth quadrennial session in Baltimore, Bishops McKendree, Roberts, and George being present. The number of delegates from each Conference was as follows: From New York, 16; New England, 14; Genesee, 16; Philadelphia, 13; Baltimore, 14; Ohio, 13; Kentucky, 11; Missouri, 5; Tennessee, 9; Mississippi, 3; South Carolina, 11; Virginia, 9; in all, 134. After the usual opening exercises, Bishop McKendree in the chair, Thomas L. Douglass was made Secretary *pro tem.*; and committees on "public worship" and to draw up "rules" were appointed, and the Conference adjourned until Monday. At the next session, the body organized by electing John Emory, Secretary. The Rev. Richard Reece, as messenger, and the Rev. John Hannah, his companion, from the Wesleyan Methodists of England, were then introduced to the General Conference, and delivered impressive addresses. Committees on Episcopacy, boundaries, itinerancy, local preachers, the Book Concern, missions, churches and parsonages, people of color, revisal, and education, were appointed. A special committee was appointed on Canada affairs. Two more days were consumed in arranging business and adopting rules. To the writer—the youngest member of the body—it was an imposing spectacle. Bishop McKendree observed the action of the body with great solicitude. In a few days petitions and addresses began to pour in, declaring that "the *people* were the source of legislative authority;" "the power of the Bishops to be found nowhere else but in popes;" "we have no constitution;" "the restrictive parts of the Discipline not binding on succeeding General Conferences after 1808, nor upon the laity, as they were made by a legislative body, without the design or authority to adopt a constitution;" "let the *Church* try and expel her own members;" "laity to have an equal representation," etc. Several remonstrances were made against Presiding Elders as needless, and doing "a work of supererogation," etc., etc. And among others, on the same topic, one asking that "no slave-holder shall be a member of the Church." Such were the memorials from cities, towns, and country; from quarterly-meetings, Sunday-schools, and other official bodies, as well as unofficial petitioners by scores and hundreds of subscribers. Ten or more of them were from the West, or South. It was astounding to hear such attacks upon the very fundamental principles of our economy. Could they find advocates in a Methodist General Conference?

Of course, the reports of the various committees, to whom these papers were referred, brought up all these topics for discussion. That upon Episcopacy was about the first which was reported:

1. Approving the conduct and character of the Bishops.

2. Bishop McKendree continue in his present relation—*i. e.*, without regular work.

3. That it is necessary to strengthen the Episcopacy by the election of two more Bishops.

4. The Bishops, if necessary, to lay off Episcopal departments.

Attempts were made to modify each of these items of the report, except the second, but the principal opposition was made to the last two, some contending we had as many Bishops as was needed. The motion to recommend was lost by a vote of 54 to 60. The fourth item was discussed at considerable length. It was contended that the General Conference had authority to lay off the work in departments temporarily—some wanted the Bishops' work laid off for four years. Wm. Winans said, On this question there are three different opinions: his own was, the Bishops have the prerogative to divide their work for their own convenience and the good of the Church; and, as one of the restrictions upon this delegated body is, that "they shall not destroy the plan of our itinerant General Superintendency;" and, inasmuch as the exercise of the authority by the delegated body in limiting, and thus localizing the Bishops, violates the plan of our itinerant General Superintendency, it is, and must be, a violation of the constitution of the Church. He said it was absurd to deny that we have a Church-constitution. By what authority do members occupy their seats here as delegates, or the Bishop his chair, but by the constitution? These restrictive articles, adopted by a convention of the whole body of ministers in 1808, are as truly a constitution to the Church, (and to this body,) and for the expressed purpose of restricting this delegated body, as the Constitution of the United States is to this nation. In short, if these articles do not constitute a part of the organic law of the Church, in all its departments, we have *no* constitution, and this body is lawless. This speech was thrilling. The report was adopted, leaving it discretionary with the Bishops to divide their work temporarily.

Friday, May 20th, another question of importance came up, called "the constitutional test," the object of which was to prevent hasty action, violative of the constitution, by giving the Bishops a qualified veto, with an ultimate reference of the question to the Annual Conferences. It involved constitutional questions only. The Bishops, anticipating some action of the kind, had agreed to unite, and, if desired, present to the Conference the following amendment to the sixth Article of the "Limitations and Restrictions," adopted by the General Conference in 1808, signed by their own hands, and by two others, to wit:

Resolved by the delegates of the Annual Conferences in General Conference assembled, That it be recommended, and is hereby recommended to the several Annual Conferences, to adopt the following Article as a provision, to be annexed to the sixth Article of the Limitations and Restrictions, adopted by the General Conference in 1808, to wit: "*Provided, also,* That whenever the Delegated General Conference shall pass any rule or rules which, in the judgment of the Bishops, or a majority of them, are contrary to, or an infringement upon, the above Limitations and Restrictions, or any one of them, such rule or rules being returned to the Conference within three days after their passage, together with the objections of the Bishops in writing, the Conference shall reconsider such rule or rules; and if, upon reconsideration, they shall pass by a majority of two-thirds of the members present, they shall be considered as rules, and go into immediate effect; but, in case a less majority shall differ from the opinion of the Bishops, and they continue to sustain their objections, the rule or rules objected to shall be laid before the Annual Conferences, in which case the decision of all the members of the Annual Conferences present when the vote shall be taken, shall be final. In taking the vote in all such cases, in the Annual Conferences, the Secretary shall give a certificate of the number of votes taken in the affirmative and negative, and such certificates shall be forwarded to the

Book Agents in New York, who, with one or more of the Bishops who may be present, shall be a committee to canvass the votes and certify the result."

We recommend the adoption of the above resolution.

W. McKendree,
Enoch George,
R. R. Roberts,
Thos. L. Douglass,
Wm. Capers.

Whether the subject was brought into Conference by the presentation of this document, or by another series of resolutions, the writer cannot say; but the discussion of the subject was upon substantially a similar, if not an identical, presentation of the question.

A motion to lay on the table was lost by 61 to 65.

J. Soule said: "The General Conference is not the proper judge of the constitutionality of its own acts. The course of the last General Conference, in the case of the suspended resolutions, shows it thought thus. If the General Conference be the sole judge in such questions, then there are no bounds to its power. The General Conferences held and exercised unlimited power until 1812, because they met *en masse*, and not by virtue of their election or delegation. This was felt to be a dangerous state of things, and unfair to the more distant portions of the work. And one great, controlling motive in introducing the representative principle was, to lessen the danger of sudden and violent changes in the fundamental polity of the Church, by establishing a delegated legislative body, under restrictions—thus insuring stability to the organic institutions, and equality in representation. It matters not by what name these restrictive rules may be called; the design and effect were to take the questions enumerated from under the control of the delegated Conference, except in the way and manner specified." *He* called it a *constitution.*

L. McCombs and James Smith opposed the resolution at considerable length, and W. Winans replied in one of the strongest, most analytical, and effective speeches ever delivered on the floor of the General Conference. The question was carried by a vote of 64 to 58.

A heavy load was lifted from the heart of the senior Bishop. His face put on a subdued smile, and he breathed freer. But the subject which had in some form or other agitated the body since 1808, and which had, in 1820, culminated in the adoption of certain resolutions, which were subsequently reconsidered and suspended, and hence were known as the "Suspended Resolutions," was yet to come up. No questions had so long and so deeply disturbed the entire Church as those involved in these resolutions. Their purpose was to diminish the power of the Bishops, by the *election* of the Presiding Elders, and investing them with the *stationing* prerogative. In 1820, it was carried as a *compromise*, or *peace-measure*—many voting for it as such who really disapproved it. But no sooner was this done than the real and baneful tendency of the measure began to be perceived, as already stated in a preceding chapter; and so general was this conviction, that it was suspended until 1824. The great and avowed cause of opposition to it was, that it was an infringement on the constitutional authority of the Episcopacy—who nevertheless agreed to submit it to the several Annual Conferences, and, if they should sanction it, to consider it passed. It appeared that Bishop McKendree had done this at the Conferences he had attended, and probably the other Bishops had done so too; but some Conferences had voted against it and some for it, while several had failed or refused to vote on it at all. It was evidently against the wish of a majority of the members of the Annual Conferences. A motion was made on the 24th of May, declaring the suspended resolutions *null and void.* Almost the entire day was spent in discussing the matter, and upon taking the vote, it stood 63 for and 61 against the motion. But as there was a complaint that several Conferences had not voted, whose votes, if in the affirmative, might carry the question, there was a disposition among the majority to hold the decision in abeyance until these Conferences might have another chance to vote, and if there then should be a majority in favor of these resolutions, they should be considered as adopted. To this it was replied, The *principle* is now lost, and the resolutions themselves are not of so much importance.

On the 28th, Lewis Myers moved "to take up

the motion on the subject of the suspended resolutions." Dr. Capers said there was a division of sentiment on these resolutions. "A majority of the members of the Annual Conferences, as well as of the Conferences themselves, have said they are unconstitutional. There is a division of sentiment among the Episcopacy, and if things are left as they are, will not the Bishops be delicately situated? May it not produce confusion in the administration? For surely they will not give practical effect to the measure, after what has transpired."

Dr. Winans wished the resolutions to be considered "unfinished business."

It was finally moved by the writer, and seconded by Dr. Capers, that "the suspended resolutions, making the Presiding Elders elective, etc., be considered as unfinished business, and they shall not be inserted in the new edition of the Discipline nor go into operation before the next General Conference."

In putting the question to vote, (Bishop Roberts in the chair,) the quorum was broken twice; but, under the remonstrances of the venerable Freeborn Garrettson and the chairman, at last it was carried, and the Conference soon after adjourned *sine die.*

After the decision that the resolutions so often referred to were null and void, the reason for the refusal of Joshua Soule to submit to consecration being thus removed, it was greatly desired by his friends to have him reëlected to the Episcopacy; and as two were to be inducted into office, Joshua Soule and Elijah Hedding were elected Bishops.

And on the 27th, after a sermon by Bishop George, they were solemnly ordained as Superintendents of the Methodist Episcopal Church in the United States of America. These two men were in many respects eminently qualified for the high positions assigned them, and proved themselves worthy and useful shepherds of the Church.*

When it was evident that the Conference was ap-

---

* Joshua Soule was a native of Maine—born in Bristol, Hancock county, 1781. He entered the itinerancy in 1798, having been converted the year previous. He died in Nashville, Tennessee, March 6, 1867. His long ministerial career was crowded with labor and eventful scenes. He enjoyed the esteem of Bishops Asbury and McKendree, and deserved it. When shall we have his biography? It is to be regretted, that in the very valuable and usually fair and liberal "History of the M. E. Church," by Dr. Stevens, written since the Bishop's death, the author, in sketching his character, could find so little, comparatively, to say about him, and of that little, so much that is depreciating.

Elijah Hedding was born in the county of Dutchess, New York, June 7, 1780; was converted December 27, 1798; admitted on trial in 1801; elected Bishop in 1824; and died April 9, 1852. He had been a faithful and efficient laborer in the Northern and Eastern section of the work, and was highly respected for his purity of character, his amiability, and his talents. He was a large and venerable-looking man, and lived and died with a spotless reputation. During the General Conference of 1824, the writer heard him preach in Light Street Church, Baltimore, on "*God is love.*" He illustrated the great truth in the text as exhibited in creation, providence, and grace. It was clearly and fitly spoken, but seemed not to make a very strong impression. In his Episcopal duties he was popular, and much revered for his wisdom, piety, and fidelity. His labors were not extended to the South-west. Dr. D. W. Clark has given us an excellent biography of him.

proaching its close, the senior Bishop determined to carry out his meditated purpose of giving to its members a brief address. Mr. John Summerfield, the renowned and justly popular Anglo-Irish preacher, (between whom and the Bishop there existed the strongest feelings of attachment,) was requested to join the writer and take down the address in short-hand. We accordingly prepared ourselves, and recorded every word he uttered as it fell from his lips, and, after comparing our notes and making out a copy of his address, handed it to him. It was a striking and touching scenic presentation. There he stood before the assembled representatives of the Church, with every one of whom he was acquainted, and with some of whom he had been a fellow-soldier on many a moral battle-field for about forty years—whose thin hairs were white as his, and whose bodies, like his, were wasted and worn with unceasing toil and care. The moment he arose, noise and motion ceased in the crowded house. He paused awhile, and then, in a low and hesitating voice, began. After saying that he would avail himself of the present opportunity to state his views upon a subject on which some brethren had misunderstood him, the following were his words:

"At the last General Conference, unexpected circumstances led to a development of our situation in certain matters, which was of a serious and painful nature; after which difficulties were to rise out of this which affected the peace and harmony of the Church. Soon after, I understood that brethren supposed me to have said that I considered it my right and prerogative to negative the laws of the General Conference. This surprised me, for I had disavowed this principle above thirty years ago, and had never changed my sentiments, but have disavowed it at all seasonable opportunities, and do still. This I supposed quite sufficient to satisfy those who know me; and yet I perceived the other day, from the statement of a brother in this Conference, that this sentiment still lives, and was again attributed to me. If I had at any time, in the multiplicity of cares and of business, suffered any thing to escape me which by possibility could be construed to have this meaning, I should still have thought that my disavowal, so frequently made public among you, would have been sufficient to guard against such a construction. I therefore add, that in my estimation no construction of this kind can be legitimately drawn from any thing I may have said. After Conference, I took a course in this business which has been objected to by many. I have no hesitation in saying that the act was not within the limits of our restricted powers; but I was induced to do it from a precedent which had been once set by that venerable man, Bishop Asbury, who may perhaps be considered as the father of the American Connection. Soon after I was ordained a Bishop, an objection was made against an act of the administration, and the objection was on constitutional principles. Asbury deplored that our Discipline made no provision for adjusting such a controversy, and determined to lay it before the Annual Conferences. The first that met was the Baltimore Conference. After it had been submitted to them, he carried it forward to the Philadelphia, New York, New England, and Genesee Conferences, in each of which it was acted on, and the difficulties were adjusted. This was the plan on which I acted: unapprehensive of any evil tendency, I laid this matter before the Annual Conferences. Look now at its tendency. I viewed it on constitutional principles, and my reasonings are still in existence. I thought from the first, and I do still think, that the Annual Conferences have the power of determining the question; and if they had said, 'We think them constitutional,' (*i. e.*, the suspended resolutions,) I was bound to submit. However, as they did not, I simply advised them to recommend it to the General Conference. In all this I saw no evil tendency whatever.

"At the commencement of the present General Conference, your Bishops consulted together, to devise some way to harmonize the brethren and the Connection at large. It is true they have had *their* difficulties—and I would ask if any three men could unite their views on every subject for eight, or even four years. Yet, after all, when they came together, they were anxious to agree upon some plan which would harmonize the body. They thought they saw a plan open, and they entered in. The plan was to invite the brethren on both sides to vote a *peace-measure* which should meet the wishes of all. In order to guard against a recurrence of like disagreements, they agreed to recommend to the General Conference a *constitutional test* which should for ever settle these things. I was pleased with an adjustment which is calculated to heal the past by the peace-measure proposed, and to guard against a recurrence by the constitutional test."

Having concluded this topic, he spoke of the importance of the present time in the history of our Church, the extension of the work, and the increase in the number of the Conferences; thence deduced and maintained the necessity of an efficient Superintendency, and the importance of leading on the thousands of our Israel to inward and outward holiness, and of training up the hundreds of thousands of the rising generation. He enlarged on the necessity of united counsels and exertions to carry on this great work, and expressed his anxiety to see his brethren go hence to their work in perfect harmony. He rejoiced to know the differences of opinion would produce no division in the Conference. He said the office of a Bishop among *us* is not an enviable station; that in truth it is an accumulation of toil, labor, and privation, superadded to the "care of all the churches;" and that any one who would desire the office of a Bishop "as a good thing," for any other motive than to increase the general happiness of man and the glory of God thereby, had not counted the cost. He briefly adverted to his age and infirmities, and the probability that he would not live to meet them four years hence. He then proceeded to advert to the labor and anxiety they had endured through the long session about to close, and congratulated them upon the measures adopted, and the degree of harmony and brotherly respect which had generally prevailed. He exhorted them to love the Church and each other, to avoid strife, to cultivate deep personal piety and an unwavering devotion to the high ends of their holy vocation. Finally, after expressing a joyful hope of renewing in heaven the friendship and sanctified affection begun on earth, he invoked the blessing of God upon them all, and in tremulous tones—his cheeks moistened with tears—bade them, as he supposed, a long farewell. The whole audience continued awhile in profound silence, interrupted only by partially suppressed emotions. He concluded his address with the apostolic benediction, and retired.

Various other measures were adopted by this Conference, which, upon the whole, was one of the most important sessions of the body ever held in the United States. Bishop McKendree was especially gratified. His well-known opinions upon several vital issues had been sustained, his course fully vindicated, an untrammeled Episcopacy and primitive itinerancy perpetuated, and two able and trustworthy colleagues had been added to the aged but excellent college of Bishops. The Church, especially in the South and West, was delighted at what was regarded, and has proved to be, virtually a peaceable disposal of harassing and dangerous attempts at innovations, and the preachers felt renewed confidence in the recuperative energy and perpetuity of their beloved *Alma Mater*.

Thus closed the memorable General Conference of 1824.*

---

* There are several discrepancies between the notes made by the writer *at the time* and Dr. Bangs's valuable History—viz.: He says, on page 277 of Vol. III., the election of the two Bishops occurred on the 26th, and their consecration on the 27th. My notes, made at the time, say the election was on the 28th, and the consecration on the 29th, of May. Again, he says Bishop McKendree preached the ordination-sermon: my record says Bishop George preached it. On the first balloting, Wm. Beauchamp was next to Soule, Hedding next, and Emory last. Emory withdrew his name on the third balloting, and Hedding was elected by a small majority.

CHAPTER III.

The Bishops divide the work for four years—Bishop McKendree starts on a tour of three thousand miles—His letter to Dr. Sargent—His route from Baltimore to the Wyandotte Mission—Bishop Soule and family—Jacob Crist—Finley meets him at Columbus, Ohio—Visits and preaches to the Indians—Weary—Bear-skin bed on the ground—Gets to Kentucky Conference at Versailles — Attends the Missouri Conference — Returns to Tennessee very feeble — His letter to Bishops Roberts and Soule, resigning the active duties of the Superintendency—Resumes his travels in the spring of 1825 — B. T. Crouch's letter—Mr. Summerfield.

Immediately after the close of the General Conference of 1824, the Bishops agreed to a division of the work among themselves for the ensuing four years, conformably to the views expressed by that body. For the first two years Bishops Roberts and Soule were to attend the Western and Southern Conferences, and Bishops George and Hedding the Eastern and Northern, and to exchange their fields of labor for the ensuing two years—thus enabling each of them to attend every Conference before the next General Conference.

After spending a few days in Baltimore, and at the residence of his long-tried and devoted friend, Dr. Henry Wilkins, then living in the vicinity of the city, and finding his health and strength a little improved, he resumed his travels, intending, if possible, to visit the Indian missions and the North-western and Southern Conferences—a distance of more than three thousand miles.

From Sharpsburg, Pennsylvania, he wrote to Dr. Thomas Sargent, President of the Philadelphia Missionary Society, in reply to a note just received from him, and, after several suggestions as to the application of missionary funds to the various Indian missions, and especially in aid of New Orleans, he proceeds to say:

"Our Church-politics is strangely embarrassing. The course I took relative to the suspended resolutions was not to defeat them, but to bring them into operation conformably to the constitution, and thereby confirm the '*peace-measure*' and harmonize the preachers. To this the preachers who prefer the old system are willing to submit for the sake of peace. On the commencement of the late General Conference, the Bishops took the subject into consideration, and unanimously agreed to recommend the introduction of the suspended resolutions so soon as they should be recommended by those Annual Conferences which had not already authorized the change. This the old side—the majority—I understand, are willing to do. But this our reformers refused to do. The majority, still desirous of an amicable adjustment of differences, would not destroy the resolutions, but perpetuated their suspension. This is my view of the matter. Hence this change in our government, which was dictated by the reformers, is defeated by the reformers. It is said by authority to be relied on, that nothing short of investing the Annual Conferences with authority to constitute the Presiding Elders, independently of the Bishops, and to make the Presiding Elders thus appointed a committee to station the preachers, in which the Bishop shall have only the casting vote, will satisfy the Northern brethren. This change would, in my estimation, effectually 'destroy our itinerant General Superintendency;' and I am deliberately of the opinion, that an effective General Superintendency is as necessary to the preservation of *our itinerancy* and the harmony of the Annual Conferences, as is the General Conference itself. Both one and the other rise out of the division of our work into so many Annual Conferences, which are equal in power and independent of each other. Could all our preachers meet in one Annual Conference, the itinerant plan might be preserved in America without either a General Superintendency or a General Conference, as it is in England. I expect to be at the Ohio Conference, at Zanesville, in September, when I hope to receive a letter from you."

The following extract from his Diary will show the route he took from the General Conference:

"At the Baltimore Conference, Jacob B. Crist was appointed to travel with me. I went to the Philadelphia Conference, and at its close returned to Baltimore. From there we went, in company with Bishop Soule and his family, as they were moving, to the State of Ohio. On Sabbath we both preached at Hagerstown. Thence we went to

Sharpsburg and Uniontown, Pennsylvania. Bishop Soule and family go on, and we stopped. Preached at Brownsville, Washington, Wheeling, Barnesville, and Zanesville, and spent the Sabbath at New Lancaster. On Monday we reached Columbus, where Brother Finley was waiting for me, and the next day we set out for the Wyandotte Mission. The weather was very hot, and one of my horses having been lamed at Lancaster, I had undertaken to go on horseback. I suffered considerably, and was greatly fatigued, but arrived safely at the mission about the 7th of August. Preached to the Indians on Sunday—spent several days visiting the Indian families, and rode sixty miles in two days, to Urbana. I had to lie down and rest, in a house, if we could find one; if not, a bear-skin on the ground made a very good bed. When musquitos were plenty, we would strike fire, raise a smoke, and rest comfortably. From Urbana we attended the Ohio Conference, at Zanesville. Thence we visited Springfield, Xenia, Ridgewell, Hillsboro, Chillicothe, Lebanon, Dayton, Cincinnati, and Lexington, Kentucky, on our way to the Kentucky Conference, at Versailles, October 11, 1824. Besides preaching in the towns and societies in the country, we attended quarterly-meetings and camp-meetings, rendering such services as we were able."

It has been already stated that he attended, with Bishops Soule and Roberts, the Missouri Conference, which succeeded the Kentucky. His route was through Louisville, crossing the Ohio, through Indiana to Vincennes, through Illinois to Padsfields, attending the Missouri Conference in November, returning through Southern Illinois into Kentucky, visiting Hopkinsville and Russellville, and passing into Tennessee. During all this long journey, he was so feeble as to need assistance to get in or out of the carriage. The roads were very bad, the streams high—frequently the horses were near swimming, and once, in crossing a deep and dangerous stream on a cold day, the water came over the backs of the horses, and wet the Bishop above his knees. His clothes were soon frozen, and in this condition he had to ride four miles to reach a house.

The Bishops were greatly delighted at the change which had resulted from the labors of the missionaries among the Wyandottes, both in the temporal and spiritual condition of this people. Their religion had consisted of paganism and some of the ceremonies of the Roman Catholic Church. They were really pagans, although baptized by the priests and claimed by them as Christians. They kept up their heathen worship—their feasts, songs, and dances; and so strong was their belief in witchcraft, that numbers had been put to death as witches, under this belief. Drunkenness, poverty, nakedness, and misery abounded. The chase was their chief, if not their only resource, for a living. But now a large majority had renounced their old faith and practices. Many had joined our Church, and were strictly attentive to the means of grace. The tomahawk and the scalping-knife, the rifle and the bow, had been substituted by the ax, the plow, and the hoe. The habits of Christian, social, and domestic life prevailed. At the manual-labor mission-school a fine farm was in full operation, supplying abundantly the wants of the mission family and school with corn, wheat, oats, rye, flax, and a great variety and profusion of vegetables. The Indians were imitating this model establishment. On the Sabbath both of the Bishops preached to a large assembly, through the interpreter. By appointment, they met a number of the leaders of the Nation—the chiefs and the Moderator of the National Council. Bishop McKendree, after addressing them, invited them to inform him of their views in relation to the mission and the general interests of the Nation. Menoncu, Punch, Gray Eves, Peacock, Between-the-logs, Driver, Washington, and Big Tree replied. They gratefully adverted to the change in the creed, manners, morals, and condition, which had resulted from the mission, and earnestly asked that it might be continued. "Bishop McKendree," says Bishop Soule, "continued visiting from house to house, attended by an interpreter," explaining experimental religion and enforcing its practical precepts. On the 14th of August they left, impressed and delighted with the visit. Bishop Soule, who had never before been among the Indians, was especially surprised and pleased; and both of them, through the remainder of their lives, often adverted to the scene, which seemed to linger in their memories like the echo of an enchanting song heard "long time ago." It awakened a deeper sympathy for "the poor In dian."

On their route from the Missouri to the Tennessee Conference, to be held at Columbia, they arrived on Nov. 21st at the Rev. Nathanael Moore's, the brother-in-law of Bishop McKendree, and found his sister, Mrs. Frances Moore, in a very feeble state of health from consumption. Having attended the Tennessee Conference and returned to the house of his brother-in-law, he yielded to the advice of friends and the entreaties of his sisters and relations, not to venture farther during the winter. Indeed, his health was very infirm, and the succeeding Conferences were likely to be so well supplied with Episcopal supervision, that it was alike unreasonable and unnecessary for him to try to go. Bishop Soule went on his way to the Mississippi Conference, and Bishop McKendree now fully devoted himself to instruct and soothe his dying sister.

Having already alluded to this subject, suffice it to say, that after a protracted and terrible scene of physical suffering, and occasionally of mental depression, she became exceedingly happy some weeks before her departure, and died while her beloved brother was by her bedside soothing and encouraging her to trust all to Jesus. Her last struggle was triumphant; her last word was "*Glory!*" This occurred January 3, 1825. The remainder of the winter of 1824–5 the Bishop continued in Tennessee, visiting among his old acquaintances, and preaching as he had ability. Besides his brother-in-law's, the Rev. N. Moore's, and his brother's, Dr. James McKendree's, his principal resting-places were Jos. T. Elliston's and H. R. W. Hill's, Nashville, and T. L. Douglass's, near Franklin, Tennessee.

The excessive fatigue and exposure he had undergone in his late tour, and his consequent debility and suffering, deeply impressed him with the conviction of his inability to perform effectively the active labors of an itinerant General Superintendent; and while laboring under the depression produced by this conviction, the following letter was addressed to Bishops Roberts and Soule, in which he proposes to retire from the duties and responsibilities of the Superintendency, with suggestions as to certain important items which he commends to their special attention; and although several preceding General Conferences had authorized him to do so, and notwithstanding this formal announcement of his purpose, yet so soon as his health and strength were a little recruited by rest and kind nursing, he was again on the wing around the Continent, striving to build up the Church and save souls from death.

Nashville, Dec. 12, 1824.

MUCH-RESPECTED BRETHREN:—Two considerations incline me to retire more effectually from the important duties and high responsibilities of the Episcopal charge:

1. My infirmities are such that I can neither bear the fatigue of traveling from Conference to Conference, nor perform the duties when present.

2. The Episcopal duties can be discharged as well without me; yet I am as much as ever disposed,

whether present or absent, to render all the assistance in my power.

Having made these remarks, suffer me to suggest a few things for your consideration, which have occurred to me as points deserving serious attention:

The importance and utility of our missionary operations are sufficiently demonstrated by the success with which they have been attended. To carry the design into complete effect, much depends, as I conceive, upon the Bishops. By them the attention of the last General Conference was invited to the establishment of a mission at Liberia, with an eye of thus opening the way for the gospel among the native Africans.

You, doubtless, recollect that the General Conference approved the design, and authorized the Bishops to send out a missionary or missionaries immediately; but as yet nothing has been done.

Can it be that a suitable man cannot be found among all our ministers? or, is the failure attributable to us? Dear brethren, let us strive to effect this grand object. The Lord will surely smile upon the undertaking.

That some of our missionaries are not sufficiently attentive to the instruction of the Indians, is evident to some of us. Should we not inquire, not only whether they are faithful in preaching and meeting the classes, but also whether they visit them with a view to instruct and incite them to agriculture and housewifery?—a very important part of their duty. It is scarcely necessary to caution our missionaries against entering into any questions involving civil politics.

Can you not devise some means by which our people and friends can be more effectually roused to the importance of sustaining and enlarging our field of missionary operations? Would it not be well to converse freely with the Presiding Elders on the subject, and strive to excite them to use their best efforts within their respective limits to raise societies and collect funds? or would it answer better to appoint suitable persons to travel and raise funds exclusively for this object?

One thought more, and I will conclude. What has been intimated relative to the laxity of the preachers in missionary operations, may apply in some degree to the "duties of a preacher," "the building of churches," "the doctrine of holiness," and conformity to the world.

Remember, dear brethren, that it is our duty, as General Superintendents, "to oversee the spiritual and temporal business of the Church," and we are holden jointly responsible for the administration. Let us, therefore, discharge our duties faithfully; then shall we not be ashamed at our approaching examination, but be able to render up an account to the General Conference with joy and not with grief. Yours affectionately,

W. McKendree.

During the summer of 1825 he attended several quarterly and camp-meetings, and preached to the edification of thousands. In the latter part of the summer he passed into Kentucky. The following letter to the writer from the Rev. B. T. Crouch, Sr., shows his habits on such occasions — alas! the worthy author, and recently his excellent widow, and his noble son and namesake, as well as the Bishop, have since all gone to the grave:—

"In the autumn of 1824, my health being very poor, my brethren persuaded me to take a superannuated relation; but not being disposed to rest, my labors were not abated, and the Presiding Elder of the District having to be absent several weeks on business, employed me to attend a whole round of his quarterly-meetings in his stead. I think in June, 1825, at one of those meetings, Bishop McKendree came up, greatly to our surprise and joy. He was on a pastoral tour eastward and northward, and hearing of the quarterly-meeting, he came to it, intending to avail himself of the Presiding Elder's company for several weeks. The absence of the proper incumbent of the District, the Rev. Wm. Adams, of precious memory, did not change the Bishop's purpose. He took me for his traveling companion, and favored us with his services at four successive quarterly-meetings. Truly, this was to be remembered! During that time I enjoyed the constant companionship of a grave and dignified man, whose godly example, spiritual wisdom, sanctified science, and rare piety, filled up my idea of a Bishop of apostolical times and New Testament type. I traveled with him over hills and valleys, labored with him in the pulpit, at the altar, occupied the same room, and often shared with him the same bed; retired with him, when other convenient places failed, to the same grove for prayer, and witnessed by day and night his sore afflictions of body and deep travail of spirit for Zion's peace; and surely of patience, meekness, calm submission, forbearance, and, in a word, every grace, every virtue, exhibited on a most exalted scale, and amidst extraordinary afflictions and sufferings, gave evidence of a pious mind and a mature Christian: his claim to that character was fully vindicated, and his living credentials entitled him to the first honors.

"It is now twenty-nine years since the events transpired which furnished the matter of this record, and the gems of knowledge then received, and the lessons of piety and propriety which his example and conversation taught, have never been forgotten. On the division of the powers of government and administration-law, as comprised in the ecclesiastical polity of Methodism, Bishop McKendree held some views which did not accord with the politics of some of our expounders of Church-law. He did not indorse the doctrine that a superior officer had a right to claim the place, or even to take it, except for special reasons, and to perform the appropriate and law-prescribed duties of an inferior during the term for which the inferior officer is held responsible for those duties, and while he is recognized as the legal incumbent of the work and place assigned him. He did not hold that the presence of a Bishop superseded the official relations, and nullified the authority, for the time being, of all inferior officers, from the Presiding Elder down; so that a

Bishop, because he is present, is *ex-officio, de jure,* Presiding Elder, and every thing else, even to the Omega of the official list. He believed that such a policy might become the source of great confusion; that it would defeat the ends of government by overleaping the checks and balances of power which distinguish the several departments and proportions of Methodist polity.

"The Bishop was drawn out fully on this point of ecclesiastical discipline by an occurrence which brought the subject directly to view. The Presiding Elder was absent; his proxy was attending a series of quarterly-meetings for him; but while it was competent for the proxy to take the place of his principal in the pulpit, in the altar, at the sacramental-table, and yet, in the absence of the Presiding Elder, placed the preacher in charge of the circuit in the chair of the Quarterly Conference, and therefore the proxy could not preside over that body.

"But there was a Bishop present, and the preacher in charge, as well as the proxy, urged that he—being a superior officer—should preside in the Quarterly Conference. To this, however, the Bishop objected; and, in stating his reasons, taught substantially this important lesson: a Bishop has the right, under law, to displace or remove a Presiding Elder, and either to preside in the vacated place himself, or to appoint another to do so; and a Presiding Elder has a right, in common with a Bishop, to remove a preacher from his charge in the intervals of the Annual Conferences, and either in person to perform the duties of the vacant charge, or to appoint another to the charge; but no Bishop has a right, in the face of law, to usurp the position which, for a definite time, has been assigned to an under-officer until that definite time shall have expired, or the under-officer, for sufficient cause, shall have been displaced. He allowed, indeed, that a superior officer might accept, as a courtesy, the place of an under-officer; but that even this should not be done where the harmony and safety of judicial proceedings might thereby be jeopardized; as, for instance, where such an act might subject an officer to the necessity of presiding twice over the adjudication of the same case: first, in the court of original proceedings; and secondly, in the appellate court.*

"Being the subject of an inveterate dyspeptic habit, he was very particular in his diet. Plain corn-bread, or cold wheat loaf, with very little, if any, butter; seldom any flesh, choosing a small relish of broiled bacon; sometimes a cup of tea, but more frequently a glass of milk or cold water, completed the good man's richest variety of table luxuries.

"He possessed the happy talent, when in a talking mood, of making his conversation interesting and instructing. And while his usual themes were the doctrines and institutions of the Bible, eccle-

---

* Is it not possible that the Bishop's position on this point was misunderstood, in part? Certainly it does not accord with his carefully-written address to his colleagues in 1833, which see.

siastical history and polity, and the preacher's duties as teacher and pastor, occasionally he would narrate interesting incidents, or discuss natural phenomena. He had traveled much in frontier settlements; had seen much, and heard more of Indian character, and felt the liveliest concern for their welfare. Their sagacity and strategy struck him forcibly. I shall not soon forget an anecdote he related, as illustrative of their shrewdness. I do not know but it has gone to print before this, nor whether he claimed originality for it, but it impressed and amused me. It ran thus:

"A party of Indians, on a hunting expedition, had pitched their tents near a white settlement, in the backwoods, when one of them found his tent had been robbed of some meat: he started in pursuit, and presently meeting a white man on horseback, inquired if he had seen an old low white man, with a short gun and a stump-tail dog. 'Yes,' said the horseman, 'I met just such a man.' 'He stole my meat,' said the Indian. 'How do you know it was a white man stole it? Might not an Indian have stolen it?' 'No; when Indian walk, he toes turn in; when white man walk, he toes turn out. Man stole my meat he toes turn out—*he* white man.' 'How do you know he was an old man that stole your meat? May it not have been a young man?' 'No; he old man. Young man active—step long; old man stiff, he step short. Man got my meat step short—he old man.' 'But why do you think he was a low man?' 'Why? Meat not high—he got block to reach my meat; high man no want block to get my meat—he low man.' 'And how do you know he had a *short* gun?' ''Cause, while he get my meat, set he gun on ground and lean it against tent-pole log, and make mark. I measure it; it short gun.' 'Well, how on earth do you know he had a short-tail dog?' 'Well, while man get meat, dog set down out there, look at man and shake he tail in snow; make short mark—he short-tailed dog.'

"After relating this amusing incident, the Bishop remarked that this and many similar things give us some idea how the children of the forest make an effort to compensate the lack of the knowledge of letters."

Mention has been made, in connection with the Bishop's address to the General Conference of 1824, of the name of John Summerfield; and, from the correspondence between them, it readily appears that, while the Bishop felt a tender and fatherly affection for this highly-gifted and eloquent young minister of Christ, it was reciprocated by a deeply reverential and filial affection. A number of letters before us attest these facts. Few, if any, of his years have so arrested public attention and been so much admired and loved as Mr. Summerfield. He was born in England, Jan. 31, 1798; was carefully trained by devoted parents, and enjoyed the advantages of a good literary education. His father having moved to Ireland in 1813, he was there converted to God in his seventeenth year, and immediately began to hold meetings, and to labor for the salvation of souls. In 1819, he was admitted on trial in the Irish Conference. Such were his zeal and pulpit eloquence that, notwithstanding his youth, he was chosen to act as missionary through the country. His constant labors and devotion to his work, in less than three years impaired his health, and, after a short absence in England, where he was greatly admired, he emigrated with his father and family, and landed in New York in March, 1821. He was at once admitted on trial in the New York Conference, and began a brief and brilliant career of ministerial usefulness in this country. His first public address was at the Anniversary of the American Bible Society, and excited the admiration of a large and intelligent audience. His unpretending modesty and simplicity of manner, the catholicity of his spirit, his chaste style, and the subdued fervor of his devotion, combined with the unbroken flow of an elocution resembling a beautiful, transparent river, gliding equably onward to its destination, riveted the attention and moved the hearts of his hearers. His youthful appearance, and the traces of suffering in his pallid face, added to the effect of his sermons, by exciting the apprehension of an early death. The sympathetic emotions which usually arise between the hearers and the speaker, were toward him of a peculiar character. Always willing and ready to preach, or to labor in any way, and anywhere, for his divine Master's glory, and ever doing it so humbly, so modestly, and yet so well, prejudice, rivalry, and pride were abashed under his ministry; and he seemed the ideal of purity, the impersonation of the genius of our loving and holy Christianity.

Mr. Summerfield's labors in the United States were abundant—too abundant for the frail and delicate tabernacle of such a soul. He was in demand everywhere—now in New York, then in Philadelphia, and then in Baltimore, Washington City, and in the towns and regions adjacent. Ministers, old and young, of all denominations, pushed through dense crowds, and sat with respect and rapture under his sermons, and invited him to their pulpits; some pastors of other denominations doing, as did Bishop Soule in Baltimore, who, when he and Mr. Summerfield had appointments to preach at different churches at the same hour, dismissed his congregation, and said, "Come, let us go and hear our beloved John," and hastened to sit and weep under his ministry. The writer feels it a privilege to have been drawn, through the influence of our mutual and venerated friend, Bishop McKendree, into close association with this godly and guileless man, and to have heard him repeatedly for a month in the pulpit, and in addresses at Missionary Anniversaries, and to children in Sunday-schools. Never can he forget hearing him for the first time in Baltimore, May 9, 1824. He confesses, too, to have had a feeling somewhat akin to prejudice, of which he soon became ashamed. Everybody was extolling Mr. S. in terms of the highest eulogy. He could but suspect that such popularity must excite the vanity, and work to the injury, of the young man, and that it was unreasonable to suppose there could be solid ground for such laudation of any one whose mind must be so immature. And yet his excellent and intelligent hostess, Mrs. W., praised him; Bishop Soule admired and loved him as a son, and, I feared, was a little proud of his pet; and even Bishop McKendree spoke of him in his quiet way in a manner which showed his high esteem and profound affection. So I resolved to hear and see for myself. To do this, I got a ticket for the love-feast, to be held in the Caroline Street Church, Baltimore, before preaching, and found the building nearly full—quite so, except the galleries. The whole General Conference seemed there—visitors, citizens, strangers—all who could get tickets had come, and a vast crowd thronged about the church. The love-feast closed, that crowd literally rushed in, and in a few minutes every foot below and in the double galleries was closely occupied, while the aisles, the doors, the sidewalk in front, and on each side of the house and the street back to the opposite side, was covered with a compact mass, eager to see the preacher, or catch a word from his lips. I could but deeply feel the responsibility of his position at the minute he appeared, but there was no chance to enter at the front, so his friends took him to the rear, and lifting him upon their shoulders, he crept through the window near the pulpit. He entered it without looking around at the immense audience, and fell upon his knees. Presently he gave out his hymn in a low but inexpressibly clear and sweet voice. It was a grand and familiar old hymn, but the reading developed both sentiment and beauty I had never before observed in it. A short, solemn, sweet prayer followed, and then the sermon. The hymn was, "Away, my unbelieving fear," and the text was Phil. iv. 6, 7. The skeleton of the sermon may be found by turning to the second of his published discourses; but, alas! it is merely the skeleton. The living, pale, but beautiful little *man* is not there. His clear, sweet voice, not loud and startling, but low, distinct, and musical as the melancholy notes of an Æolian harp, are not heard; the expressive, dove-like eye; the symmetrical, diminutive form, weighing not over 110 pounds; the pallid face, at first wearing a cast of sadness, then beaming with intellect, and presently half radiant "with thoughts that breathe;" and the few gestures in which the whole man speaks out, and give emphasis to the "words that burn"—all are wanting. The sermon was simple and practical; and while it was evident that he suppressed his imagination, yet a few flashes of chaste and thrilling imagery seemed spontaneously and irresistibly to burst forth. The effect was, the vast concourse retired instructed, impressed, and edified. The following year he fell, by consumption, into a state of great debility, which neither a sea-voyage, nor the genial climate of Southern France, nor the best medical skill, could arrest. On June 13, 1825, he died in peace, and went to rest.

Nearly fifty years have transpired since this "bright particular star" rose in splendor and beauty in our ecclesiastical sky, and, after attracting the eyes and winning the hearts of thousands, sunk beneath the horizon in cloudless effulgence. Truly does the poet Montgomery describe him as "the delight of wondering, weeping, and admiring audiences wherever he went."

Such was the holy man whose many letters—written neatly and correctly to his "dear Bishop"—now lie before me, and such the gifted and sainted genius who called forth the fatherly affection of his venerable friend. Who can doubt they have long since met and embraced each other again in their "Father's house"?

CHAPTER IV.

Richard Reece and John Hannah messengers from England—Mr. Reece's letter—Bishop McKendree's reply—He goes through Kentucky—Rests five days in ninety-five—Attends Kentucky Conference with Bishop Roberts—J. B. Finley and Dr. M. Ruter—Thence to Jonesboro, East Tennessee—Attends the Holston Conference—Lynchburg—Hez. G. Leigh—Portsmouth—Attends the Baltimore, Philadelphia, New York, and Genesee Conferences—Thence to South Carolina—Virginia in the spring of 1827—Baltimore—Philadelphia—Thence west to the Wyandotte Mission, through Ohio—Kentucky Conference—Winters in Tennessee—In 1828, he and Gwin go to the General Conference at Pittsburgh—Retrospect—A true, apostolic "*episcopos*"—Jesse Walker—Bishop McKendree's characteristics—Old Gray—Another round—Philip Bruce—Jefferson and Adams die—South Carolina Conference in Augusta, January 11, 1827—Roberts and Soule there also—Back to Baltimore—Sick—Gets to the Wyandottes, then to Nashville—His skeptical doctor convinced—Freeborn Garrettson's death—Indian letter—Henry Smith's letter—Letter from Lewis Garrett.

THE REV. RICHARD REECE, the messenger of the Wesleyan Methodists of England to the General Conference of 1824, was an aged, dignified, and worthy representative of the body which deputed him, and manifested the liveliest interest in the spiritual welfare of American Methodism. His companion, the Rev. John Hannah, was a much younger man, but was a profound and able minister. The former long since closed his consistent and useful life—the latter more recently, after having filled repeatedly the presidential chair of the Conference, and of one of the famous Wesleyan Theological Schools. They closely observed the operations of our system of Church-government, and after they returned to England, Bishop McKendree received the following interesting letter from Mr. Reece, dated September 27, 1825:

Reverend and Dear Sir:—I reflect with sincere pleasure on the few months which I spent on the American continent, and the free and affectionate intercourse which I had with the members of your Church, or, in English phrase, "of your Society." The kind attentions which I everywhere received, from the preachers and the people, have laid me under additional obligation to do and to say all that I can to promote the individual happiness of my friends, and to advance the prosperity of Wesleyan Methodism, which is the cause of Christ—with this cause all our happiness and usefulness is identified. Can I do this more effectually than by stating what has appeared to me to be a difference between our system of discipline, or action, and yours, and then leaving you to determine whether the peculiarity of your circumstances renders a conformity to our plan impracticable, and your own better adapted to spread and establish scriptural Christianity through your vast country?

1. With us it is an indispensable duty of the pas-

toral office to see the individual members of our society every quarterly visitation *at least*, to know how their souls prosper, and then to renew the quarterly ticket, with suitable advice, admonition, and reproof, and also to receive the quarterage which every one gives. This brings the pastor and his flock into close and immediate contact and intercourse; and while the one acquires a knowledge of the spiritual state and improvement of the souls committed to his care, the others have an opportunity of freely stating their cases, and opening their hearts to him who is appointed to watch over them as one that must give an account to God. By this the parties are mutually endeared, and the public ministrations of the preacher are more acceptable and more efficient. The delivery of the quarterly tickets is peculiarly, exclusively, and indispensably the duty of the preacher.

2. In addition to this, we are bound to meet the societies every Sunday evening, after preaching, when we speak pointedly to them on the discharge of relative duties—the government of their families, the religious instruction of their children, their diligent attendance on all the ordinances of God, their observance of the rules, and many other subjects which have an important influence on the formation of the Christian character. I have feared that your custom of beginning public worship so late as eight o'clock must greatly hinder this, if it do not supersede it. I grant, the labor of the preacher is greatly increased, but to these we are inured.

3. Our *band-meetings* have a most powerful influence on the experience and improvement of our people. The deep things of God form the subject of their conversation at these meetings, and the freedom and openness with which they speak upon them promotes their intellectual growth, so that these often become the most exemplary and useful members of our societies, furnishing male and female leaders of a high and excellent character. Mr. Wesley was aware of the importance of this part of Methodist discipline, and he used to say, "Where there are no bands there is no Methodism."

4. The leaders of our classes are required to collect *weekly* what each member can give to the support of the work, according to the rule, and to mark it down in the class-papers, and at our weekly leaders' meeting to pay this into the hands of the society-steward—by which means a supply is provided for the support of the preachers; and, as the sum is small which is individually subscribed, it is not felt a burden by the poorest of our members, nor does it excite discontent on complaint—on the contrary, the people are more alive to the interests of a cause which they support.

In your scattered population, it would be difficult for the preachers to carry the whole of the Methodist discipline into effective operation; but in those cities and towns which I visited, I could see no insurmountable obstacles. All that I could perceive wanting was a vigorous and united determination among the preachers to act in concert in carrying the point. Many of the people with whom I had intercourse greatly long to see these things established among them, convinced of the general advantage which would result from them to the body, and indeed to the country at large.

I thought of multiplying these remarks, but at present will desist.

It has afforded me much satisfaction to learn that the spirit of innovation, which prevailed when I was with you, has subsided, and is likely to evaporate without doing much evil.

I wrote to Dr. Jennings on the subject of his publishing Mark Robinson's pamphlet, and sent him a copy of a review which places that subject in a proper light, claiming, on the ground of "mutual rights," that it might be inserted in that publication. English Methodism will then be presented in a more correct light before our American brethren—which we are anxious should be the case. Whether he will comply with my request, I have not heard; but as the review was quickly afterward sent to your editors, in our July and August magazines, possibly they may insert it in their publication. If we can mutually benefit each other, and contribute to the greater efficiency of Wesleyan Methodism on both sides of the Atlantic, the great end of our more frequent and free intercourse will be answered.

I send you a copy of the Minutes of our last Conference, from which you will see that the increase of our members has been but small—for which we are not able to assign any reason, as the general state of our societies is prosperous as it regards stability and a deepening of the work of God. However, our prospects are encouraging. A glorious revival has commenced in the Isle of Man since the Conference, and is now extending very much. Many sinners are awakened and converted to God, and many of the believers have received a deep baptism of the Holy Ghost, preparing them to be "vessels unto honor, meet for the Master's use," in extending and establishing this work.

We have lost two most valuable men, in the vigor of their life, since the Conference—highly gifted, eminently holy and useful men—removed suddenly from the work and their families. The dispensation is mysterious, but the rod has a voice, and speaks impressively, "All flesh is grass, and the goodliness thereof as the flower of the grass," etc. Others, it is true, are raised up to supply their places, but their knowledge, experience, and godly influence are not soon acquired; their loss is therefore painfully felt.

We are looking forward to the next Conference with pleasure, when we expect to receive our American brother, the messenger of the Churches, and are praying that he may come in the fullness of the blessings of the gospel, and bring us glad tidings of your prosperity. May his coming be a blessing to us, and contribute to our encouragement and edification! I beg to be kindly remembered to all my American brethren and friends with whom you may meet in your travels. I remember them with growing affection, and hope to meet them in a better state, where there are no separations. I am, reverend and dear sir, your affectionate friend and brother, R. REECE.

To which the Bishop replied from Baltimore, July 10, 1826:

REVEREND AND DEAR BROTHER:—Your kind and truly interesting letter of September 27, 1825, did not reach me till the 4th instant. This will account for what otherwise might appear to be unjustifiable delay in reciprocating your favor. Accept my thanks for your letter and the documents accompanying it. I shall always rejoice to hear from you. Letters, or pamphlets, addressed to the care of Armstrong & Plaskit, of this city, will hardly fail to reach me.

Your friendly visit to this country could not have been more pleasing to yourself than to the American preachers and societies who were favored with a personal acquaintance with you, or had the opportunity of enjoying the benefit of your ministerial labors. In addition to every personal and individual consideration, your visit to us was rendered deeply interesting, as it was the pledge of union, in doctrine, discipline, and affection, between the Wesleyan Methodists throughout the world; and I trust that I shall not cease to pray to the God and Father of our Lord Jesus Christ, who is Head over all things to the Church, that the same faith, and order, and brotherly love may continue and abound more and more. That there has been and still is considerable laxity in regard to discipline among us, in the particulars which you notice, is certain; and the effects are to be deplored. For it is very obvious that as the rules of the societies are neglected, or the administration let down in accommodation to the wealth, influence, habits, or education of men, or from whatever other cause, there will be a loss in experimental and practical holiness—in inward and outward conformity to God. Two circumstances have had very considerable influence in producing and perpetuating this laxity. The first is the *vast extent* of our field of labor. We occupy, with pretty closely connected circuits, Districts, and Conferences, the whole of the Atlantic States, extending from the Bay of Fundy to the Gulf of Mexico—a distance of more than two thousand miles, on the most direct post-roads—and have spread over the frontier States and Territories situated from five hundred to one thousand miles from the ocean. Occupying such an extensive country, where the inhabitants are collected from nearly all the civilized nations of the world, and where the emigration from one State to another is perpetual, it is extremely difficult, not to say impossible, to establish and preserve the discipline of the Church as effectually as might be done in a condensed and permanent state of society. *The infancy of our ministry* is closely connected with the extent of our labor, and tends to render the administration of discipline inefficient. Most of the preachers in this country enter the Connection very young, and without any extraordinary advantages of education; and, in general, the means of improvement in their circuits are very limited. Locations are frequent; consequently, we have comparatively very few men of age and experience in the itinerant work. In many instances, we are compelled to commit the charge, not only of circuits, but of Districts also, to young men of too little experience for such stations. But, notwithstanding this state of things, we have ground to hope for better days, especially since the last General Conference. Among the preachers generally, there appears to be a conviction of the necessity of a more *uniform* and *diligent* attention to a strict observance of the rules. It has become a subject of serious interest in the deliberations of the Annual Conferences; and many thousands of our members, especially those who have seen both the *former* and the *latter* times, are earnestly desirous of the same thing.

The appointment of a messenger to visit your Conference the present year (as you will have heard before this letter arrives) has failed; but I am happy to say that the failure was not occasioned, even in the most remote manner, by a want of disposition to cultivate the most friendly and harmonious intercourse with our brethren in England, but from causes altogether extraneous and local. But, although we have not been able to accomplish this desirable object the present year, I indulge the hope that it will be effected the next; and I trust that the visitation will not be unacceptable to our British brethren on account of a year's delay.

We have much cause of gratitude to God for the increasing prosperity of the work generally, through these States. The increase of members the last year, commencing with the Mississippi and closing with the Tennessee Conference, was upward of *twenty thousand*, and the increase of preachers for the same period *eighty-one.*

There is cause to believe that the exertions which have been made to produce disaffection to the government and discipline of the Church, will fail to accomplish the desired effect to any considerable extent, and that, in the ministry and membership, we shall still preserve the "unity of the Spirit in the bond of peace." The history of those who have separated themselves from us and set up "altar against altar," is not calculated to afford ground of gratulation or encouragement to adventurers, but rather marks the enterprise as hazardous. The itinerant ministry, preserved in the "demonstration of the Spirit and of power," will be our *salt*, and the *salt* of the earth. The great body of local preachers and members are identified in doctrine, spirit, and order with the great *itinerant system.* Attacks have been made upon us, and will be repeated. Men, ambitious of rule and restless under the administration of wholesome and godly discipline, will not cease to complain of injured rights, grievances, and oppression; and in every extensive community individuals will be found to respond to these complaints. Such individuals have appeared among the Methodists on both sides of the Atlantic; but hitherto the great body of the ministers and members has been firm and steadfast, and I trust will continue to be "strong in the Lord, and in the power of his might," and to "abound more and more in the unity and fellowship of saints."

The success of our missionary labors is cause of encouragement, gratitude, and joy. Although the number of our stations and our means of supplying them are small, compared with those of our British brethren, we are (thanks be to God!) accomplishing a great and blessed work. Thousands of the poor and scattered population of the States and Territories are through this means receiving the blessing of the gospel of Christ. Most of our missions among the Indians have succeeded far beyond the most sanguine expectations of their warmest friends at the commencement. You will be in possession, it is probable, of the latest official reports from the missionaries and the Board of Managers, before this reaches you, in which you will have a more circumstantial account than could well be furnished in a private letter.

In view of the great and marvelous work which God has wrought, in the four quarters of the globe, by the instrumentality of the Methodists, since the day on which he raised up that "*burning and shining light*," the Rev. John Wesley, of most precious memory, it is very meet that we should be *humble* and *thankful*, and, as regards the future, that we should *strive together* in the *meekness* of Christ, and in steadfast dependence upon divine agency, till truth and righteousness fill the whole earth.

As it respects myself, the time of my departure cannot be far off. I have entered the seventieth year of my pilgrimage, and now tremble, leaning on my staff. Goodness and mercy have followed me all the days of my life, and *the witness of the Spirit* and the "*hope of the gospel*" are the solace of my age.

Grace, mercy, and peace be multiplied to thee and to the Church of God, through our Lord and Saviour Jesus Christ! Amen.

Yours affectionately, W. McKENDREE.

So soon as the roads became passable in the spring of 1825, the Bishop started from his brother's, in Tennessee, and resumed his labors in visiting the Churches and preaching. On the 15th of April he left home, or—if that term does not apply to a man who, like his Lord, never really had a home on earth—Fountain Head. He reached Slaughter's, Kentucky, in the rain, on the 16th; preached there on the 17th, from John iii. 19–22; preached in Russellville on the 20th; at Cook's Meeting-house on the 22d, from Matt. v. 6; preached Fell's funeral-sermon on the 24th; on the 26th, preached from Matt. xi. 30; traveled through "a great rain" to James's; through rain again, to Staley's and Taylor's; another funeral-sermon, May 1st, from Isaiah lxv. 22; funeral-sermon next day, from 1 Sam. xii. 23; then to Barret's, Owen's, Mount Zion, and so on, through Hardinsburg, to Lebanon, preaching or traveling every day. Thence he proceeded to B. McHenry's, Springfield, Puller's, and Ferguson's, and preached nearly every day, until June 3d, when he reports himself sick. But in a day or two he is on his way again, twenty miles, to a quarterly-meeting. Thus on he goes, through Harrisburg, Lexington, and Georgetown, by Leroy Cole's, etc., etc., until he reaches Cynthiana, June 17th, resting only five in ninety-five days. Pretty good work for an old, afflicted man! Most of our young preachers would think it hard work.

On this tour he falls in with Brother B. T. Crouch, and spends a month with him, as already related. Then we lose sight of him for a short time, but presently he is found in Shelbyville, attending the Kentucky Conference with Bishop Roberts at Russellville, September 22, 1825, and we find among his papers regular Minutes of the whole proceedings of the body—Appointments and all. There he gets a long letter from the Rev. J. B. Finley, the laborious and useful missionary to the Wyandottes. He answers with a heart warm to his correspondent and full of love to the Indians. He almost shouts in the letter, saying, "The Lord is *very* good to me. My spiritual strength is renewed; I am growing in grace, and ripening for heaven; for which I desire to be deeply thankful, and entirely devoted to God." There, too, he gets a kind letter from that noble and devoted servant of the Church, the Rev. Martin Ruter, who threw himself, from the purest religious motives, into the active duties of the missionary work, and fell a martyr to the cause in Texas, where his remains and his memory are honored by his brethren.

Whether the two great bodies of American Methodism, which separated in 1844, will ever again unite, is very uncertain. At present this seems improbable, not to say impracticable; but certainly there are ties which tend to amity and fraternity of a strong and peculiar nature. A common origin, similarity of creed, Church-polity, and usages, and a strong affection and sacred reminiscences of many honored and precious names, equally dear to both, must exert an attracting influence upon them. Among many other names, Dr. Martin Ruter's is one.

From the seat of the Kentucky Conference he takes our old route over the Cumberland Mountain, and through East Tennessee to Jonesboro, where the Holston Conference held its session. Thence crossing the Alleghany Mountains, he reaches Lynchburg, Virginia, attends a quarterly-meeting with Hezekiah G. Leigh, of honored and precious memory, and hastens down through the snow to the quarterly-meeting on old Greenville Circuit, where he exercised his early ministry, and where are found "our most disaffected members of this District." He reaches Mecklenburg, December 5th, to recruit and write letters—one of them to Bishop Soule, in Milledgeville, Georgia. Portsmouth brings him to a short halt: from there to Baltimore, Philadelphia, New York, and Genesee Conferences, and returns to the South in the fall. The following winter he spent in attending the South Carolina and Virginia Conferences, and came back to the Baltimore and Philadelphia Conferences in the spring of 1827. At the close of the Philadelphia session he returns to Baltimore, and in May starts back to the West; crossing the Alleghany Mountains by way of Cumberland; passing into Ohio to visit, for the third time, his beloved Wyandottes and their faithful missionaries. Returning, he again passed through Urbana, and visited many of the towns in the southern part of Ohio, and attended the Kentucky Conference in Versailles in October. Thence he went down into Tennessee, and spent the winter among his friends, visiting the societies, and preaching as he was able.

In March, 1828, he set out with two delegates of that Conference—one of them his old friend, James Gwin—for Pittsburgh, the seat of the General Conference, and arrived there a few days before it began.

Having thus given a concise account of his travels and labors for the past four years, and up to the session of another General Conference, we have reached a point from which it is proper to retrospect the past. We see a man who has been granted a superannuated relation for the last eight years, and requested to do only such service as his health and convenience might justify, now over seventy years of age, enfeebled by forty years' incessant toil, afflicted with rheumatism, piles, hernia, vertigo, and asthma, and yet making the circuit of the United States annually, not in stage-coaches over macadamized roads, nor on railroads, but generally on horseback—slowly traversing Indian territory, climbing mountains, fording and sometimes swimming swollen streams, through muddy roads and swamps, often lying in miserable huts and open, dirty cabins, subsisting, frequently of necessity, on coarse and badly-cooked food, going through malarious regions under a burning sun, and then through the rains, and sleet, and snows of winter; of a temperament peculiarly sensitive, carrying on a correspondence with persons in every part of the country, and above all, oppressed with "the care of all the Churches." And yet he never willingly ceased his painful travel, nor murmured at the hardships and sufferings endured! And was not he a true "Overseer?" a Pauline "Episcopos?" a real New Testament *Bishop?* What if he could not trace an undoubted personal ordinal succession from Peter or John? Who really can? And what if any one can? Alexander VI., Leo X., John XII., Benedict IX., Sylvester III., and Gregory VII.—"horrible monsters as ever lived"—even the four popes living at the same time—each anathematizing the others, and calling them devils and antichrists—yet each and all claimed it.

Equally absurd is the claim of the *Protestant* Church of England—the Church of Henry VIII., whose "Majesty is the only supreme head of the Church of England and Ireland"—which, in severing her allegiance from the Romish Church, claimed to do so, not, of course, on the ground of succession, but of prescription—*i. e.*, a right before and independent of all written law—a "divine right"

—and yet, from the youngest proselyte to the Episcopacy, they are now claiming that they only are the successors, by virtue of their official lineage, of the apostles; while Coke, Asbury, and McKendree are not Bishops at all! Well, let the Chief Shepherd decide.

Among the many correspondents of the Bishop during 1825, he received one letter from his old friend and co-laborer, Jesse Walker, dated Sangamon, Illinois, May 18, 1825. Mr. Walker was a rare character. He joined the Tennessee Conference in 1802, and traveled under Bishop McKendree as his Presiding Elder for several years. His literary education was quite limited, and he was a married man. Bishop McKendree was an excellent judge of men, and soon selected him to take the van of the pioneer army of preachers in the West; and the result vindicated his wisdom. Jesse Walker was a brave, self-reliant, zealous Christian minister. He feared only God, and his great purpose was to be good and useful. The poor, the frontier settlements, where women and children endured the hardships of isolation from society, and were exposed to the tomahawk, the scalping-knife, and, what was worse, to the torture of fathers and sons, and the captivity of wives and daughters, excited his sympathies; and the poor pagan Indians themselves, often as "much sinned against as sinning," aroused his Christian zeal. He may have had also an inclination for adventure, and an instinctive passion for a roving life among the grand old forests and the wide, flowering prairies of the West. But his ruling passion was to preach Christ "in *the regions beyond*." For this kind of life he was admirably adapted, physically, intellectually, and morally. To a constitution of iron—a strong, compact frame, capable of great endurance — was added a calm, shrewd mind of fine common sense, and a wonderful aptitude to adapt himself to his circumstances, and thus gain the confidence and exert a controlling influence over the rude settlers of the backwoods, and the more wary and suspicious Indians. Tennessee, Kentucky, Illinois, Indiana, and Missouri were the fields of his labor. He planted the gospel in St. Louis, and by his personal effort built the first Methodist Church there. He has been styled the Daniel Boone of the Church, but he was more: his impulses were holier, his motives and ends were nobler. He had a tender and manly love for his wife, and an occasional visit to his home was relished as a religious holiday. His family enjoyed the narratives of his travels and toils, and entered into his feelings and plans for the good of souls. From his letter to the Bishop, now before us, we learn he had established missions among the Indians at Fort Clarke and Chicago, and was about to go farther north-west to other tribes. He survived Bishop McKendree only eight months, and died calmly at home in Illinois, saying, "God has been with me from the time of my conversion, and is still with me." Few preachers have equaled him in enduring hardness as a good soldier, or been so useful as a missionary on the frontiers and among the wild Indians.

Little things sometimes better develop the true character of a man than his professions or public actions, as the finer touches of the limner's pencil best reveal the original. The great ocean is made of little drops of water; the Himalaya Mountains by the aggregation of small particles: so of great characters. Bishop McKendree was not transcendently great in any thing: others surpassed him in many particulars, and yet, in the aggregate, very few equaled him. Some are great in great things, but small in little things—intellectually great, but deficient in heart, and practically useless, if not pernicious—and they resemble a huge, bare mountain, composed of blocks of volcanic rocks: not a tree or shrub hides its ruggedness, nor a single wild-flower adorns it, nor even a lichen or sprig of Iceland-moss finds foothold for its hardy roots; but the snow-crowned and ice-clad monarch is utterly barren of good, and serves only to chill the air and dwarf the vegetation around its base. So was Lord Byron. Bishop McKendree was only a man, a frail, fallen one, like all his race; but he was a full-grown and symmetrically-proportioned man, in body, mind, and heart; and the whole man was permeated and elevated by piety. He had not only a mind of rare analytical and logical acumen, of extraordinary legislative and administrative ability, but of strong and tender sympathies. No unfortunate preacher need ever be afraid to approach and tell him all his wants and woes. He was stern only toward sin, and exacting toward himself alone. The following incident will at once illustrate his kind and genial nature:

Like all the early Methodist preachers of the ecclesiastical cavalry corps, he valued his horse. He did not *swap* horses, and did not profess much skill in judging as to age, etc.: when obliged to get a horse, he usually deputed some old friend, who better understood the subject, to swap or purchase one for him; but when he got one that suited him, no money could purchase it. If his horse got sick or lame, he would leave him in good hands and buy another, and in six or twelve months would return, or send for him. An instance of this kind occurred in 1825, on one of his long tours, and, from a letter before us, he had written back to Tennessee for his nephew to go for him and take good care of him until he should return. It was his famous "*Old Gray*." He had ridden this horse again and again around the circuit of the United States. His qualities as a riding-horse suited his aged master. They suited each other, and there was a strong mutual attachment. Gray was almost as well known by thousands as was his owner. In the Bishop's last will and testament, he bequeathed to Old Gray money sufficient out of his little savings to furnish him a plenty of food, a good stable, a nice bluegrass pasture for life, and an honorable burial. The last time we heard from Old Gray, he was about thirty years old, and was fat and flourishing in a gray old age.

The events of 1826 were too important to be passed over cursorily. We have followed Bishop McKendree from the West to Virginia, and through the snows of the winter of 1825–6, making his toilsome journey to Portsmouth: there meeting Bishop Soule, they presided over the Virginia Conference, Feb. 15, 1826, where the project was initiated for the establishment of a literary institution of high grade, which ultimated in founding Randolph Macon College. On March 8th, the Baltimore Conference was attended by the same Bishops. The Philadelphia Conference followed, April 12th; and on May 7th, Bishop McKendree preached and dedicated Willett Street Church, in New York, Bishop Soule preaching in the afternoon, and Bishop Hedding at night. May 15th, the seventh Anniversary of the Missionary Society of the Methodist Episcopal Church was held in old John Street Church, New York, Bishop McKendree presiding, Bishops Soule and Hedding, Dr. Bangs, Dr. Luckey, Dr. Fisk, Samuel Merwin, and Freeborn Garrettson, taking parts in the meeting. It was an exceedingly interesting occasion. The place in which it was held—the cradle of American Methodism—the venerable and talented ministers who bore a conspicuous position in it, as well as the great object of the meeting, all conspired to give it dignity and interest.

The New York Conference began May 10, 1826, attended by the three Bishops named; and the Genesee Conference began at Palmyra, New York, June 7th, Bishops McKendree and Hedding presiding. A camp-meeting, attended by ten thousand persons, was held in a grove at the same time. Bishop McKendree preached at ten o'clock Sunday to this immense concourse.

May 10th, the Bishop's old colleague and long-tried friend, Philip Bruce, died in Giles county, Tennessee, in the triumph of Christian faith. He entered the itinerancy in 1781—seven years earlier than the Bishop—and died a superannuated member of the Virginia Conference. He was a wise, holy, and useful man; assisted greatly in laying the foundation of the government of the Church, and was always true and faithful to its interests. The Bishop mourned his death as a brother.*

After attending the Philadelphia Conference, in

---

*When Philip Bruce became an itinerant preacher in 1781, there were only about 20 preachers, and less than 10,000 members in America. (See Minutes, 1780.) He is said to have been teaching school in North Carolina when the war of the Revolution occurred—quit his school, raised a company of volunteers, acted gallantly in the great battle of King's Mountain, and became distinguished for his zeal and usefulness as a preacher. He was for many years a Presiding Elder in the Virginia Conference; bore a conspicuous part in forming the constitution and polity of the Church, and was regarded by Asbury and McKendree as a wise and trusty adviser; and, after he had become superannuated, he came to Tennessee, and resided at his brother's. The writer knew him well, and revered and loved him greatly. He was indeed a holy, cheerful, and useful preacher. Dr. G. D. Taylor, who was with him at his death, says the night before he died he requested "to be left alone with God." And when the doctor entered his room, at the early dawn of day, and asked how he was, and how he had spent the night, his countenance brightened, and he replied: "O doctor, I am perfectly happy! I have been almost in heaven all night! Such views of God—of Christ and glory!" And thus, in perfect rapture, he passed from earth to heaven. Like McKendree, he never married, but gave his whole life to God and Methodism; and, like him, he died happy. He professed to enjoy the blessings of sanctifying grace; he preached it; lived an exemplification of it, and

June, he returned South by way of Baltimore, arriving in Washington City soon after the 4th of July, upon which day Thomas Jefferson and John Adams died, just fifty years after they subscribed the Declaration of Independence. Thus its author and its ablest advocate "were not in death divided."

August 29th, Bishop McKendree leaves his old friend Foxhall's, Georgetown, to go South and attend the South Carolina Conference, at Augusta, Georgia, passing through and preaching (1 Thess. v. 21–24) in Fairfax, Fauquier, and Culpepper counties, to Madison Camp-meeting, where he preached twice, (Isa. xlv. 22;) thence to Timberlake's, in Fluvanna, where he preached three times at a camp-meeting, (Matt. v. 6, Matt. xi. 28–30, Eph. vi. 1–4.)

He attended and preached three times the next week at a camp-meeting in Nelson county; the same the following week at the Buckingham Camp-meeting; then at a camp-meeting in Mecklenburg, and spent a few days among his old friends—Edmund, Howell, and Allen Taylor—preaching nearly every day. Thence, crossing Roanoke, through Granville and Person counties, North Carolina, to a camp-meeting in Halifax, Virginia; and thence, resuming his route, through Caswell and Guilford, North Carolina, stopping to rest a day at Menden-

---

died its witness. He resided in the immediate neighborhood of my father; baptized, married, and buried several of our family, and was a great blessing to the community, even in his extreme old age. His memory is dear to many, and to none more than to the writer. What a state of society must that be in heaven, made up of such as he! But a greater and lovelier than he is there!

hall's, after riding thirty-four miles the previous day, attending several meetings. Crossing Pe Dee River, he pushed forward to Columbia, South Carolina; thence to Charleston, Dec. 9, 1826. Here he rested a few days — if preaching, writing, and visiting daily, may be called resting; and, after attending two quarterly-meetings, and preaching four times on the way, he arrived in Augusta, Georgia, Jan. 8, 1827.

The South Carolina Conference commenced here January 11th, Bishops Roberts and Soule being present. The three Bishops, after the close of the Conference, left in company: Bishop Roberts went home, and the other two traveled back to Baltimore together, going through Camden, Fayetteville, Raleigh, Fredericksburg, and Georgetown, arriving at Baltimore, March 27th; and, after attending and presiding at Conferences and Anniversaries in Baltimore, Philadelphia, and New York, Bishop McKendree gets back to Baltimore, May 4th, and reports himself *sick*—and no wonder.

Thus, in his seventieth year, did he go on—on, in his never-ceasing round of travel and sufferings.

We have already referred to the fact that his next move was for his Indian friends; and, after a long and wearisome ride, he again gets to the Wyandottes, June 16, 1827; thence back again to Tennessee, where winter overtook him and compelled him to lie up until spring. Here, in the society of his relatives, and at Nashville, in the hospitable mansions of Joseph T. Elliston—whose excellent wife had been the widow of his beloved and lamented co-laborer,

Learner Blackman—and H. R. W. Hill, both of whom kept a room known as the Bishop's room, where he was ever welcome and most kindly treated, he passed much of his time during the winters spent in Tennessee, always busy writing or reading. An incident occurred about this time at Mr. Elliston's, which is perhaps worth recording. He was very sick, and suffering exquisitely. A doctor was called, and, upon examining his venerable patient, became alarmed, and also greatly surprised, that under such torturing pain he was so quiet and uncomplaining, and referred to it, saying, "Bishop, how can you bear such pain so quietly?" The old gentleman opened his eyes, and looking with a smile at the inquirer, answered, "Doctor, does your philosophy explain how a Christian can be perfectly happy while his body is in agony? Must there not be a soul in him?" The doctor was silent, for he was skeptical, and then said, "Bishop, *it must be so.*"

On Sept. 27, 1827, Freeborn Garrettson, another of the Bishop's old fellow-laborers, and a most laborious, useful, and lovely man, died in New York. He was a native of Maryland; born 1752; converted in 1775, and began to preach the same year. His labors extended throughout Maryland, Pennsylvania, New York, and New England, Virginia, North Carolina, and Nova Scotia. His faithful and highly useful life as an itinerant preacher was continued to his death, covering an eventful period in Methodism of fifty-two years. His piety was profound and uniform; and few men have done more for Methodism and for the conversion and salvation of souls. He had recently parted for the last time from the Bishop at the New York Conference. The year previously, Bishops McKendree and Hedding had visited and rested several days at his hospitable house at Rhinebeck; and, just before his death, he had been again elected a delegate to the General Conference of 1828, but his long and arduous labors were succeeded by perpetual rest, and his spirit went to God who gave it. He lived and died professing perfect love, and his life and dying testimony vindicated the truthfulness of his profession. He was greatly and justly respected in life, and his name and memory are honored by all who knew him.

Throughout the whole ministerial life of Bishop McKendree, we are impressed with his devotion to the cause of missions. The frontier settlers, Africa, the slaves in America, and the Indians, all shared in his sympathies and efforts. Here we find him again enduring another long and tiresome journey to visit the Indians; and that this affectionate concern for their spiritual welfare was appreciated by them, the following letter demonstrates:

Upper Sandusky, Sept. 5, 1825.

FATHER:—On the 5th day of the first fall month we are assembled together, and all of us salute you in the Lord; returning thanks to God that he has spared us all alive, and that all the leaders that you saw here when you were with us last, are still alive, and have good health, with most of our Nation.

Bishop McKendree, Father in the Church, we, your brethren and children, send you this letter to let you know some of the good that has fallen to us through your exertions in sending us the most blessed gospel. We still are watching and laboring, and are determined to do so till the end comes. Many of our people are still on their way to heaven, and are happy in the love of God; and we, your leaders in the Church, are still going from house to house, and trying with all our might to banish all evil from amongst our people.

But, father, we must tell you the bad with the good. Some of our people slid back. This we know will not be so pleasant for you to hear; but you must pity us and help us by your prayers: though we are not out of heart, for we still believe the Lord will hear our prayers, and the work we will never give up. Although we have many difficulties to encounter, the Lord helps us, and we are much encouraged, and we think we are gaining strength. One of our chiefs—Warpole—that did not belong to us, has joined, and this day was received into full connection, and appointed one of the leaders. We hope he will prove faithful, and make us a strong stake.

The school is still prospering, and our children are like the buds of the trees in the spring; and although we have not yet tasted the ripe fruit, we see the blossoms, and rejoice in expectation, and believe we will not be disappointed. We still pray that you continue your care for us and our children; and through you we return our thanks to all our friends that have contributed to help forward this great work among our Nation. We hope they will not get tired, but as they have helped us to wake out of our deep sleep, and on to our feet, they will still help until we can walk and gather food for ourselves.

In our farming business we are still on the march, and go the slower because we are poor and unacquainted with the business; but our condition is altered very much for the better. Father, when we last took you by the hand, you told us you was old, and did never expect to see us again. This made us very sorry, but we still hoped God would bring you back this last summer; but we heard you do not expect to get here. It may be God will appoint a day for us to see one another on earth again; but if not, we are determined to do as you told us, and hold fast until we meet in heaven. There we hope to meet you, and all your brothers in the ministry. Father, we cannot express our minds to you and your brothers (the Bishops) as we feel for the gospel; and we do thank you all, and want you to know that we pray for you all, and we hope you will not forget to pray for us.

BETWEEN-THE-LOGS, his × mark.
JOHN HICKS, his × mark.
MENONCUE, his × mark.
PEACOCK, his × mark.
GEORGE PUNCH, his × mark.
SUMMENDERWITT, his × mark.
HARREHOOT, his × mark.
JAMES BIG TREE, his × mark.

This letter was dictated by Between-the-logs and Menoncue, and interpreted by Isaac Walker, United States Interpreter, and written by myself as interpreted.

Certified by me. J. B. FINLEY.

We cannot forego the pleasure of inserting here the following letter to the author from the Rev. Henry Smith. He entered the traveling connection in 1794, and was associated with the Bishop, both in the Atlantic and Western Conferences, for many years. It was written in 1855, having heard that the writer had been requested to prepare and publish the life of the Bishop. He was then residing near Baltimore, and was among the oldest, if not the very oldest, of living itinerant Methodist preachers, being eighty-five years of age, and about sixty years in the itinerancy. He has since gone to rest. The greater part was written by a lady-friend at his dictation—the remainder by his own aged and trembling hand. It is a valuable memorial of its venerated author, as well as an affectionate tribute to the memory of his beloved old col league and friend.

To Bishop R. Paine:

REVEREND AND DEAR SIR:—I am truly glad that we are at last to have a Memoir, or Life, of that extraordinary man, Bishop McKendree. I think the Conference has been happy in their selection, and have reason to believe it will be a fair and impartial history of that excellent man and his times. I fear you are not furnished ample matter to enable you to do justice to your subject. Our early preachers seemed to have lived and labored not for history, but for the generation they were appointed to serve: a Garrettson and Watters have left something to perpetuate their memory, but of the talented E. Cooper and his associates, the present generation knows very little.

Now, dear Bishop, it would give me pleasure, and I would esteem it an honor, to furnish you with some material to make your Life of McKendree complete; but alas! my sight and memory are greatly impaired: withal, I am troubled with vertigo, and my kind doctor forbids me to read or write much; but when my old and esteemed friend Bishop McKendree is concerned, I am inclined to disobey the doctor, and venture to furnish you with a few scraps: perhaps you can pick something out of them.

Of Bishop McKendree's early history I personally know nothing; and yet I think I can correct Dr. McClintock in one thing which he says in his sketch of McKendree, on page 69. That William McKendree was a patriot of high order, there remains not a doubt; but from what he told me while riding over the ground in October, 1820, he belonged to a company of country volunteers, raised, I presume, in his immediate neighborhood. They were at the siege of Yorktown, and he pointed out to me the place where they were encamped, and where they were drilled; but what rank he sustained in the army, or what part he bore on that memorable occasion, I never heard him say; but McKendree could not be hid, nor found in the rear of any important enterprise. I never saw McKendree until May 4, 1800, at the Baltimore Conference, held at the Stone Chapel, about five miles from where I write. He preached to a crowded house, while Jesse Lee preached to a still greater crowd out of doors. His sermon showed plainly that he was "a workman that needeth not to be ashamed." On the General Conference floor, on the 6th of May, I first heard him exhibit his peculiar talent for debate: he certainly had a remarkable gift for analyzing and sifting a subject to the bottom. His clear, penetrating, far-seeing mind, qualified him for this. After this, I never saw Bishop McKendree until October 21, 1802, when he appeared as our Presiding Elder in Kentucky. We needed at that time just such a man. We had then a Bush, a Wilkerson, a Kobler, a Sale, a Page, and other worthy men; but still just such a spirit as our McKendree was needed. He succeeded in bringing a firmer union between the local and traveling ministry, and more fully getting our preachers and people to profit by the great revival which had just commenced. His charge was heavy, his responsibility great; but he never shunned responsibility where the cause of God was concerned. Though naturally a man of keen sensibilities, if he saw a storm coming, could shut up his feelings, as he used to call it, and calmly and boldly meet every difficulty; and then his clear, comprehensive mind and sound judgment developed itself. Those who had the pleasure of seeing and hearing Mr. McKendree can never forget him, and the present as well as future generations should gratefully remember his labors of love in the West. His administrations were judicious and wise, and were crowned with success. I presume Mr. McKendree was then in the prime of his life and usefulness. In the pulpit he was original, his method and oratory entirely his own; nothing artificial about it; natural and fascinating. His voice, though not loud and thundering, could be heard in the open air by thousands. His preaching was often attended with a soul-searching, melting, subduing influence, that bore down all before it. Christians were made too happy to jump and shout—yes, more than shouting happy—while sinners were cut to the heart. I saw and heard Bishop McKendree in his prime, and shall never hear or look on such another.

In the General Conference of 1808, he distinguished himself in favor of a delegated General Conference. I did not hear the sermon he preached in Light Street Church, in Baltimore, at this Conference, which Bishop Asbury said would make him a Bishop. The records will show that he was elected to the Episcopacy by an overwhelming majority.

At the first delegated General Conference, May 1, 1812, Bishop McKendree drew up a plan of business, to be brought before the Conference; but as it was a new thing, the aged Bishop Asbury rose to his feet immediately after the reading of the paper by the Secretary, and addressed the junior

Bishop to the following effect: "I have something to say to you before the Conference." The junior Bishop also rose to his feet, and they stood face to face. Bishop Asbury said, "This is a new thing. I never did business in this way, and why is it introduced?" The junior smiled, and promptly replied, "You are our father, and we are your sons: you never had need of it. But I am only a brother, and have need of it." The senior Bishop said no more, but sat down with a smile on his countenance. The scene is now before my mind.

The action of the General Conference, which met in Baltimore in 1820, relative to the Presiding-eldership question, greatly afflicted our worthy Bishop—the more so, as his colleagues differed with him in opinion on the subject. I had several conversations with one of them on the subject; and so far as I could learn, they were both, so far as personally concerned, satisfied with the rules as they were, but thought it best to yield this point for peace' sake—for they feared a split in the Church. Bishop McKendree conscientiously believed that as an important principle was involved, the measure was an infringement of our constitution, and fraught with mischief. All this bore heavily on his constitution, already broken by labor and care. I sympathized with him, and became his traveling companion, as he wished to travel for his health, and visit the Churches and families of his old friends. I knew the man in the vigor and tide of usefulness, and I now saw him almost a wreck; but his concern for the Church and his zeal for the cause of God were not at all abated.

On the 19th of June he left the house of his old friend, Dr. Henry Wilkins, and made a visit to Virginia, calling on many families, and preaching as often as he could. Upon our return to Baltimore, we called at a camp-meeting on Frederick Circuit, where the Bishop preached, and was divinely aided. The sermon had a prodigious effect, for he rose above his weakness, and it reminded me of former days. That sermon is still remembered and spoken of by a few of the many who heard it, the most of whom have passed away.

Very frequently we were on our way before daylight, and stopped by the wayside to refresh ourselves with what we had brought with us—and in this he rebuked many of the present race of preachers. He tried to imitate his Master, "who went about doing good."

I must here conclude by saying that I am sorry I can afford you so little aid. I should like to have a copy of your work, should I live to see it published. I am as well as I could expect to be, after passing through eighty-five winters. My general health is better than it was forty years ago, but weakness and the infirmities of age attend me; yet still "the Lord is the strength of my heart and my portion for ever." Respectfully and very affectionately, yours in the bonds of the gospel,

HENRY SMITH.

Pilgrim's Rest, Hooktown, Baltimore co., Md.,
February 6, 1855.

The Rev. Lewis Garrett, Sr., who died in peace, some years since, in Canton, Mississippi, sent the author several communications, from which the following extracts are made. Lewis Garrett entered the itinerant ministry at the same time with Henry Smith, in 1794, and, like him, traveled with the Bishop, both in Virginia and the West. He was a preacher of unusual power and force of character. He was Editor of the Western Methodist, published in Nashville, Tennessee, and wrote an interesting little volume of "Biographical Sketches," chiefly of Western preachers.

"In the autumn of 1795, I was called by Bishop Asbury to go from Holston to the Virginia Conference. On my way, at the house of a brother, I first saw Mr. McKendree. His plain and affable manner interested me. At the Conference he was appointed Presiding Elder of a District east of James River, and placed in charge of Williamsburg Circuit. I was appointed to Orange Circuit, in that District. In 1797, he presided over the same District enlarged, and extending from Gloucester to Greenbrier. In 1799, he presided over a District in the northern part of Virginia, embracing Alexandria. In 1800, he was on his old District, and I on Gloucester Circuit. We met at the General Conference, in Baltimore, May 1, 1800. The small-pox was very prevalent. I was inoculated—he knew it. Late at night he came to my room. I had had a chill—was covered up, and had a high fever. He jerked off the cover and alarmed me, showing much concern for my safety. He was a kind friend. In the fall of 1800, he was sent to Kentucky, where there was no Presiding Elder, and in 1801, presided over the whole Western country. Having lost my health in the lowlands of Virginia, I obtained leave to return to the West, and met him at the Western Conference, held at Earnest's, on Nolichucky, East Tennessee, October 1, 1801. He being appointed to the same District, and I to Lexington Circuit, Kentucky, we traveled together to Kentucky. This was an interesting journey to me, because I never met with a more agreeable traveling companion. Always prompt and 'at the time,' economical of time, and careful in preärrangement, a loiterer or one devoid of forecast would be left behind. He was also social and communicative.

"William McKendree had no talent for getting up or carrying on a revival; and yet his discourses were animating and instructive in a high degree. The great revival of 1800 had awakened inquiry. The dogmas of Calvin and Antinomian delusions had received a shock, and controversy was prevalent. Mr. McKendree was the man for the times. He was then robust and of commanding personal appearance. I have seen him enchain for two hours the attention of large crowds, with his ingenious, argumentative, and animating sermons. Though modest and retiring, when duty called he was prompt and fearless. In 1804 and 1805, I traveled Cumberland District, and he remained on the Kentucky District. In 1805, I located, and he succeeded me on the Cumberland District. We met again at the Western Conference, held at a camp-meeting at Liberty Hill, October, 1808. He was then Bishop. I love and respect his memory, and desire to see his successors imitate him in zeal, purity, and usefulness."

CHAPTER V.

General Conference of 1828 at Pittsburgh—Bishops' Address—Suspended resolutions lost—"Wesleyan Repository"—"Mutual Rights"—McCane and others expelled—Memorial—Report upon it by Dr. Emory—Dr. Thomas E. Bond and Dr. Emory defend the Church—Canada question settled—Action of the General Conference—Inferences—Dr. Capers elected delegate to the Wesleyan Methodist Conference—Dr. Fisk—Bishop McKendree's account of this Conference—A crisis in the history of the Church—The Bishop's Journal—Travels back to Tennessee—Attends quarterly and camp-meetings in Kentucky and Tennessee—His route to Georgia over Lookout Mountain—Preached to an Indian Council—Gets to Athens, Georgia—At Asbury Hull's—Sick—Ordains Stephen Olin—Sketch of him.

We have seen that Bishop McKendree had arrived at Pittsburgh, Pennsylvania, a few days before the General Conference began its session there on May 1, 1828. One hundred and twenty-five delegates were present, out of one hundred and seventy-seven elected, and all the five Bishops were there—McKendree, Roberts, George, Soule, and Hedding. The senior Bishop opened the session, as he had done since the death of Bishop Asbury. Dr. Martin Ruter was elected Secretary, and the quadrennial Address of the Bishops was read and referred to the committees. It referred gratefully to the general prosperity of the Church, and especially to the extensive revivals during the past three years, to the importance of sustaining the missionary work, the Sunday-school and Tract Societies, and to the administration of the government of the Church. The Bishops regretted their failure of sending a delegate to the British Conference, asserting it had not been owing to any want of affection for their British brethren, nor of respect for the expressed will of the last General Conference; and, without stating the cause of this failure, they suggested that the Conference itself should select and send one. The General Conference of 1824 requested and directed the Bishops to select and send a preacher as a representative from the American Methodists to the British Conference, and the senior Bishop had endeavored to get all his colleagues together to make the selection. This was found difficult to accomplish; but the principal impediment had been that three of them nominated Dr. Wm. Capers, of South Carolina, for this mission, and an objection had been made on account of his connection with slavery; and so, after several ineffectual attempts, the matter was dropped, and the true reason was not stated. It also appears that Dr. Capers declined the nomination, giving as his reasons the responsibility of the office and his dread of crossing the ocean, as well as the time it would take him from his work and his family.

Bishop McKendree, in common with many others, felt no little solicitude as to the course this

General Conference would pursue in reference to several important measures. "The suspended resolutions," which were calculated to diminish very seriously the authority of the Episcopacy, in the appointment of the Presiding Elders and stationing the preachers, were expected to come up for final action; but the subject had been so generally discussed, and opposition to the measure had been so decidedly expressed by the Annual Conferences, that it was lost by an overwhelming vote. Indeed, many who, at the last General Conference, had been inclined to favor these resolutions, after they saw the violent spirit which its leading advocates exhibited, and finding it was to be only the "entering wedge" of innovation, became alarmed, and withdrew their names and influence from the measure.

Between 1824 and 1828, the spirit of innovation was strongly and dangerously exhibited in claiming the *right* of the laity to an *equal representation* with the traveling preachers in the Annual and General Conferences. A periodical, styled "The Wesleyan Repository," was started in Trenton, New Jersey, avowedly to agitate this subject, which soon became bitterly personal. The contributors were mostly anonymous, and the course pursued became so unpopular that its publication was discontinued. Shortly afterward another originated in Baltimore, styled the "Mutual Rights," advocating the same principles, which had the sanction and influence of a few traveling preachers, and of several well-known local preachers, as well as a good many laymen. But, as in all such revolutionary associations, the more violent and factious spirits soon took the lead, drawing after them those not so fully imbued with their temper. It culminated in the expulsion of a notorious local preacher—Alexander McCane—who had published an outrageous attack upon the government of the Church, implicating and slandering its founder and fathers. Other expulsions and withdrawals followed. A society of "Associated Reformers" and "Union Societies" were formed, and a convention was held in Baltimore in 1827, constituted of preachers and laymen. Thus the line between the friends and foes of the Episcopal form of our Church-government was distinctly drawn; and, a memorial having been presented from this convention to the General Conference of 1828, brought up the subject. Several members of the convention, who had been honored and useful traveling ministers, attended the Conference, who were invited to seats, and received appointments to preach.

The chairman of the committee to whom the memorial was referred—Dr. John Emory—brought in the report, which was read amid profound silence. It was such a document as few could write, exhibiting a thorough comprehension of the whole question, set forth in the simplest language, and in the clearest and most convincing manner. The points were distinctly made, and argued fairly, logically, and in a conciliatory spirit. The writer watched the countenances of the Rev. Asa Shinn and of his *confrère*, the Rev. N. Snethen, who represented the convention, during the reading of this report, and thought then, as he does now, that they appreciated it, and were convinced by its unanswerable arguments. But, alas! they had too far committed themselves. Dr. Bangs deserves the thanks of the whole Methodist Episcopal family for inserting it in full in his valuable "History of the Methodist Episcopal Church." The moment the reading of it was concluded, Mr. Shinn sprang to his feet, and proposed that five thousand copies be printed. Of course, the report was adopted by a vote nearly or quite unanimous; and as it provided, upon reasonable terms, for the return to the bosom of the Church of those who had withdrawn, it was believed and hoped by many that this would end any farther serious alienation; and, although this very desirable result was not fully realized, yet this action of the Conference greatly tended to check the disaffection, and diminish the asperity of feeling which had, unfortunately, arisen. The "Appeal" to the Methodists in opposition to the changes proposed by the Reformers, by Dr. Thomas E. Bond, and the "Defense of our Fathers," by Dr. Emory, were timely and masterly vindications of the polity of the Church, and contributed much to the same end. May we not hope that now, after the lapse of more than forty years, when nearly all those who took part in this division, have passed away, with the prejudices and passions of the occasion, a reünion may take place?

Bishop McKendree was a close observer of these acts of the General Conference, and when he found that these perplexing and dangerous questions had been adjusted with great unanimity, he thanked God and took courage. He had suffered much anxiety, and labored long for the great principles involved in these controversies, and when he saw them settled in accordance with his views, he felt reässured of the prosperity and permanency of his beloved Church.

He also felt a good deal of solicitude as to another delicate and important question which came before the Conference. It was what is called "the Canada question." The case was simply this: When our preachers had extended their work to the northern limits of the United States, they were invited into Upper Canada. They went and formed circuits and stations, and were requested to continue and extend their labors. The question came up whether the Bishop had the right to appoint preachers to labor out of the limits of the United States, inasmuch as the Church only claimed to be "the Methodist Episcopal Church in the United States of America," and Bishop Asbury disclaimed the authority to do so, and sent none but *volunteers*, with the understanding that it was done by agreement or compact between the Canadian brethren and our preachers. His successors took the same view, and acted conformably to it. But after awhile it was found that our preachers laboring there, were subjected to great disabilities; they were regarded not as citizens, but foreigners, and could not celebrate the rites of matrimony even among the members of their own charges. Various other difficulties grew out of the position which our preachers and members occupied, and prejudices naturally sprung up to limit the usefulness of our ministers. Difficulties, too, occurred between our preachers and the English Methodist ministers. A petition from our people there, borne by a delegation from the Canada Conference, was presented to this General Conference, stating these and other facts, and asking to be set off as an independent body, and the ordination of a Bishop for their work. A committee was appointed to consider and report upon the request. Dr. Emory and others, including the writer, were placed upon the committee, and reported in substance that, as our relation to the Canadian brethren was founded upon a *compact*, and not upon our right to organize and govern a Church in Canada; and inasmuch as one of the parties to the agreement now asked that the compact be dissolved, the General Conference should agree to its dissolution, and consent that the Canada Conference organize and elect its own Bishop. And farther, that our Bishops, or any one of them, be authorized to ordain a Bishop for Canada whenever one shall be elected and presented for this purpose.

The following extracts from the Journal of the General Conference show the action of the body upon this subject:

May 17, 1828, William Ryerson offered the following resolutions, viz.:

Whereas, The Canada Annual Conference, situated in the province of Upper Canada, under a foreign government, have, in their memorial, presented to this Conference the difficulties under which they labor in consequence of their union with a foreign ecclesiastical government, and setting forth their desire to be set off as a separate Church-establishment; and

WHEREAS, This General Conference disclaims all right to exercise ecclesiastical jurisdiction under such circumstances except by mutual agreement; therefore,

Resolved by the delegates of the Annual Conferences in General Conference assembled, 1. That the compact existing between the Canada Annual Conference and the Methodist Episcopal Church in the United States be, and hereby is, dissolved by mutual consent, and that they are at liberty to form themselves into a separate Church-establishment.

Resolved, etc., 2. That our Superintendents or Superintendent be, and hereby are, respectively advised and requested to ordain such person as may be elected by the Canada Conference a Superintendent for the Canada Connection.

Resolved, etc., 3. That we do hereby recommend to our brethren in Canada to adopt the form of government of the Methodist Episcopal Church in the United States, with such modifications as their particular relations shall render necessary.

Resolved, etc., 4. That we do hereby express to our Canada brethren our sincere desire that the most friendly feeling may exist between them and the Methodist Episcopal Church in the United States.

Resolved, etc., 5. That the claims of the Canada

Conference on our Book Concern and Charter Fund, and any other claims they may suppose they justly have, shall be left open for future negotiation and adjustment between the two Connections.

G. R. JONES,
MOSES CRUME.

The question on the first resolution was decided in the affirmative—104 for, and 43 against it.

The other four resolutions were, on motion, referred to a special committee, to consist of five members.

May 21st, it was, on motion,

Resolved, That the subject of the petition from the Canada Conference be resumed; whereupon the resolutions, as reported by the last committee appointed on that subject, were read.

It was then resolved that the subject shall now be considered and acted on.

Samuel H. Thompson moved, and it was seconded, that the resolution, as reported by the committee, be adopted. The question being taken, it was decided in the affirmative, 108 voting in favor of adoption, and 22 against it.

N. Bangs moved, and it was seconded, that the following be referred to the consideration of the same committee:

That, if the Canada Conference should be set off, so as to become independent of the Methodist Episcopal Church in the United States, the General Conference be recommended to make such alteration in the Constitution of the Missionary Society of the Methodist Episcopal Church as shall authorize the Board of Managers to make an appropriation, to a certain amount, of the funds of that institution for the support of the Indian Missions in Upper Canada. And the motion prevailed.

The principle involved in this decision is truly an important one.

The following conclusions seem to follow from the action of the Conference in the premises, and the opinions expressed by leading members of the body:

1. That the Church cannot rightfully claim ecclesiastical jurisdiction beyond her territorial limits, except by consent of parties.

2. That therefore she has not the *right* to ordain a man for an independent or foreign Church.

3. That the General Conference can authorize its Bishops to ordain a man for an independent or foreign Church, after he shall have been selected and presented by that Church, with the understanding that his functions are to be limited to that Church.

4. That to "set off" a Conference as an independent Church, and within its territorial jurisdiction, without the consent of the laity as well as the preachers, would be an unjust and dangerous precedent, except, perchance, for *moral* cause, such as heresy, defection of morals and practice, after proper efforts to reclaim them.

5. That it is competent to ordain and supervise men as missionaries in any country, and to continue to do so, even after the missions shall have been

organized into Conferences, so long as it may be done by mutual consent—the absolute right to do so being another question.

The writer does not say that these opinions were announced *ipsissimis verbis*, by the Bishops, Dr. Emory, Dr. Bangs, and others; but he lays them down as his own deductions, from what was said and done, and is persuaded that they harmonized in the main with the sentiments of the Bishops and Conference. He doubts not they did with Bishop McKendree's. It will be seen that these views fully apply to a Church which, by its assumed and legal title, is limited to a specified territory, as "in the United States of America." The expediency of omitting such a limitation, and to what extent, if any, such a change of title would modify the deductions stated above, may be subjects of reflection.

The Church of England has authority coëxtensive with the dominions of the crown, because it is "*by law established;*" but it required the consent of George III. and an act of Parliament to authorize her Bishops to consecrate Bishop White for America, and then his functions were expressly inhibited as to the possessions of Great Britain. As yet our country is free from a legalized ecclesiastical hierarchy. May it ever remain so!

The Bishops having failed to comply with the request of the last General Conference, to select and appoint a delegate to the Wesleyan Methodist body in England, and having invited the Conference to make a selection and carry out this purpose, the

Conference proceeded to elect one, and the Rev. W. Capers was chosen. Dr. Capers was then in the prime of life. His *personnel* was handsome and impressive, his literary and theological attainments, his refined and dignified manners, and his well-known abilities and earnest devotion to God and his Church, conspired to render him well adapted to this responsible office, and vindicated his previous nomination by Bishops McKendree and Soule.*

Dr. Wilbur Fisk, who received the next highest vote, was considerably his junior, and consequently less known. He first came conspicuously into notice at this General Conference, and soon attained a very high and deserved reputation as President of the Wesleyan University, a scholarly and able divine, as well as a lovely and liberal-hearted man. His reputation was based upon talents of a very high order, and he was among the few who could rise above early impressions and prevalent prejudices, and take an enlarged and independent view, with moral courage to act upon it. Methodism suffered a great loss in his early death. But more of him hereafter.

The fifth session of the delegated General Conference closed on May 24, 1828. It was a session remarkable for its general harmony, its rapid dispatch of business, and for the final settlement of several important questions which had long and deeply agitated the Church. No new member was

* Bishop Roberts agreed to his nomination when it was first made.

added to the Episcopal College, and it was thought it was not necessary, and therefore would be improper.

The following brief account of this session is all that the Bishop says about it:

"On the 1st day of May, 1828, the General Conference was organized. The appearance and spirit of the members savored more of simple-hearted Christians than of determined controvertists. The suspended resolutions were taken up, and the vote taken without debate. They were voted out in a peaceable manner. The memorial from the local convention was treated in a formal and respectful manner: upon examination, it was found the advocates for changes in the government were very few —not more, perhaps, than one in a hundred, if that. They were treated with lenity and tenderness. From the conduct of their representatives who were present, it was hoped the breach would be healed; but it turned out otherwise, and time must declare the ultimate result. These eventful cases having been disposed of, the Conference concluded in peace. A few subjects of interesting importance were introduced, but concluded peaceably."

The General Conference of 1828 marked an historical crisis in the Church, and the preachers and members, who truly loved its old landmarks, felt like those in a vessel long buffeted by stormy winds and threatening waves upon a dangerous coast at last emerging into calm and open waters, and gliding smoothly and safely beneath a sky serene under a gentle and favorable breeze. Thus, it seemed, our ecclesiastical ship had weathered the tempest without serious damage to hull or sail, and the glad passengers looked back with gratitude and forward with hope.

The Bishop's narrative proceeds:

"From Pittsburgh I came in a steam-boat with many preachers to Maysville. With their help I formed a plan to visit the Churches as far as Missouri this summer, and return with the Conferences in the fall; but upon farther consultation, they judged it altogether inexpedient, if not impracticable, for me to accomplish the undertaking: it was therefore given up. Brother Tydings conducted me to Lexington, Kentucky; I attended the quarterly-meeting at Frankfort, and the Kentucky Conference in Shelbyville, October 23, 1828; then a three-days' meeting on my way to Elizabethtown, where Brother Crist met me. Hitherto I have had the company and help of friends; have preached considerably, and hope good has been done. We attended a meeting at Bowling-green, at Fountain Head, a camp-meeting at Carr's, Goose Creek, and another at Woodward's. After this, Crist was taken with the fever, and declined going farther. My nephew, John McKendree, left his business, and came to me at Smyrna camp-meeting. I was at a camp-meeting at Douglass's, one near Murfreesboro, a quarterly-meeting in Nashville, and another camp-meeting near Shelbyville. Thence I set out for Georgia, crossed the Tennessee River safely, and reached the foot of Lookout Mountain; but having arrived there sooner than my friends, who were to meet me, expected, I placed my nephew at the wheels to scotch the carriage, and undertook to drive it myself. It was hard work for man and beast, and in some places dangerous. Indeed, the undertaking was objected to as dangerous and impracticable by travelers; but we surmounted the difficulties without any serious injury. After resting awhile, we began to descend the mountain, and met Brothers Coody and Scales, with a black man and a yoke of oxen, coming to take us up the mountain, having been informed by a traveler we were on the way. We rested at Brother Ross's on Friday, saw and conversed with the missionaries from Brainard, about fifty miles distant, and preached on Sunday to a small congregation of Cherokees: hope our labor was not in vain. In the evening we rode home with Brother Scales, a missionary from the Tennessee Conference. Mr. Ross and an old Indian were moved under preaching, for the first time, as their acquaintances said. Tuesday, Brother Scales set out with us for the place where the chiefs of the Nation were assembled in grand council. We visited an afflicted native woman on the way, and from the manner we were received, I hope she will make a happy end. We lodged at the house of the Widow Hicks, a disciple of the Moravian missionary. Next day we arrived at the 'Indian National Council;' preached to them Thursday night; on Friday, went to the missionary station and camp-ground, and preached to a large congregation. Saturday, rode to Mr. ——, and established a school. Here Brother Gunter, the interpreter, and Turtle Fields, the Indian traveling preacher, met us. Sunday, we preached in the school-house to a considerable number of people. Gunter returned to the Council, and Turtle Fields went with us to Mr. ——, where we lodged that night, and accompanied us next day to Mr. Betts's, on the Georgia Road. In the evening the neighbors were collected, and we held meeting. Tuesday, we left our friends, and set our for Georgia, in company with a man, his wife, and son, in a carriage, who were returning from a visit to their friends in the West to their home near Athens, Georgia. They had a tea-kettle and a coffee-pot, and we as well as they had provisions; so we fared pretty well. Through the day we were at home in our carriages, and at night in taverns. We were ever received and treated kindly in the Indian Nation. In Athens, Georgia, we put up with Brother Asbury Hull, and preached there the last Sunday in October, 1828; and the first Sunday in November preached at the Cherokee Corner, at Lexington; attended a three-days' meeting at Greensboro, and on Monday a brother kindly took me in his carriage to Eatonton. I was unwell. Doctors visited me in the evening, and took a pint of blood: two hours afterward returned, opened the same orifice, and took another pint. Tuesday, I was feeble. Wednesday, I must needs be taken in a carriage to the meeting-house, to be seen at least. There was a congregation, and I commenced speaking—forgot myself, and preached an hour—a feeling time. Thursday, I rode to Brother H.'s. Next day it rained — rode, in company with

Brother Hodges, to a quarterly-meeting at Warren—preached twice. Thence I went to Milledgeville—put up with Brother Hodges—preached and visited considerably—ordained Brother Olin. Next went to Sparta — preached; Powelton — preached; preached at Washington; crossed Broad River; passed through Petersburg to Brother Rembert's, where I rested a day or two. In the fork of Broad and Savannah Rivers there is a considerable space without preaching. The land belongs to rich men. There are few white, but many colored people. The gentlemen engaged to support a single preacher, if one could be spared. From Rembert's we crossed the Savannah at his ferry, his carriage and family going with us about eight miles, to a meeting-house, where I preached, ordained a brother, and lodged with Brother ——. Next day I traveled, and preached in ——town — stayed all night. Thence to Mount Ariel—rested Saturday, preached Sunday. Recrossed the Savannah, and proceeded on to Augusta, Georgia — attended their quarterly-meeting. Stayed over the second Sunday, including Christmas—preached and visited considerably. Left Augusta December 27th—Saturday, got to Brother Wade's. Here Brother Hill met us, and continued to Conference. Sunday I preached to a large congregation—an impressive time."

Among the names mentioned in the above extract of the Bishop's Journal, which deserve more than a passing notice, is that of one who attained a high and well-merited reputation for extraordinary talents, ability as a preacher, ripe scholarship, and usefulness as an educator. The Bishop notes the fact that at Milledgeville, Georgia, November 20, 1828, he "ordained Brother Olin." This was the Rev. Stephen Olin, at that time, and for six years subsequently, Professor of Ethics and Belles-lettres in Franklin College, Athens, Georgia.

Dr. Olin was a native of Vermont, born 1797; graduated at Middlebury College, 1820, with a constitution shattered and ruined by excessive study in his senior year; went to South Carolina for his health; taught an academy in Abbeville District—Mount Ariel, now Cokesbury; was converted; became a Methodist preacher in 1822. In 1823, he was appointed Professor in Middlebury College, but declined it, because he would not become a Congregationalist. In 1824, he was admitted into the South Carolina Conference, and stationed in Charleston; but after six months' efficient labor, his health failed, and he was never afterward able to perform the duties of the pastorate in the regular ministry. In 1826, he was elected Professor of Ethics and Belles-lettres in Franklin College, Athens, Georgia—*i. e.*, the University of Georgia. In 1828, he married Miss Mary Ann Bostick, of Milledgeville. In 1833, he resigned his professorship at Franklin College, and in 1834, entered upon the duties of the Presidency of Randolph Macon College, Virginia, with L. C. Garland, Edward D. Sims, and Professor Duncan, as associates in the faculty. His health failing, he sailed for Havre in 1837, and traveled extensively through Europe, Egypt, and the Holy Land. He lost his wife at

Naples, in 1839. In 1840, he returned to the United States, and succeeded Dr. Fisk as President of Wesleyan University, Middletown, Connecticut. In 1846, he attended the meeting of the Evangelical Alliance, in London, and in 1851, closed his useful and eventful life by a calm and triumphant death.

Dr. Olin was gigantic in stature, mind, and heart—a great sufferer from nervous prostration—a profound thinker, a clear and elegant writer, and unsurpassed as a preacher. It is doubtful whether Methodism in America has ever produced a greater mind. He was a delegate to the General Conference of 1844, when the separation of the Church occurred, and expressed the conviction that it was inevitable, under the circumstances; and perhaps few members of that body deplored the necessity more truly and deeply than did he. Indeed, such was his mental agony on that occasion, that he was compelled to leave the General Conference before it closed. He was one of the few truly great and good men with whom it has been permitted us to become acquainted. We thought *then*, he should have imitated the example of Bishop Soule, in vindicating his claim to the highest moral courage; but he did not think so, and we have long since concluded to let him judge for himself, and to love and respect most highly his precious memory.

When, in 1834, he became President of Randolph Macon College, Virginia, he was associated in the Faculty with Langdon C. Garland, Edward

Drumgoole Sims, and Professor Duncan—each of them singularly adapted to the responsible task of instructing and training his charge to the highest intellectual and moral standard of education. Professor Garland succeeded Dr. Olin as President of Randolph Macon College, and afterward became President of the University of Alabama, and, upon the destruction by fire of its buildings, by Federal soldiers, during the late war, accepted the Professorship of Physics and Astronomy in the University of Mississippi, at Oxford, which he now occupies; in all which places and positions he has deservedly gained the highest esteem, as a profound scholar and superior instructor, as well as an earnest and working layman of the Church. The Rev. Edward D. Sims was for several years the intimate and beloved friend of the writer, and his associate in the Faculty of La Grange College — then for some time a student in the universities of Germany. Upon his return to the United States, he became a Professor in Randolph Macon College, and afterward in the University of Alabama, where he suddenly closed his life, regretted and respected by all who knew him, as a man of rare purity, learning, and amiability. Professor Duncan, the veteran Professor of Ancient Languages, has left his impress upon hundreds, as a thorough and successful teacher of ancient Greek and Roman literature, and bequeathed to the rejuvenated College a son, who worthily fills the position once held by Dr. Olin.

CHAPTER VI.

McKendree at Augusta — Savannah — Preaches to whites and blacks — Conference at Charleston — Bishop Roberts absent— Not able to preside—Returns to Lynchburg, to the Virginia Conference—To the Baltimore and Philadelphia Conferences— Thence, through Pennsylvania, Ohio, and Kentucky, to Tennessee—Douglass's Camp-meeting—His voice—Conversion of a mute—Bishop George's Death—Sketch—The Bishop's homes at Nashville: J. T. Elliston's and H. R. W. Hill's—Down the Mississippi River—The Colonel—His Plan—Liberia.

We resume the Bishop's Journal:

"*Thursday*, January 1, 1829.—Preached to a number of the colored people, in presence of the whole family, in an apartment of the dwelling-house. The Lord was present.

"*January* 2d.—We rose early, to start for Savannah, and were called to prayer and breakfast by candle-light; but I was taken so sick I was obliged to lie down. I lay until eight o'clock A.M., and set out without eating any thing. Brother Wade took me fifteen miles in a remarkably easy carriage. We accomplished our journey of thirty-odd miles before sunset, and reached Savannah next day. Here we stayed and preached two Sabbaths—through the week visited the brethren, met the society, and received visits. The Presbyterians seem disposed to be friendly with us. Next week we left Savannah. Brother Hill accompanied us, by the Sisters' Ferry, through the Black Swamp Circuit, to Brother Lowery's. In addition to his own, he manages an estate of a wealthy planter who invites preaching among his colored people. There are several such men in this neighborhood. They wish their slaves to be instructed in the Christian religion. On Sunday we preached to a large congregation of white and colored people. Brother Hill gave them a night-meeting. It is hoped our visit is not in vain. The way is opening to have the gospel preached to the slaves.

"We arrived safely in Charleston on the 20th, and found the preachers, their families, and our brethren in health. We now had a few days to rest, and to visit the societies and friends. This is an agreeable and profitable part of a minister's duty.

"Bishop Roberts was to have attended the Conference; we waited in expectation. On the 28th of January, the Conference began according to appointment—Bishop Roberts not arrived." Afterward he adds, "He did not come at all."

In reference to this Conference, and his ability to preside, he says:

"Being the only Bishop present, the business necessarily devolved on me. Having received no information from either of my colleagues as to their absence, it seemed providential that I had come. I commenced with considerable confidence in my ability to perform the duties, but the experience of the first day convinced me of my utter inability to bear the labors of my office."

This no doubt greatly mortified him, as it evinced that his days of extensive travel and active usefulness were nearly over. No one who has not been thus tried knows the feeling of sadness incident to such a state. No man ever felt more acutely this sensation than the good old Bishop. But he was not the man to succumb, and soon resumed his course. Quitting Charleston, he goes through Georgetown, Fayetteville, Raleigh—attending the North Carolina Conference—thence to Petersburg, Richmond, and Lynchburg. Here he meets the Virginia Conference. Thence he goes back to Richmond, and proceeds to Portsmouth and Norfolk, and from thence to Baltimore on the 14th of March, 1829. And after attending the Baltimore Conference, he goes through Philadelphia, to Trenton, New Jersey, and there attends the Philadelphia Conference Back again he travels to Baltimore, and goes thence to Washington City, Hagerstown, Sharpsburg, and Uniontown—making one hundred and thirty miles in four days—to Barnesville, Ohio, July 25th. And after attending the Ohio Conference at Urbana, and the Kentucky Conference at Lexington, he gets back to Nashville, Tennessee, and spends the winter of 1829–30 there.

The Bishop confessed that the anxiety and labors of the General Conference fatigued him, and that his health was not so good at its close; and yet we have followed him through an unceasing tour of several thousand miles, everywhere preaching and trying in every possible way to do good. His power of endurance and his moral courage were wonderful!

The Bishop alludes to his having been at a number of quarterly and camp-meetings during the summer and fall of 1828, in Tennessee. Several of them were in the Nashville District, of which the writer was then the Presiding Elder. At Douglass's Camp-meeting there was an immense concourse, and the Bishop preached for me at eleven o'clock, September 7th, to at least six thousand people; and, although his voice seemed feeble, yet was it so distinct and penetrating, and so perfectly silent was the vast crowd, that after the first five minutes he could be heard by all. In order to regulate his voice properly, he requested me to take my position near the outskirts of the assembly, and, by signals, let him know whether he could be heard; and after he understood that he spoke loud enough, he continued in the same key to the close. He was in his proper element, and preached with great logical clearness and spiritual power.

The lesson was a valuable one to public speakers, teaching that the distance at which the voice can be distinctly heard depends not so much upon the volume of sound as upon distinctness of articulation. Preachers often bring on a premature ruin of voice and health by not practicing upon this lesson, and some of them commit a species of suicide. If Bishop McKendree had not learned this lesson, his usefulness, and, perhaps, his life, would have terminated twenty years before he died.

An incident occurred at this camp-meeting which interested him greatly. While he was preaching the sermon alluded to, there were sitting immediately before him, and near the pulpit, an intelligent and worthy family, by the name of Tullis. The father and mother were members of the Church, but one of the daughters was deaf and dumb. The family being in good circumstances, she had enjoyed all the advantages of education possible; had a sprightly mind and a fine person, but she was not pious. Her attention was soon riveted on the venerable preacher, and she seemed to understand his speaking face and significant gestures. She became absorbed in thought and bathed in tears; and, when mourners were invited, she arose and knelt. The Bishop, with her parents and friends, gathered around her, and offered prayers for her conversion; and, after an apparently severe mental struggle, in which penitence and prayer were clearly indicated by her tears, her countenance, and her actions, she suddenly arose, and with a face radiant with joy, embraced her parents and the venerable preacher. She was converted!

Nor is this the only instance of the kind the writer has known.

The Bishop attended several other camp and quarterly-meetings within the Nashville District during this year, at all of which, as well as at the writer's own home, he enjoyed the pleasure of his society; and he can never cease to feel toward him, and Thomas L. Douglass, his father in the gospel, the profoundest respect and love.

The death of Bishop George occurred in this year. He was born in Lancaster county, Virginia, 1767 or '68; became a traveling preacher in 1790; was ordained Bishop in 1816, and died August 23, 1828, at Staunton, Virginia. Having traveled two or three years in the Virginia Conference, at the call of Bishop Asbury for volunteers for South Carolina, he went there, and labored in that State and Georgia four or five years. Finding his health much impaired by incessant labor and the sickliness of the climate, he returned to Virginia and located, believing he could not render efficient service, and feeling unwilling to become a burden on the Conference. Thus thrown out into the world sick, poor, and incapaciated for ordinary worldly business by his past exclusive devotion to his vocation, he "resorted again to his old alternative—school-keeping." Having despaired of being able to continue in the itinerant ministry, he married a lady of "piety, industry, sympathy, and sincere affection," who died in 1816, leaving four children—one of them only a few weeks old. He never married again. The field of his labors, as a Bishop, required him to travel into Canada and through the United States; and, during the twelve years of his Episcopate, he faithfully attempted to perform all his arduous duties.

Parting with Bishop Hedding at the close of the New York Conference, he started for Jonesboro, Tennessee, to hold the Holston Conference; and, having been taken violently ill of dysentery at Staunton, Virginia, after a few days of great suffering he breathed his last. He died not only resigned, but willingly and joyously, exclaiming, "Glory to God!"

As a Christian, he was devout and holy; a man of much prayer and strong religious feelings; as a preacher, he excelled in pathos. He preached "in the demonstration of the Spirit and with power." What he felt deeply he spoke with great simplicity and sensibility. Having heard him repeatedly, the writer can attest that he never heard any one who surpassed him as a pathetic preacher. At our first visit to a Conference in 1817, held in Franklin, Tennessee, he and Bishop Roberts attended, and he preached at eleven o'clock on Sunday, in the Methodist Church. His text was 1 John v. 4, "This is the victory," etc.; and he had scarcely got through his exordium before he and all his hearers were in tears. It was indeed a "pathetic, powerful, and useful" sermon. His appearance, voice, and manner, as well as his matter, conspired to excite and overpower the audience. He was a weeping prophet. *He* wept, and everybody caught the spirit of the preacher. His way of removing the tears which blinded his small and deeply-seated eyes, by running his finger behind his spectacles, and uttering in soft and subdued tones, "Glory!" was peculiar and impressive. He was low of stature, with a broad chest, a short neck, large head, long, flowing hair turned back; his face broad and short; his eyes twinkling like diamonds beneath an expansive forehead and heavy, overhanging brow.

In private, as in public, he avoided ostentation,

and was simple and affectionate in private intercourse. He detested an assumed dignity, and won the respect and love of all with whom he had intercourse by his urbanity and unstudied dignity. He was not a learned man; and his early literary opportunities had most probably been confined to "the old-field schools" of Virginia; but he had traveled much, mingled in the best society among our people in Virginia and Maryland, and spoke correctly and fluently. He had no fondness for office or notoriety, but was humble and strictly conscientious.

As a Bishop, while he loved the Church, and strove to do his whole duty, yet his want of method and inattention to the rules of order, occasionally involved himself and the Conference in confusion. He wanted the administrative talent of the senior Bishop. The latter had an analytical and remarkably logical cast of mind. His office was to instruct, and to legislate, and to govern. The former, endowed with stronger feeling and more sympathy, carried by storm the citadel of the heart. They were both rare men, but differed in the spheres in which they moved and shone. McKendree, like Asbury, could read character, foresee the results of movements, and adopt means to frustrate or advance them with remarkable astuteness and success. George, not so prescient nor such a tactician, and more timid, was easily affected by his views of the apparent and present. Both were equally honest, and worked for the same ends. Bishop McKendree could have made a prime minister, or the king of a nation, and would have made it greater and happier. Bishop George was adapted to the rostrum of a popular assembly, and might have been a leader in a time of excitement. But they were holy men and Christ's ministers; and therefore, while McKendree assisted to make a great Church out of a little one by his administrative ability, George contributed to the same end by his impassioned pulpit eloquence. Bishop McKendree's throne was the chair in Conference and council; Bishop George's throne was the pulpit. McKendree taught, George moved his audience. Both excelled in their spheres; both were necessary, and God gave both to the Church.

It is worthy of note here that each of these Bishops was awakened and converted under the preaching of that great revivalist, John Easter, and were inducted into the ministry by Philip Cox. How many others became preachers and members of the Church through the labors of Mr. Easter, eternity alone will reveal. Let Methodists, and especially Methodist preachers, beware how they depreciate revivals; for if, in our pride of higher intellectual attainments, and our boast of colleges and universities, our graduates and doctors of divinity, we undervalue and speak of them as merely *sensational* and of *transient* influence, may not God curse us with spiritual barrenness, and leave us like potsherds, to strive with potsherds, without the aid of the Holy Ghost?

During the winter of 1829–30, Bishop McKendree passed the greater part of his time in Nashville and its immediate vicinity. The residences of H. R. W. Hill and J. T. Elliston, where he had homes, and where every comfort and kindness which, in his debility and sickness, he could need, were his principal places of staying.

Both of these gentlemen deserve a passing notice. Mr. Hill was converted at Conference in Franklin, Tennessee, in 1817. His mother was a devout Methodist of the old Virginia type; and, at the time of his conversion, he was a clerk in a store. His business capacity was remarkable, and he accumulated a fortune by merchandising in Nashville, and as a commission merchant in New Orleans. A crisis in monetary matters occurring, his house in New Orleans failed to the amount of about three millions of dollars, owing to his having entered into acceptances for planters, who did not meet their engagements. Upon his return to his family shortly after his failure, he said to the writer, "I have lost every thing, and am in debt three millions—all is gone except my character and *what I have given away.*" He lived, however, to pay his debts, and died a wealthy man; but, notwithstanding his liberality, his cares injured his piety. He never stinted his benevolence. Not only did he afford Bishop McKendree a home, but when Bishop Soule came to the South, he gave him a comfortable house and valuable little farm near Franklin, worth from three to five thousand dollars. He liberally assisted in erecting an excellent house in Nashville for the occupancy of a Bishop, known still as the Bishop's house, in which Bishop Soule resided awhile, and where a worthy colleague now lives. In New Orleans he was equally generous, having, under the leadership of that princely layman, Hon. Edmund McGehee, of Woodville, Mississippi, given ten thousand dollars at one time toward the erection of the McGehee Church.

His wife was a sincere Christian lady, plain and devout. Both have passed from earth.

Joseph T. Elliston was also a man of fine business talent, and, by foresight, tact, and economy, amassed a fortune, but never speculated, nor sought wealth by hazardous means. He was a plain, unpretending man, of great prudence and common sense; happy in his domestic and social relations, and always at work as trustee or steward for the benefit of the Church. He was the person to whom, principally, is due the honor of erecting the McKendree Church in Nashville, as well as the parsonage and Bishop's house.

His excellent wife was in every respect a worthy helpmeet to her devoted and noble-hearted husband. They, too, have gone to rest.

Is it not fit that an old friend, who has often enjoyed the hospitality of these laymen, should chronicle their names in connection with the life of one who so often enjoyed their hospitality? For, although not preachers, they were truly their friends and comforters. And may we not trust that He who rewards "a cup of water" given to a disciple, will not fail to reward those who give them food and shelter, and, like ministering angels, watch over them in age and affliction? Without such friends, what must have been the fate of many an old and feeble man, whose youth and strength have been spent in preaching the unsearchable riches of Christ! Such deserve to be classed with the house of Stephanas, who "addicted themselves to the ministry of the saints."

In their quadrennial Address to the late General Conference, the Bishops made no suggestion as to the necessity of increasing their number; but in reply to an inquiry made by the committee, through S. G. Roszel, as to the propriety and necessity of doing so, they said that if any more Conferences should be made, it would certainly be necessary to strengthen the Episcopacy; whether it was necessary to elect any more unless this should be done, the Conference could judge. The four efficient Superintendents had evidently enough to do. The death of Bishop George had reduced them to three, and consequently their tasks were onerous. To contribute what he could to assist his colleagues, Bishop McKendree resolved to visit the societies and to attend as many Conferences as his health would allow.

In conformity with this purpose, he resolved to go South during the winter, and embarked on a steam-boat at Nashville. From a letter to J. B. Finley, dated January 29, 1830, we learn that he was then "on the steam-boat Nashville, at the mouth of the Cumberland River, to visit the Churches as low down as New Orleans, and as extensively as possible;" that he expected to return in March; and that as soon as the roads would allow, and he could procure suitable assistance, he would visit the Churches in the West; that he had written to his old friend Abbott Godard, to induce him to go with him to Illinois, upon a visit to his old friends—and he concluded it by sending his love to Brother Spencer, Brother Smith's family, his Newport friends, and especially to his beloved Brother Holliday. It appears that he stopped at Natchez, with Dr. Henry Tooley, and spent some time there, preaching and paying pastoral visits, and enjoying the company of W. Winans, B. M. Drake, Thomas Clinton, B. Pipkin, and other valued and beloved friends. The greater part of his time was spent in New Orleans, where the necessities of the Church required his influence and counsels. He also paid a visit to Bayou Sara, and to Woodville, Mississippi, where, in the family of his greatly respected friend and brother, Judge Edward McGehee, he was always a most welcome and honored guest. Thus passed away the winter.

Upon this steam-boat trip to New Orleans, he had the company of A. L. P. Green, then associated with James Gwin in the Nashville Station. The well-known genial temper and social qualities of Brother Green rendered him always a most desirable companion to the Bishop. He had a high esteem and reverential affection for Bishop McKendree, and to the close of the good man's life was his attentive, tender, and trusted friend. It was on this trip to New Orleans that the incidents occurred which are narrated in Dr. Green's admirable sketch of the Bishop, in the "Biographical

Sketches of Itinerant Ministers," edited by Dr. Summers, in 1858. I hope I may be pardoned for making the following extracts from this work, which ought to be circulated throughout the whole Methodist community. Dr. Green says:

"I think, in the year 1830, while descending the Mississippi on a large steamer, crowded with passengers, the weather being cold, we were compelled to live in close community about the stove. The company was a mixed one—old and young, ladies and gentlemen—so that various subjects of conversation were up from time to time, until an old lawyer and politician, who no doubt mistook the Bishop's character in part, (thinking that the Church had made him Bishop on account of his goodness and lamb-like nature—never once supposing there was any of the lion in him,) concluded, no doubt, that he would make some capital by a controversy with him on Church-government. A greater mistake no poor man ever made, for the Bishop would have been his equal on any subject; and upon Church-government he was too strong for any one, for he had given to that subject extraordinary attention. Having been a little troubled in that direction in his youth, he had threshed, fanned, and sifted it with his powerful intellect for years, until there was not a comma, a crossed *t* or a dotted *i* in the whole empire of Church-government which he did not have by heart and at his fingers' ends. The old Colonel commenced by saying to the Bishop, that he differed with him on Church-government; to which the Bishop answered,

'So, so.' The Colonel, finding he had not got the Bishop to his liking, said next, that he thought the Bishops of the Methodist Church had too much power. The Bishop answered by saying, that he wished he had more power than he had; that he once had power enough to travel around this continent in a year, but now he had hardly power enough to walk. This produced a laugh around the circle, which was any thing but comfortable to the Colonel; so at once he commenced an argument against the government of the Church and the power of the Bishops. Finding that nothing else but a controversy would do him, the Bishop met him promptly, with a force that evidently overpowered him. The Colonel rallied and came again to the attack, but was again routed, with great slaughter of his arguments. Next he attempted to escape without calling for quarter, by saying he had not words to express his ideas, or he would make it appear very different. But the Bishop had determined that as nothing but a contest would do him, he would make him cry out. The Bishop repeated slowly the words of the Colonel—'*Words, words,*' said the Bishop, 'to express your ideas! Words,' said he, 'are the signs of ideas, and you cannot have ideas without signs. Now, friend,' said he, 'if you have any ideas that you have not conveyed, you have received and retained those ideas by a certain set of signs. They may not be the best signs for the purpose; but do you use just such signs as you have, and I will undertake to understand them. Now,' said he, 'use your signs,' and dropped his head. All sat in perfect silence for half a minute, waiting for the signs to be given; but not one word was said. The Bishop then looked him fiercely in the face and said, with a manner of earnestness not common to him, 'Use your signs,' and another pause ensued—and to the poor Colonel it was an awful pause—but no signs were given. Then said the Bishop, 'Friend, you are mistaken; it is the want of ideas.' I felt too badly for the poor Colonel to laugh; but the sympathies of the circle were with the Bishop, and the controversy closed with a burst of laughter at the Colonel's expense. After awhile, when the Bishop and myself retired to the state-room for me to read to him, (which he requested me to do at stated periods,) I said to him, 'You treated that gentleman too badly.' He answered by saying, 'Let him let me alone.'"

From New Orleans he wrote to the Book Agents at New York:

"I intend to stay here some ten or twelve days, then take steam-boat for Bayou Sara, then land and visit the Churches as entensively as I can, to Natchez, then go by steam-boat to Nashville by the last of March. From Nashville I intend to resume my course of visiting the Churches, through the lower part of Kentucky, Indiana, and Illinois; thence return, with the Conferences, from the West across the mountains, and visit the Atlantic States and Conferences. From Philadelphia, where Brother Emory left me last spring, I set out to visit the Churches through Virginia, Pennsylvania,

Ohio, Kentucky, and Tennessee, where I expected to take up my abode for the winter. I have attended three Annual Conferences and ten or twelve quarterly-meetings. I have seen great and very good times, and rejoiced in the prosperity of Zion. For want of a steam-boat, I failed to attend the Mississippi Conference."

Thus his soul could plan and his zeal could dare to try and execute; but his strength enabled him to effect a part only of his programme of labor.

Having concluded the object of his tour to Mississippi and Louisiana, he returned in the early part of the spring, and was at his brother's on the 20th of April, 1830. There he received a respectful and affectionate letter from his old friend and fellow-laborer, Abbott Godard, regretting his inability to accompany him, as requested, on account of his poor health. He then again called on J. B. Crist to go with him, who, in his usual kind and respectful manner, readily consented. Preparations were soon made, and he started to visit and preach at popular meetings and in towns through the West. About this time he received an official communication from the Board of Managers of the Missionary Society, through their committee, (S. Merwin, S. Luckey, and James L. Phelps,) calling his attention to the subject of a mission in Africa, and suggesting Liberia as a suitable site for such an establishment, and promising "the means for such mission or missions." The writer is fully aware that for eighteen years, at least, the Bishop had been anxiously looking around for the men and means to send the gospel to Africa; and he received the letter with high gratification. The result, and the mission of the lovely and lamented Melville B. Cox to that benighted region, and his heroic and untimely death, will appear hereafter.

CHAPTER VII.

Begins his tour in 1830, in feeble health—Friends protest—Breaks down at Jonesboro—Returns—Discontinues his Diary—In 1831 starts again—Spends the winter in Baltimore—General Conference of 1832—Bishops' Address—Action of the General Conference as to Bishop McKendree—J. O. Andrew and John Emory elected Bishops—Sketches—Emory as President.

WHEN Bishop McKendree started, in the spring of 1830, to accomplish his proposed campaign of pastoral duties, it was evident to others, as it was presently to himself, that he was physically unable to endure the labor of so great an enterprise. He was no longer the Jupiter of our ecclesiastical system, the largest and brightest in the Episcopal train, and sweeping along a vast orbit, but, like Mercury, moving in a smaller circle, seldom seen, but ever near the sun. Instead of making the tour through the West, South, and East, as he had proposed, he had to confine himself to a small part of the West during the spring and summer; and even that was effected in great pain and weariness. In October, however, he was present at the Kentucky Conference, in Russellville. It seems that he had not yet fully made up his mind to relinquish his cherished project, and it required the earnest and repeated protests of his old friends to dissuade him from attempting it. At last, however, he consented to a compromise. He was to cross the Cumberland Mountains, attend the Holston Conference, at Ebenezer, Greene county, East Tennessee, November 4th, and thence travel east, if his strength should allow, across the Alleghanies; but should he find himself greatly exhausted, he agreed to return from Ebenezer to Nashville. The tour began. Slowly and painfully he journeyed over the mountains, for about the sixtieth time; and before he reached the seat of the Conference, he could neither get in nor out of his carriage without assistance. Frequently he had to be carried in the arms of others—his sympathizing and faithful traveling companion, J. B. Crist, being often constrained to shed tears over his precious and suffering charge. Yet he complained not, except occasionally by an involuntary, half-suppressed moan. No murmur escaped his lips. Upon the second day of the session he arrived, pale, haggard, and utterly exhausted. The preachers were struck with amazement and admiration, and gathered around him, some in tears and some with smiles. He was confined to his bed nearly the whole session—visiting it but once, and but for a few minutes. But it still required the earnest advice of his friends to divert him from his proposed tour. At last he yielded, and with tears welling in his eyes, said, "I approve your judgment, and *submit.*"

Sad, sick, and very feeble, the good old Bishop began the return tour soon after the close of the session. He could not venture to remain there during the winter, already setting in. He was at the base of the highest mountain range in the United States; and the long and severely cold winter must greatly aggravate his asthmatic and rheumatic complaints. It was death to stay, and little less to go. The distance was nearly four hundred miles, over as mountainous and rough a road as could be found. He had accomplished nothing by coming, except to convince himself that the circle of his future movements must be a constantly diminishing one, with constantly increasing pain. Yes, he had doubtless learned also that it is both duty and pleasure, "In age and feebleness extreme," to be able to say, "*Thy will be done!*"

Recrossing the Nolichucky River, and passing through Greenville, and down the Valley of the Holston to Knoxville, and thus on, and over the mountains, and down to Nashville he came, reaching his brother's about Christmas. Who can imagine what that trip cost him, when motion itself was wearying, and every root, and rut, and rock over which the carriage jolted, was an instrument of agony!

The Bishop was accustomed to keep a diary for each year—some portions are lost, but others have assisted in tracing his footsteps and delineating his character. We have no such traces during this era of his sufferings—not a line from his own pen. He seemed to act on the principle that his bright days and active labors for the Church should be scored down and remembered, but that days of sadness and suffering should be left unrecorded and unremembered. The fact is, from the spring of 1830, no regular diary has been found.

From his return home to the ensuing spring he remained in winter-quarters, not venturing to go far, nor taxing his strength very much, having become convinced that unless he could get stronger, he could do but little in future. Of course he preached, and visited in the neighborhoods of his temporary residences, as he had opportunity. This prudent course revived him considerably; and, in the spring of 1831, he went forth again. His course was through Kentucky and Ohio, passing over the mountains in the fall, and spending the winter in Baltimore, staying principally with his old friend, Dr. Henry Wilkins. Throughout this tour he, as usual, attended quarterly and other meetings, and preached frequently

The following letter from Dr. Emory was received at this time:

New York, April 17, 1832.

Dear Bishop:—Your favor of the 14th instant reached me last evening. I am much gratified to learn that you will visit us on the 20th instant, and will meet you with a carriage at the boat.

Permit me to add that a large and beautiful new church of ours, in a central part of this city, is to be opened on Friday next, 20th instant, at four o'clock P.M., the opening sermon to be preached by Brother Fisk, of Middletown, and one in the evening by Brother Merwin. A joint committee of the trustees and preachers have requested me to supply the pulpit on the first Sabbath morning, viz., the

22d instant, at half-past ten o'clock, with the privilege of inviting any other person to supply my place at my discretion; and knowing, as I do, the great satisfaction it would afford to have your services on that occasion, I beg that you will have the goodness to accept the appointment and allow me to have it announced, (as may very conveniently be done on Friday evening,) that you will preach there, the Lord willing, at that time. A line from you, by return of mail, signifying your assent, will very much oblige me. Should you be too much fatigued to write yourself, some friend will do it for you on your dictation.

It may be proper to inform you that our Missionary Anniversary is to be on Friday, the 27th instant, at five o'clock P.M., and not on the 25th.

With great respect, very affectionately yours,

J. EMORY.

In the latter part of March, 1832, he passed from Baltimore to Philadelphia, and lodged with his old and long-tried friend, Dr. Thomas Sargent, where unremitting and affectionate attention was ever shown him by the kind and amiable family.

The General Conference of 1832 began, as usual, on the 1st day of May, in Philadelphia: 223 delegates had been elected by the 23 Annual Conferences, viz., New York, 20; New England, 14; Maine, 11; New Hampshire and Vermont, 11; Oneida, 12; Genesee, 6; Pittsburgh, 11; Ohio, 15; Illinois, 7; Holston, 8; Kentucky, 13; Missouri, 3; Tennessee, 13; Mississippi, 7; Georgia, 12; South

Carolina, 9; Virginia, 14; Baltimore, 17; Philadelphia, 18; and Canada, 3. After the organization of the body in the usual manner, the Bishops presented their Address, and it was referred to appropriate committees. This Address congratulated the Conferences that the troubles and dangers which had threatened the peace and prosperity of the Church had nearly passed away; that, whilst these troubles had elicited a more general and careful attention to the economy of the Church, the result had been a clearer conviction of the excellency of our polity, and especially of the efficiency of our itinerant system; and consequently, peace, harmony, and reciprocal confidence had been greatly increased and confirmed. They therefore suggested that the chief business of that assembly was to preserve this state of things, and to devise measures for the more extensive and efficient operation of that system which has been so remarkably successful.

The attention of the Conference was invited to the subjects of missions and temperance, with various other topics, particularly to the necessity of "strengthening the Episcopacy in view of the death of Bishop George and the enlargement of the work."

Bishop McKendree was greatly delighted with this representation of the condition of the Church, and of the peaceful and harmonious indications in the Conference.

Bishop McKendree, having been solicited to preach the funeral-sermon of Bishop George and preside at the ordination of the Bishops elect, delivered an appropriate and impressive sermon on May 25, 1832.

The following extract from the Journal of the General Conference of 1832, shows the action of that body conformably to a Report of the Committee on Episcopacy in relation to Bishop McKendree's work and compensation for the next four years:

Philadelphia, General Conference, May 24, 1832.

In consequence of the age and increased infirmities of our venerable and beloved Bishop McKendree, it is recommended that his present relation be continued, and that the sum of $250 be allowed him annually for extra expenses, and to defray the traveling expenses of a traveling companion, and $100 for the allowance of said traveling companion, and that he be authorized to draw this amount from the Book Concern.

"He was too feeble to attend constantly the sessions, but occasionally would be seen walking up the aisle and taking a seat by the side of his colleagues, but would remain in the room a short time only. His last visit to the Conference was made the day before the adjournment. Having remained as long as his strength would allow, he arose to retire. He was but too conscious of his approaching dissolution to expect ever to meet his brethren again in another General Conference. Leaning on his staff, his once tall and manly form, now bent with age and infirmity, his eyes suffused with tears, his voice faltering with emotion, he exclaimed, 'Let all things be done without strife or vainglory, and try to keep the unity of the Spirit in the bonds of peace. *My brethren and children, love one another.*' Then spreading forth his trembling hands, and raising his eyes to heaven, he pronounced, in faltering and affectionate accents, the apostolic benediction. Slowly and sadly he left the house to return no more." *

The whole assembly rose and stood till he disappeared. It reminded the writer of Joshua's farewell to the assembled elders and people of Israel at Mount Ephraim: *our Moses* had departed in 1816, and now his successor takes his last, fond look at "the heads of the tribes"—his old and tried fellow-soldiers on many a moral battle-field—and bids them *adieu!*

In compliance with the suggestions of the Bishops and the Report of the Committee on the Episcopacy, the Conference proceeded to elect two more Bishops; and James O. Andrew and John Emory were elected on the first ballot—the former by a vote of 140, the latter by 135, out of 223 votes cast.

The two persons elected to the Episcopacy, were eminently fitted for the office. James O. Andrew was about thirty-eight years of age. He was admitted on trial in the South Carolina Conference in 1812, and had faithfully and usefully filled many important appointments in South Carolina and Georgia. He was in the prime of life, and of

---

* Larabee, p. 228.

a spotless reputation, both as a man and a minister. In his private and social intercourse he was cordial, sincere, and affectionate; and as a preacher, he was earnest, strong, and useful, grasping his subjects firmly, and often presenting his thoughts with peculiar force and effect. His strong common sense, combined with his piety, intelligence, and undoubted devotion to the Church, pointed him out as a suitable man for the office. How he has fulfilled its duties, we must let his future biographer tell. He still lives as the superannuated senior Bishop of the Methodist Episcopal Church, South, honored and beloved by all who know him, as a man and a Bishop, without guile or reproach.

John Emory was a native of Queen Anne county, Maryland, born 1789. He received a classical education, and devoted himself to the study of the law with ardor and success. Before he had reached his majority, he obtained license as a lawyer, and soon secured an honorable position in his profession. His parents were Methodists, and belonged to the best class of the community. He joined the Church at seventeen years of age, and entered the itinerant ministry, in the Baltimore Conference, in 1810. In person, he was below the medium height, thin, not weighing over 120 pounds. His features were indicative of intelligence, benignity, and thoughtfulness. His manners were easy, grave, and always dignified. His early classical and professional training had developed a mind naturally clear and vigorous. His piety was steady; his sense of duty strong. In debate, he seized upon the point at issue at once, cleared it of all extraneous verbiage, and discussed it logically. Such was the estimate placed upon his character and abilities, that he was sent, in 1820, as a representative of the Church to the British Conference, and in 1824 was elected Book Agent with Nathan Bangs. Mr. Emory had filled every position with great propriety and success, and brought to the Book Agency the very highest capacity for the management of that difficult work, and, in association with his laborious and worthy colleague, effected great and useful results. Take him all in all, as a scholarly and thoroughly trained mind, he had no superior in that General Conference. He had therefore rare qualifications for his office. This was tested severely immediately after his consecration. It is a custom, which would be "more honored in the breach than in the observance," to place the newly-elected Bishop in the chair the first session after his ordination. In Bishop Emory's case this happened to be the closing session of the body. It was moreover a night-session, the members were impatient, had arranged to leave early next morning, and there was a great deal of unfinished business and some perplexing matters to adjust. I think I never saw a General Conference session which threatened to be more difficult to control, and I truly sympathized with our Episcopal novitiate when the elder Bishops placed him in the chair that night. But, to the surprise of all, he had not occupied it five minutes before there was perfect order. He was calm, self-possessed; understood thoroughly the "Rules of Order," and applied them promptly, impartially, and to the admiration of all present. Thus a great amount of business was dispatched quietly and intelligibly; delicate questions were settled; notices given; and late at night the largest body of our ministers which had ever convened in the United States, adjourned in good order, to meet in Cincinnati, Ohio, May, 1836. It was the most harmonious and conservative session held since the organization of the delegated body in 1808.

CHAPTER VIII.

Bishop Emory's visit to the South—His death—His letter to Bishop McKendree—Both died the same year—Bishop McKendree takes final leave of old friends—Gets back to Tennessee on a bed in a carriage—Letter from Bishop Morris—Dr. Adam Clarke's letter—Melville B. Cox—His account of himself—Goes as missionary to Liberia—Dies.

Bishop Emory returned to New York the day after the close of the General Conference, and the writer having a lady in charge, had the pleasure of his company. He had known him for eight years, but had not been much with him, except in General Conferences and committees, and was much pleased with his affable manners and gravely genial spirit. Upon arriving by steam-boat at the New York wharf, there was as usual a great crowd, and a rush of hack and cab-drivers for baggage and passengers. The Bishop advised me to stand by our baggage until he should select a conveyance, and then we must take it, and leave the management of the baggage to him until he should come to us. When all was ready, we were surprised to see him get in too, and order the driver to carry us to a certain private boarding-house. It was nearly night, and we knew that his family resided out of the city, and remonstrated against his taking the time to accompany us out of his way. He persisted, introduced and committed us to his friend, and then left for his own home, promising to call on us at our far-distant Southern home "some day." This promise he made good during his only tour to hold the Southern Conferences, greatly to our surprise and gratification; for late one afternoon in 1833, who should ride up to our home in La Grange, Alabama, but the Bishop? He had traveled on horseback pretty much alone the whole distance from his house to Alabama, and was *en route* to the Mississippi and Louisiana Conferences. With us he tarried and rested about a week. Knowing his peculiar temperament, and that he could not sleep unless all was silence and darkness, he was domiciled in a retired room, and at night all his fire was extinguished, the doors and windows tightly fastened, and the utmost quietude was enjoined—even the watch-dog was interdicted from barking. While here, he wrote out his plan for a four-years' course of study instead of two, with various other important suggestions upon this and kindred subjects, as explained in his letter to Bishop McKendree, written at this time and place. He visited and preached for us, and the writer went some distance with him when he left. His visit taught us to love him deeply: we had respected and admired him before.

The ensuing year (1835) he was thrown from his carriage, and was found on the turnpike near Baltimore, bleeding and dying. Then the Church suffered a great loss, and we mourned over his early death as for a brother beloved. The writer has perpetuated his name in his own family, and his memory in his heart.

The following is his interesting letter to Bishop McKendree, just referred to above:

La Grange, Ala., October 28, 1833.

Dear Bishop:—If your health will allow it, as I hope it will, I beg your consideration of the following thoughts, and your judgment on them, at your convenience.

It has long been my conviction that our course of study for young preachers should be the *same* in *all* the Conferences; that it should be more simple and Methodistical than it has been in some of them—the *indispensable* books being such as all the candidates can everywhere and at all times obtain—and the measures for examination to be more efficient. A sketch of this sort may be found in the course proposed by Bishop Hedding and myself to the Philadelphia Conference in April last, and very unanimously adopted. It is contained in the Christian Advocate and Journal of May 10th; and though it was drawn up in haste amid the business of Conference, yet I beg leave to refer you to it as an outline of what I propose for the present, subject to the improvements of experience and time. The course is there divided into *two* years in reference to the present rule for admission into full connection; but I shall hope that we may agree to recommend to the next General Conference the extension of it to *four* years in reference to graduation to the full powers of eldership; by which means also the course may be made more comprehensive, and elders be trained up who will be prepared to advise and examine others on doctrine, discipline, and government, as well as on language, history, geography, etc. The necessity for such a *uniform* course of study of the *same* standard works for both traveling and local preachers—as you will presently see my plan embraces—appears to me the most obvious, not only from the mere fact of the great annual increase of our members spread over so great an extent of country, but also from the multiplication of books and the many speculations which are issued from the press—whether our own or others—through the periodicals or otherwise. I propose, also, that the committees of examination be always appointed at the Annual Conference preceding; that each member of the committee be informed on what particular branch of the course he will be expected to examine; that the candidate be required to meet the committee in the morning of the day before the sitting of the Conference; that the members of the committee be *in part* changed annually, so as to circulate the work of examining through the Conference, and thereby to excite the older members to study in order to prepare themselves for this duty; and also that we ourselves in the General Superintendency, on whom the effective administration rests, make ourselves familiar with the course as far as may be convenient—which may the more readily be done when it shall be the same in all the Conferences—attend the examinations when practicable, and give such advice and assistance as we may judge expedient; thereby exciting both the candidates and examiners to greater diligence, promoting uniform views and practice, acquainting ourselves personally with the qualifications of those whom we have to station, and on whom to lay hands, not to mention the improvement (which I feel much the need of myself) which we ourselves may derive from being present on these occasions, and thus assisting to teach.

And now in reference to the local order—the great nursery for the itinerant connection—why may we not, through the Presiding Elders or otherwise, recommend to all the Quarterly-meeting Conferences to require attention to the *same* course of study, suitably divided, on the part, for example, of all those applying for license to preach, or for renewal of license, or recommendation of orders, or to travel, that they shall, in these respective cases, have previously acquainted themselves with such a part of the course as shall have been prescribed? This, in the first place, will tend to check the licensing of wholly unfit persons and the recommending of such either for orders or to travel; and, in the second place, local preachers who had previously gone through this uniform course of training, would, in case of their admission into the traveling connection, find their subsequent progress easy; and the way would be also thus prepared for a future enlargement and improvement of the course. Indeed, I see no reason why the Annual Conferences and the Quarterly-meeting Conferences, by consent, on our advice, might not now act on these principles, preparatory to the establishment of some such uniform and efficient measures by the General Conference. In all cases of committees for examining local preachers on the course, I should think it desirable that one or more of the preachers of the circuit or station should be of the committee, and that the Presiding Elder should be present, and give his advice or assistance as he might judge expedient—in the same manner as is proposed to be done by the Bishops in the case of itinerant preachers—thus securing or promoting, as far as practicable, a harmony of views and practice between our two great ministerial bodies. One other great point which I have much at heart, believing it vitally important for the preservation of our economy, and to both spiritual and temporal prosperity, is, the effecting of a greater uniformity in the administration of discipline throughout our wide-spread charge. In this I fear there is not only increasing neglect, but great variety, if not contrariety: as a preventive, or a remedy in part, I think of proposing to the Bishops—

1. That we severally keep a record of all decisions made by either of us, and of all those of a general nature made by any Annual Conference which we may attend, and that we communicate them to each other at the close of our respective rounds of Conferences, or oftener; that we may sustain each other when we agree, or endeavor to convince each other and come to an agreement when we differ.

2. That we direct the Presiding Elders to keep a record of all of their decisions and those of any Quarterly-meeting Conferences which they may attend, and to furnish us with a copy when they meet us at our respective Annual Conferences.

3. That all preachers in charge be directed to consult their Presiding Elders in all cases of difficulty or doubt, and the Presiding Elders, in cases of difficulty or doubt to them, to consult the Bishop most convenient; and if we ourselves individually doubt, to consult each other by letter, giving such temporary instructions in the meantime as we shall judge most prudent. I had once indeed thought of proposing that one of us be designated to whom all such communications should be made in the interval of Conferences, and that one to communicate with the rest in cases of difficulty at such time as he should judge proper. This would obviously throw on such an individual great labor, and I am not sure whether it would be the best plan; yet, if any one of the Bishops be willing to take it, I should heartily concur, or should even be willing to render any service in this way in my power, if desired, rather than to fail in the object.

4. That the Bishops agree to meet always several days (perhaps a week would be little enough) previously to each General Conference, then and there to discuss all points remaining unsettled in our proper province; by which means also we would be better prepared to make such farther recommendations as we should judge requisite.

With best wishes and prayers for your health and happiness, Very affectionately,

J. EMORY.

P. S. The Conferences which I am next to attend, the Lord willing, will be at Natchez, Mississippi, November 13th; Montgomery, Alabama, December 11th; Washington, Georgia, January 8th; Charleston, South Carolina, February 5th; after which, to Baltimore; and shall at all times be happy to hear from you, and to receive your counsel, or any suggestions which may occur to you. J. E.

The foregoing letter, whatever opinions there may be as to some of his suggestions—and the writer is free to say he sees no serious objections to any of them—exhibits strongly the characteristics of this great and good man's mind. Many of his suggestions have been adopted in the Methodist Episcopal Church, South, and, it is believed, in the Methodist Episcopal Church, also. In thinking of Bishop Emory, and of his equally talented son Robert, and of their early death, the exclamation involuntarily rises to our lips, Why, O why, were such men taken so soon away? We must wait for the answer until the day of judgment. Until then, we must bow with submission to the providence of a wise and good God.

The death of Bishop McKendree and Bishop Emory occurred in the same year — 1835 — the former, like the evening star, slowly and majestically sinking below the horizon of a cloudless sky; the latter, as if

The brightest star in all the train,
The glory of night's diadem,

should rush from the meridian, and become suddenly extinct. But they are *not extinct*—they have risen in another hemisphere to shine *for ever!*

"The General Conference of 1832 having closed, the senior Bishop took an affectionate leave of his friends, and especially of the preachers, expecting to see them no more until he should meet in the heavenly city." With mingled emotions of sorrow and joy, this final farewell was uttered—they "sorrowing most of all for the words which he spake, that they should see his face no more;" and that, however white the wide-spread harvest-field might be, the arm that had swung the sickle so long and so effectively, was now palsied by age, and the voice that had rung its clarion shouts of "Onward!" to his fellow-toilers in the glorious work, was like the daughters of music brought low; the doors were being shut in the streets, the sound of the grinding was low, the almond-tree flourished, the grass-hopper was a burden, desire failing, and man was going to his long home. On his part, doubtless, there were tears, and sorrow, too; but could we look into the depths of his heart, we should find that this sorrow was not on account of youthful pleasure gone, nor for declining health and strength; still less for cares, and toils, and sufferings endured, but rather that he could work and suffer no longer for Christ's sake.

Returning to Baltimore, he spent a few weeks enjoying the society of many endeared to him by long years of Christian love and fellowship; then turning his face to the West, "he crosses the Alleghany Mountains, which he had so often crossed in weariness and affliction before, for the last time. Passing through the western part of Pennsylvania, the north of Virginia, the States of Ohio and Kentucky, he at last reached his friends in Tennessee. In the latter part of this journey it became necessary to fix a bed in the carriage on which he might lie down, being too feeble to sit up."

In connection with the foregoing, and as illustrative of the feelings entertained by the members of the General Conference, as well as of the Church generally, toward the Bishop, I hope I violate no courtesy which will not be conceded, by inserting the following letter from the Rev. Thomas A. Morris, now senior Bishop of the Methodist Episcopal Church, long the loved and trusted friend of Bishop McKendree, as also of the writer:

Cincinnati, Ohio, Feb. 27, 1833.

BISHOP MCKENDREE:—Perhaps when we parted in Philadelphia, I shook hands with you for the last time in the land of our pilgrimage, but am not without hope of seeing you in peace when the redeemed shall be called home. You have had your day of toil, peril, and warfare, but it is nearly gone by; and now, while you retire from the field to recount your campaigns, toils, and victories, it must be a source of much consolation to lift up your eyes, look eastward, westward, northward, and southward, and behold the land possessed by your brethren and children in the gospel. What wonders God has wrought in these latter days!

The history of our Church in this place the present year, if carried out in all of its parts, would be somewhat remarkable. Three of our local preachers have died, and many of our members. During the cholera, we lost, by removal, etc., two hundred, which reduced us far below twelve hundred. But we had more than all this to discourage us. . . . Yet God was with us, and this was enough. The work began to appear in October, among the brethren first, and then the wicked. It gradually increased, until Brother Maffitt came on the last of November, which formed a new crisis in the history of a *revival* that has now become both deep and wide. Seven hundred, at least, have now been regularly admitted on trial, and I risk nothing in saying, more than five hundred souls have been "born again." Many of the old members have obtained the full, flowing evidence of *perfect love.* Class-meetings are feasts of joy among us, and Zion puts on her "beautiful garments." Infidelity, in its various modifications, has suffered much from this work, but the Church is greatly strengthened, both in graces and members. The work still goes on, and we hope to realize a thousand new members in this station the present Conference-year. Glorious revivals are now in progress in many of the towns in Ohio. May the swelling tide roll on and increase until the glory of God shall cover the whole earth!

I trust, Father McKendree, that amidst all of your earthly sufferings, you hold on to the *sheet-*

anchor, and when your heart and your flesh shall fail you, may God be the strength of your heart, and your portion for ever!

Your obedient son in the gospel,

THO. A. MORRIS.

As there had been an interchange of delegates between the British and American Methodists at the two preceding General Conferences, it was hoped that as we had sent one in 1828, (Dr. Capers,) another would be sent by the British Conference to the General Conference of 1832; and as it was greatly desired by Bishop McKendree, as well as by others, that Dr. Adam Clarke should visit us, it appears that certain well-known ministers wrote him a letter, inviting him to visit the United States. The following highly interesting reply is found among the Bishop's papers:

To Messrs. J. Emory, B. Waugh, N. Bangs, F. Hall, and George Suckley:

GENTLEMEN AND REVEREND BRETHREN:—Having been absent in the West of England for a considerable time, your letter did not reach my hand till some weeks after its arrival. Your kind invitation to visit the United States was gratifying to me, and had I been apprised of your intention a few months earlier, I should most certainly have endeavored to meet your wishes; and by doing so, I have no doubt I should have been both gratified and profited. But the warning is too short, and I am engaged so far, both to England and Ireland, in behalf of our missionary cause, that I cannot by any substitute redeem those pledges. I had proposed also to have visited the Zetland Isles, if possible; but as I had not pledged myself to the voyage, I would have waived my purpose in favor of America—to visit which I have been long waiting for an opening of Providence. I might add, that I should have wished to have had the appointment of our Conference for the voyage.

Now, although I feel a measure of regret that I am disappointed in this wished-for visit to the American continent, yet I am far from supposing that there may not be a providential interference in the way. I am, as no doubt you have already learned, an *old man*, having gone beyond *three-score years and ten*, and consequently not able to perform the labor of youth. You would naturally expect me to preach much, and this I could not do. One sermon in the day generally exhausts me; and I have been obliged, for several years, to give up all evening preaching, as I found the night air to be peculiarly injurious to my health. My help, therefore, must have been very limited, and in many cases this would be very unsatisfactory to the good people of the United States. This deficiency, I grant, might be supplied by an able assistant, who might be inclined to accompany me; but even this would not satisfy the eye or ear of *curiosity*. But, as the journey is now impracticable, these reflections are useless.

I respect and wish well to your *State*, and love your *Church*. As far as I can discern, you are close imitators of the original Methodists, (than whom a greater blessing has not been given to the British nation since the Reformation,) holding the same doctrines and acting under the same discipline; therefore have you prospered as we have prospered. There is no danger so imminent both to *you* and *us* as departing from our original *simplicity*, in spirit, in manners, and in our mode of worship. As the *world* is continually changing around us, we are liable to be affected by those changes in our manners and in our mode of worship. We think, in many cases, we may please well-intentioned men better, and be more useful to them, by permitting some of the more innocent forms of the *world* to enter into the *Church:* whenever we have done so, we have infallibly lost ground in the depth of our religion, and in its spirituality and unction. I would say to all, Keep your *doctrines* and your *discipline*—not only in your Church-books and in your Society Rules: preach the *former*, without refining on them; observe the *latter*, without bending it to circumstances, or impairing it by frivolous exceptions and partialities.

As I believe your *nation* to be destined to be the mightiest and happiest nation on the globe, so I believe that your *Church* is likely to become the most extensive and pure in the universe. As a *Church*, abide in the apostolic doctrine and fellowship. As a *nation*, be firmly united; entertain no petty differences; *totally* abolish the slave-trade, (if it be not yet done;) abhor all offensive wars; never provoke even the puniest, and never strike the *first blow*. Encourage *agriculture* and friendly *traffic;* cultivate the *sciences* and *arts;* let *learning* have its proper place, space, and adequate share of esteem and honor. If possible, live in peace with all nations; retain your holy zeal for God's cause and your country's weal; and, that you may ever maintain your liberty, avoid, as its bane and ruin, a national debt. I say to you, as it was said to Rome of old:*

> Tu regere imperio populo, Romane, memento;
> Hæ tibi erunt artes; pacisque imponere morem,
> Parcere subjectis et debellare superbos.—*Virgil.*

But whither am I running? Will it be a sufficient excuse to allege, "The zeal of *your house* hath eaten me up"? Truly, truly do I wish you good luck, in the name of the Lord; and therefore, with my best prayers for your civil and religious prosperity, and hearty thanks to each of you individually, for the handsome and honorable manner in which you have framed your invitation, I have the honor to be, gentlemen and reverend brethren, your obliged humble servant and most cordial well-wisher, ADAM CLARKE.

Haydon Hall, Middlesex, February 6, 1832.

Melville B. Cox, a member of the Virginia Conference, who had been stationed in the city of Raleigh

* The appropriateness of this quotation, in its application to the United States, as well as its *morale*, may be questioned.

in 1831, and was a reserve-delegate to this General Conference, volunteered to go as a missionary to Liberia, on the western coast of Africa, and having been accepted and appointed, attended the General Conference on his way to his distant and dangerous field of labor. In mind and heart he seemed admirably adapted to this enterprise, while some thought his health and constitution too frail for it. Great admiration and much sympathy were excited in his behalf. He was a very promising, intelligent, and lovely man, in the prime of life, and full of heroic Christian zeal. Bishop McKendree, feeling a lively interest in the man and the cause, requested him to give in writing the incidents of his life, especially his conversion and religious experience. The following is his answer, written when on his way to embark for Liberia:

Philadelphia, May 28, 1832.

Reverend and Dear Father:—Below are the *data* of my Christian and ministerial experience, which you were pleased so kindly to inquire after. Though my life can have been of little or no consequence in this world, save that I love and am trying to serve God, still, the interest which prompted the inquiry by one so venerable in age and so high in the government and confidence of the Church, I assure you, is very grateful to my feelings. That the God whom you serve may bless and be with you, that he may particularly sustain and comfort you under the infirmities of age and the care of all the Churches, and that your life may long be preserved to us and to the world, is my sincere wish and ardent prayer.

I am now thirty-two years old. I was born in Hallowell, Maine, November 9, 1799. In 1818—the 1st of July, I think—I found peace in believing and joy in the Holy Ghost, while alone in the woods, pleading for mercy in the last language of hope, if not in despair. In a few weeks after I joined a small class of Methodists, and from that time to this my name has been among them. Early in 1820, during a gracious revival, I took charge of a class, and on December 17th of the same year I preached my first sermon. In March following, I was licensed as a local preacher by the Kennebeck District Conference, and immediately commenced traveling under the Presiding Elder. At the Bath Conference of 1822, I was received on trial and put in charge of Exeter Circuit. I traveled as an effective man until May, 1825, when I was taken sick, and was left that year as a supernumerary, with but little prospect of recovering. In 1826 and 1827, I was superannuated—passing the winter of 1826 and the spring of 1827 in Maryland and the lowlands of Virginia, where I have remained until now, except the last year, in North Carolina. In 1828, I located, and took charge of "The Itinerant." In 1830, finding myself about a thousand dollars poorer than when I commenced my editorial labors, under deep family afflictions, and with lungs too sensitive to endure the cold, I left Baltimore for a more Southern climate. The kind manner in which I was received by my Virginia brethren, and an anxiety once more to be in the traveling connection, induced me to join that Conference, and, live or die, once more to *try* to preach to sinners. As yet I have no cause to regret it. It has been a year of greater profit to my soul than any I have ever experienced. I have *suffered* much, but *enjoyed* more. Some souls were converted, and my own more filled than for years. "God was with us." At present, I am in peace. Death looks pleasant to me, life looks pleasant to me, labor and sufferings look pleasant to me, and last, though not least, *Liberia* looks pleasant to me. I see, or think I see, resting on Africa, the light and cloud of heaven. I thirst to know that the winds of heaven are wafting me there. I pray, at least, that my frail body may enrich the soil.

Very affectionately and Christianly, your son in the gospel, M. B. Cox.

On the 9th of March, 1833, he arrived at Liberia, and immediately began his labors. He found many members, class-leaders, and preachers, and organized them into a branch of the Methodist Episcopal Church. He planned three missions and an academy at Monrovia. On the 29th of March, he held the first camp-meeting ever held in Africa. But in less than five months from the time of his arrival he died, and his body rests in the soil of Africa. Nevertheless, he laid the foundation of a great mission, and vindicated his sincerity by prescribing as his epitaph, "Let a thousand fall, before Africa be given up." Alas! twenty-five *white* missionaries had died of the climate, or fled from it with ruined health, in seventeen years, while only four *colored* laborers had died in the same time.

CHAPTER IX.

McKendree attends the Tennessee Conference in Pulaski, 1833—Bishop Roberts failed to get there—Bishop McKendree unable to preside—His substitutes—Meteoric shower—He appoints T. L. Douglass Presiding Elder—Sketch of him—Bishop McKendree's address to his colleagues—His sermon—Returns to Nashville exhausted—Preaches—Resumes his Journal—Watch-night—Starts to New Orleans, January 1, 1834—His account of the tour—At Vicksburg—C. K. Marshall—At Natchez—Judge Edward McGehee and the Rev. John C. Burruss—Dr. Tooley—"Slight paralysis"—His letter to the Rev. F. A. Owen—Returns to Tennessee—His last camp-meeting and interview with Wm. Burke—His last Conference at Lebanon, Tennessee, 1834—Requested to prepare his biography—His reply—Last document.

So utterly debilitated was the Bishop by his long and painful journey from Philadelphia to Tennessee, after the General Conference of 1832, that a considerable period of repose was necessary before he could begin to move about; but, as usual, rest and kind nursing after awhile revived him, and in the latter part of the spring of 1833, and throughout the remainder of the year, he exerted his utmost ability in preaching, visiting, and attending quarterly and camp-meetings. In August, 1833, he attended at Saunders's Camp-ground an interesting camp-meeting, and, of course, preached. His kind hostess, Mrs. H. R. W. Hill, met him there, and carried him to his home in her house at Nashville. There, besides the kindest attention, he could enjoy frequent religious privileges, and the society of his friends—Elliston, Garrett, his old fellow-laborer, Gwin, another firm and devoted friend, A. L. P. Green, whose fine social qualities and reverential attachment to the Bishop always made him an agreeable companion, F. E. Pitts, and Thos. L. Douglass, upon whose fidelity, sound judgment, and love of primitive Methodism he ever relied with unshaken confidence, besides many others, who always made his stay in that vicinity most agreeable.

The Tennessee Conference met in Pulaski, November 6th. Bishop Roberts was expected to preside, but he was taken ill in East Tennessee, and did not get to Conference. Bishop McKendree arrived, but was so feeble and afflicted that, after opening and organizing the body, he despaired of being able to attend effectively to the duties of his office. Indeed, he was in bed most of the session. He informed the Conference of his inability to attend to the onerous detail of the business, and especially in making the Appointments, and that he would select two men who must act for him, subject to his general supervision; claiming, especially, the selection of the Presiding Elder and the arrangement of the Districts. He then named Lewis Garrett and the writer as his substitutes. The session closed on the 15th. It was a long and laborious one.

On the night of Tuesday and Wednesday, the 12th and 13th November, occurred the memorable meteoric shower, which is admitted to have been the most magnificent on record. The Bishop's substitutes and cabinet had been engaged to a late hour, and the writer had just fallen into a profound sleep, when he was aroused by loud calls from without. Upon going out, the most glorious scene was presented. The heavens were illumined by countless meteors. Some seemed small, gliding down like snow-flakes; others were like great fire-balls: a few of these separated into fragments, leaving long and luminous trains behind. Look wherever you might, the whole hemisphere was full of them. It was literally a great shower of meteors. The display began before midnight, increased until three or four o'clock A.M., when it became surpassingly grand, and continued, with little if any diminution, until day-break. Many displays of this kind are recorded, dating back to A.D. 902; the most remarkable of which was that seen by Humboldt and Bonpland, at Cumana, in South America, on the night of the 12th and 13th of November, 1799—the time of the writer's birth. He had just been reading the account given by these *savants* of that shower, and their speculations upon the nature of these bodies, their source, and the height of our atmosphere; and his first thoughts upon witnessing the scene of 1833, were as to these speculations. The meteors of 1799 were observed from the Equator on the south, over North America to Greenland and Labrador, and on the other side of the Atlantic to Germany; and from their bearing and course at different points, their elevation was computed to be 1,419 miles. The display of 1833 was seen over all the United States, the West India Islands, Mexico, and Canada, and their *source*, as computed by Professor Olmstead, of Yale College, could not have been less than 2,238 miles, and consequently was far beyond our atmosphere. Astronomers now, I believe, agree that they emanate from a nebulous body which revolves around the sun, and intersects the earth's orbit periodically. Their nebulous character is inferred from the fact that, though they seem to fall toward the earth with great velocity, none of them ever reach it in a solid state, but are so dissipated that nothing is found to discover their nature. It is also supposed that there are several such bodies, or streams, which periodically intersect the orbit of our planet; and that the most brilliant displays are seen while passing through the densest group of these streams. Meteors are not to be confounded with aerolites.

There was considerable religious interest in Pulaski at the time, and this awfully sublime phenomenon startled and impressed the people very greatly. The less-informed believed "the stars were falling," and the day of judgment had come. Prayers, shouts, and screams arose in many places of the town. Several preachers had asked to be located the previous afternoon: next morning all withdrew their request except one. Some one observed in the Conference, "While the stars seemed falling last night, I thought what a pity it would be to locate on the eve of the judgment!" About forty professed conversion, and joined the Church. After a long session, the Conference closed on November 15th.

The Appointments having been completed, excepting the Presiding Elders, the list was presented to the Bishop, when the incident occurred alluded to in Dr. Green's sketch of Bishop McKendree; and as it exhibits the delicate and responsible nature of this office, as well as his fitness for it, it may be properly introduced:

Thomas L. Douglass had long been known as singularly adapted to the Presiding-eldership. He was a model preacher, well-versed in the history, doctrines, and usages of the Church, administered the Discipline admirably, and dearly loved Methodism. Owing to a fall from his horse, he had been disabled, and had not been effective for four years; but his health had improved considerably, and at this Conference he became effective. A prejudice, however, had arisen against him, both among some of the preachers in the Conference and some of the stewards in his former District, simply and exclusively because he insisted that in the distribution of the "Conference-collections," and the "quarterage" on the circuits, the law of the Church gave to every legal claimant his *pro rata* share; and that in neither case had the stewards the right to constitute themselves a "committee on necessitous cases," and divide the funds at their discretion; that if a preacher was rich, this did not affect his lawful claims, and that *he* preferred to be the almoner of his own money. He admitted that the Conference could appoint a committee on "necessitous cases," who could appropriate such funds as might be obtained for this purpose; but the money raised according to the Discipline is not of this kind, and therefore by right belongs to the regular claimants. In this he was undoubtedly correct; but, on account of these views, there was said to be opposition to his being sent to his old District as Presiding Elder. Bishop McKendree, no doubt, understood it all, and coincided with Douglass as to the law of the Church, yet was distressed because by appointing him to the District he would seem to disregard the wishes of the stewards, and in rejecting him, would not only lose the best man for the position, but appear to sanction a departure from the rule of the Discipline. After revolving the subject anxiously and maturely, he felt it his duty to appoint him to the office. In this he certainly did right, and his decision was fully vindicated; for Brother Douglass was continued on the District during four years, with increasing popularity and usefulness. Then, full of years, and weighed down with infirmities, he retired from the effective ranks which he entered in 1801. In 1843 he closed his life in peace, honored for his talents and usefulness, and loved for his many virtues.

While at the Tennessee Conference, Bishop McKendree dispatched to each of his colleagues the following document, giving his views of the rights and duties of ministers, and the proper manner of trying members according to the Discipline and Scripture. It was addressed to the Bishops, and if they approved of it, to the preachers generally. We do not know whether the other Bishops concurred in his views, nor whether it was ever submitted by them to the Annual Conferences. It presents *his* matured views, and was his last attempt to bring about a consistent and uniform administration of the Discipline in the premises:

BELOVED BROTHER:—In passing through our work here and there, our attention is frequently arrested and called to notice the course pursued in the administration of discipline; and we apprehend there is a danger, in some instances, of a departure from the spirit and letter of the rule, both to the injury of individuals and the work generally. We have therefore thought it advisable that something be done, both to preserve the execution of discipline in its purity, and to maintain uniformity of procedure throughout our societies; and as the Bishops are responsible for a correct administration of the government, it would seem to us that it is our business to unite in such a course as will have a tendency both to correct errors and abuses, and harmonize the views of our preachers on this all-important subject. In view of this object, the accompanying Address has been drawn up, for the purpose of being presented to the preachers in the Annual Conferences. There may be some things needing correction not noticed in this Address, but those which are mentioned are, to us, very evidently of high importance. They are submitted to you for inspection and concurrence. Explanations of this kind cannot be given with propriety or authority, in the intervals of General Conference, except from the Episcopacy; and we shall be greatly strengthened and sustained therein by consulting and knowing that *old men* and *men of experience* approve and concur with us in those things.

With continued prayers to Almighty God that he may prosper and bless you in all your labors in his vineyard, we remain, as ever, your brethren in the love and fellowship of the gospel of our Lord Jesus Christ.

To the preachers and brethren whose duty it may be to execute the discipline of our Church:

Dearly beloved in the Lord:—It is admitted to be the glory of Methodism that it is virtually the *same* in every part of the world: our doctrines are the *same* both in Europe and America; our discipline the *same* throughout the United States; and the execution of discipline, or the administration of the government of the Church, *ought* to be the *same* throughout the societies. In this respect, however, we have found considerable difference of sentiment and practice, owing, it is presumable, to the different circumstances and situation of things in different sections of our widely-extended field of labor. It is therefore thought proper that a short explanatory view of our rules, for conducting the trials of preachers and members in our Church, should be presented to you for the all-important purpose of preserving and maintaining, if possible, a uniform practice among us, in every respect, conformable to our excellent system of discipline.

As the grand object of the gospel is to save men, consequently the design of gospel discipline is to convict, reform, and fit them for happiness, and not to destroy or render them subjects of misery. In the execution of discipline, punishment or expulsion is the last operation consequent upon man's continuance in unbelief and crime, and this is a painful work to the administrator. When our Lord pronounced sentence against the Jewish nation, he wept. Luke xix. 41–44.

St. Paul suffered much persecution from the backslidden Corinthians, but he persevered in the exercise of gospel-discipline, by applying the doctrines of justice to convict, and mercy to encourage a return to reformation, until he succeeded and triumphed in their salvation. (See 1st and 2d Epistles to the Corinthians.)

In conformity to this view of gospel-discipline, our rules and regulations are carried into operation, with the explicit understanding that crimes are divided into two classes: The first comprehends all such as are "expressly forbidden in the word of God;" (see Discipline, p. 68;) and to this class *only* is the act of punishment or expulsion extended in the first instance of the exercise of discipline. The second class of crimes comprehends neglect of duties, etc. (See Book of Discipline, p. 70.) In all such cases, the first step in the exercise of discipline is private reproof, given by some one having the charge over the supposed offender; and if there be an acknowledgment, etc., the person is to be borne with. On a second offense—that is, on the crime being repeated—one or two faithful friends are to be taken, and if the person be not then cured, the case is to be brought before the Church, as the Discipline directs; and if there be no sign of real humiliation, he must be cut off. And when a person is clearly convicted of such a crime or crimes, nothing short of expulsion will satisfy the rule, unless there be such a manifestation of genuine repentance and humiliation as will justify the extention of pardon to the offending person; in such case, the connection between crime and its punishment is dissolved. Such cases may possibly occur, and when they do, much care and prudence is necessary to guard the Church from reproach and injury, and, at the same time, save the offender. In all cases of the second class of crime, the first and second steps ought to be taken previously to bringing the offender before the Church, and the continual intention should be to "save a soul from death" and the Church from reproach, and influence of bad example consequent on holding persons guilty of crime in fellowship. James v. 20; Jude 20–25.

The Discipline, when rightly understood, in connection with the nature of our Episcopal government, very clearly points out the mode of trial to be pursued in regard to the different grades in the ministry, and also the private members; and there are some important principles closely connected with the administration of discipline which should never be forgotten.

A *Bishop*, or *Superintendent*, having the general oversight of the spiritual and temporal concerns of the Church, is, of course, authorized to attend to any and all matters, small and great, in the execution of discipline.

A *Presiding Elder*, who is, in fact, the agent of the Bishop, is, in virtue of his appointment, authorized to exercise Episcopal authority within the limits of his District, (ordination excepted;) consequently, it is his business, when present, fully to attend to every part of the execution of discipline.

The *assistant preacher* is indeed the Presiding Elder's aid, and has the more particular oversight and care of the circuit or station to which he is appointed. (See his duties as contained in the Discipline, p. 39.)

The *helper* is one placed on a circuit or station, with the assistant, and is under his direction in any thing he may do in the execution of discipline.

The *class-leader* is restricted to his own class; and, if active and zealous, may do much for God and souls in keeping up order and discipline therein.

It should never be forgotten that the privileges of our ministers and preachers of trial, by a committee and of an appeal, and the privileges of our members of trial before the society, or by a committee and of an appeal, are sacredly guaranteed to them by the Constitution of our Church.

The great object of committees is to attend to complaints or charges in the intervals of Conferences, and thereby rescue the character of innocent brethren, wrongfully accused, from injury, and preserve their usefulness by acquitting them when not found guilty; and, if judged to be guilty, to save the Church from reproach and injury, by suspending them until the ensuing Conference. The suspending power is clearly restricted to such crimes as are expressly forbidden in the word of God, and to such as are persisted in after gospel-reproof and admonition have been given. And it may be farther remarked, that neither the organization of a committee, nor any of its acts, can abridge the powers of a Conference when they afterward come to act on the same case; and should a case occur at or during the sitting of Conference, or although known of, be neglected; or if it should be of such a recent date as not to afford time to call a committee, and should then be brought before the Conference, there is nothing in discipline or reason to prevent the Conference from hearing and deciding thereon without the intervention of a committee, and especially if the person accused desire it. But, as the Conference has the entire control of all cases in which its own members are concerned, subject to the order of discipline, they may, or they may not, appoint a committee, as they may judge proper; but they cannot, in any case, transfer their *authority as a Conference.* The committee can only *acquit* if not guilty, or *suspend* if guilty; and if suspended, the Conference must finally determine the case. The accused ought always to have timely notice to prepare for trial; and, while on one hand, the administrator of discipline does not rule him to trial unprepared, so, on the other hand, he ought not to put off or lay over the trial of a case without good reasons.

The assistant preacher, in a circuit or station, is invested with full power to oversee all the concerns of the Church, as far as his jurisdiction extends, in attending to the complaints and wants of each member without partiality, and very strictly, but mildly, enforce every part of the Discipline, as occasion may require. If he obtains a knowledge of any misconduct or violation of discipline by any of his members or preachers, it is his duty, as soon as possible, to attend to the case and have it settled, without waiting for a formal charge to be handed to him. He himself must act in behalf of the Church, as God's minister appointed to that work. Ezek. iii. 17; xxxiii. 7; 1 Cor. v. 1–5; Rev. ii. 1, 2, 12–15, 18–20; Heb. xiii. 7, 17.

No person ought to be permitted to *come forward* in the character of a *prosecutor.* Such a character is not known of in all our economy. The *accuser* is to be *brought* face to face with the accused. If this cannot be done, "let the *next best evidence* be procured;" consequently, the accuser is the very best evidence in the case. An aggrieved person may be a *complainant;* but our Discipline does not recognize any one as an accuser, unless he be a witness in the case against the accused. Any and all testimony offered on the trial of a case ought to be read or heard; but if any be of doubtful character, the Church is at liberty to give it as much weight as they think it deserves. We have no rule making it illegal to admit what is called *ex parte* evidence. No accused preacher or member ought to be suspended or expelled unless found guilty by a majority of those by whom he is tried. On taking a vote, the question ought always be put in the positive. If any accused person has any well-grounded objection to any one called to sit on his trial, a prudent and judicious administrator would leave out the person objected to, and, if necessary, supply the place with another. But the right of *challenge*, so called, is not recognized in our Discipline. We do not think it advisable, or consistent with propriety or the nature of things, that a person should vote in the same case in condemnation of an accused person, both in the society or select number, or on a committee and in Conference, or in more than one Conference where appeals are taken. We think it prudent and a mark of sound judgment to pay due respect to the *opinions* and *advice* of the *aged*, who have had experience, because from such it is expected that a knowledge of *primitive usage* and *custom* may be obtained; and, in every point, there ought to be frequent recurrence to *first principles*. These are generally best expressed in the original words which contain them. Observe well the *old landmarks*, inquire after the *old paths*, and rally around the *old standards—the standards of our fathers*.

The careful reader will perceive a discrepancy between some things in the above document and Brother Crouch's remarks as to the Bishop's sentiments about his authority to preside in a Quarterly-meeting Conference—if Brother Crouch did not mistake his *unwillingness* to do so under ordinary circumstances, for an avowal of his want of *authority* to do it under *any* circumstances. I suppose our *fathers* generally agreed with the views set forth on this point in this document. Bishop Asbury, it is said, coincided with Bishop McKendree.

The Bishop was evidently much exhausted at this Conference, and returned to Nashville slowly, stopping to rest on the way at Brother Douglass's and other old homes. We hear from him, however, on the first Sunday of December, preaching a very clear and impressive sermon in Nashville, and administering the Holy Eucharist. On December 25th, he preached in the same place on Luke ii. 8–14; (see Appendix;) and again holding a watch-meeting in the same Church on the last night of the year 1833, addressing a large audience on "the goodness of God," and closing the meeting with the Lord's Prayer.

He now resumed his habit of keeping a Journal, and says:

"For several years I have not been able to travel and preach as formerly, and therefore had no matter for a Journal except my own experience as an afflicted man; but as I am yet spared, I will notice some of the displays of Divine goodness, for my own comfort and improvement.

"On Wednesday evening, December 31, 1833, I attended a watch-night in the new church in Nashville. It was a solemn time. I felt my spiritual strength renewed. I returned with Brother Hill and his family, and at four o'clock I arose refreshed, and in a comfortable state of health.

"About ten o'clock, January 1, 1834, took passage

on the spacious steamer Tennessean, commanded by Captain Thos. P. Minor. The river was low. We arrived at the Harpeth Shoals in the evening. The steamer Pacific was aground. We put off one hundred and ninety bales of cotton, and succeeded with difficulty in getting over the shoals.

"Thursday, 2d, was a cold, snowy day. We had about fifty cabin passengers—a very agreeable set—and one hundred deck passengers.

"Friday, 3d—last night was very cold: at ten o'clock at the mouth of Cumberland River.

"Sunday, 5th—the thermometer was below zero. At three o' clock, I preached to an attentive congregation, on Heb. ix. 27.

"Monday, 6th—large addition of freight and passengers. River covered with ice—breaking the paddles and arms of the boat.

"Thursday, 9th—abundance of ice coming down the Mississippi River; the captain thinks it the hardest freeze he ever saw from so short a spell; so foggy, could not run at night.

"Friday, 10th—passed Memphis; foggy.

"Saturday—foggy; laid by at night, and until six o'clock A.M.

"Sunday, 12th—preached from Romans vi. 23. The hearers serious and attentive. Hope for good.

"Monday, 13th—boat ran all night for the first time; ice in the morning three-fourths of an inch thick.

"Tuesday, 14th—at Vicksburg. The stationed preacher at this place (C. K. Marshall) came on board; had an interesting conversation with him on different subjects for nearly two hours. There is a meeting-house and a flourishing society in this town, and a circuit in the neighborhood of several hundred members. Yesterday a duel was fought across the river—a man was dangerously wounded.

"Wednesday, 15th—arrived at Natchez five o'clock A.M.; found myself in a deplorable condition. It seems of twenty-seven days there have been but two fair days; mud in the streets knee-deep—shoe-deep on side-walks.

"For my passage I paid $20; to waiters on boat, $1 75; to porter, 50 cents; waded shoe-deep in mud to tavern; for riding in dirty hack, $1. Got to my old friend Dr. Tooley's; found all well; met with a hearty welcome," etc.

Here was a trip of fifteen days from Nashville to Natchez! He was now in good quarters, but mud and weather-bound. Preached on Sunday, 19th, to white people in the forenoon, and to large colored congregation at three o'clock. A profitable time!

"Sunday, 26th—another rainy week. Dr. Tooley preached an ingenious sermon from Gen. i. 22, 23, 24.

"Tuesday, 28th—very cold for this climate; rain, snow, and sleet; but I am comfortable; excellent coffee, every morning at six o'clock, greatly relieves me of headache.

"Sunday, 2d February—got to meeting; heard the stationed preacher, Brother F. A. Owen. I administered the Sacrament; a profitable meeting. Sacrament to the colored members at three o'clock.

"Tuesday, 4th—Judge Edmund McGehee and John C. Burruss called to see me."

The Rev. J. C. Burruss was a native of Virginia, removed to North Alabama in 1819, and settled near Huntsville, where his talents and family position gave him great influence. He was a very fluent and impressive preacher, of fine address, and unusually agreeable social qualities. At the time this interview occurred, he was in charge of Wilkinson Circuit, in Mississippi, and was the father-in-law of Judge McGehee. The Bishop's Journal states at length certain events in his early history in connection with Mr. O'Kelly's proselyting and schismatical course in Williamsburg and Hanover Circuits, Virginia, in 1796–7, and the Bishop's success in counteracting his efforts, was brought to his recollection by Brother Burruss.

Under date of February 6th, he notices the fact that although he had been in Natchez twenty-two days, he had preached only twice—the state of the weather and the streets preventing—but assisted by Dr. Tooley, had paid many visits to the poor and afflicted. He says: "Our method was to introduce religious conversation at once; after this prayer; commit them to God, and take our leave. . . . The visiting of families to dine or take tea, I designedly avoided:

"1. Because I doubt if the minister's time is most profitably spent in that way.

"2. Whether social intercourse of this kind promotes family piety as much as purely religious visits.

"3. Unless the rich and poor are treated alike, the latter is liable to think the minister partial.

"Friday, 7th—Dr. Tooley took me seven miles to Washington. I put up with Brother Miles Harper—a friend of more than thirty years' acquaintance. Here I was comforted with temporal, social, and spiritual blessings.

"Sunday, 9th—preached to a large and attentive audience—Ps. xxiii. 1. Hope good was done. In the afternoon returned to Dr. Tooley's.

"At eight o'clock, Monday, 10th, left Dr. Tooley's in a hired hack for Judge McGehee's, Wilkinson county, Mississippi. Brother Owen offered to go with me; I thought it unnecessary, but he persisted. Soon I was thankful for his kind attention. For seventeen miles the road was pretty good; but after crossing the Homochitto River, the mud was very deep, and the horses refused to pull, and after taking them from the carriage, Brother Owen and the driver carried it by hand to the level of the bridge, from whence the horses took it to the next bad place. Got to Brother Grooms's, and stayed all night.

"Tuesday, 11th—we left before eight o'clock, and went fifteen miles to Judge McGehee's by three o'clock P.M., through horribly muddy roads. All glad to see us.

"Wednesday, 12th—very sore to-day from yesterday's work.

"Thursday, 13th—my *head* very much disordered.

"Sunday, 16th—preached in Woodville—Gal. vi. 9. The Church here in a very formal state.

"Wednesday, 19th—last night had another slight shock of what I consider as *paralysis*. My physicians reject this idea, but I regard it, as I have for years, as gentle visitations of paralysis, and apprehend it may terminate in death; and am therefore admonished to 'be *always ready*.'

"Sunday 23d—quite unwell: preached: left pulpit very feeble. Dined with Brother Chew; lectured at night at Brother McGehee's to a number of colored people—Isa. xii. *Weary*.

"I fear the societies in this quarter have but little of the power of religion; yet the families where I have been appear to attend regularly to the form."

His last entry in this Journal is, "Monday, 24th—my health is better—my strength increasing."

After spending a short time in Woodville and its vicinity, enjoying the princely hospitality of the Judge and his excellent family, he continued his trip to New Orleans. He had ever manifested much solicitude for the spiritual welfare of this city, which he foresaw was destined to become the great mart of South-western commerce. Having returned to Natchez, he there took passage for Nashville on the same boat—Tennessean—about April 18th. The following characteristic note was addressed to the stationed preacher, and shows his constant vigilance as a supervisor of the preachers and the Church generally:

Natchez, Miss., April 16, 1834.

DEAR BROTHER OWEN:—For a stationed preacher regularly to attend to his appointments for preaching, class-meeting, and visiting the sick from house to house, is his indispensable duty. But the spirit of enterprise will carry him farther. Were you to select proper places for preaching and prayer-meetings in private houses, much good might be done; and if the flat-bottom boats were to be visited with sermons, the good effects are beyond calculation. On these boats there are some religious persons, and some well disposed to religion, that would be instructed and built up, instead of losing their good desires; and seed might be sown among the careless to bring forth fruit and spread the gospel in their neighborhoods on their return home. The correctness of these sentiments has been realized among us. You have a fair opportunity to make the experiment, and I think it will be inexcusable if you do not.

Brother Owen joined the Tennessee Conference in 1822, was a superintendent of the missions to the Cherokee Indians, a delegate to several General Conferences, Agent of the Southern Methodist Publishing House, besides filling many important appointments in the regular itinerant work. He is yet a member of the Memphis Conference, and doing service in the Mississippi Bottom District.

On May 10, 1834, the Bishop preached an unusually long and interesting sermon in Gallatin, Tennessee, and he officiated at the communion, and was in pretty good health, for him. Through the spring and summer he continued to preach, and visited as much as he could, and Dr. Green gives a very interesting account of his last camp-meeting:

"It was in Sumner county, at Old Salem; and we were also favored with the presence of the Rev. Wm. Burke. I had the pleasure of seeing them meet. They held each other's grasp for some time, the Bishop saying, 'I am very happy to see you once more at camp-meeting,' while Mr. Burke says, 'We have camped together before, Bishop.' Tears came into their eyes. They talked together by the hour of other days, with an evident pleasure which was refreshing to observe. Mr. Burke was not at that time in connection with the Methodist Episcopal Church, but was the pastor of an independent congregation in Cincinnati; yet I put him up to preach, so that the thousands that attended the meeting had the great pleasure of hearing each of these old veterans preach once a day for three successive days; and I would perform a pilgrimage now to enjoy such a privilege.

"Soon after this meeting was over, the Bishop said to me, 'I would like to live until next General Conference, for one thing.' 'What is that, Bishop?' 'I want to see Brother Burke back again in his place in the Church.' Although the Bishop did not live to attend the Conference, Mr. Burke was restored, and died in the Church."

The last Conference this good and venerable man of God attended, was the Tennessee, held in Lebanon, November 5, 1834. It was an affecting sight to witness the reverence and filial affection of the Conference toward him. He had set apart most of the members to the work of the ministry —had baptized many of them in their infancy.

Their fathers had known and loved him. He had been the organizer and defender of Methodism in the West—a pioneer Presiding Elder in 1800, when his District was an empire in extent, embracing all "the Western country." He had submitted cheerfully to the privations of frontier life, whether traversing the wilderness, in the wigwam of the Indian, or in the cabin of the white pioneer—to unceasing travel over mountains and plains, through the rains, snows, and sleets of winter, and the drought, heat, and malaria of the South in summer. He had instructed, guided, and governed the young and feeble, animated the desponding—had been always in the front rank, charging against the strongholds of sin and Satan—himself never dismayed or despondent, but ever brave and true. Far-seeing, calm, and unselfish—their oracle in Church-polity; and never descending to draggle himself or others in the cess-pool of partisan politics; "without partiality and without hypocrisy;" loving devotedly the Church—the whole Church—its doctrines, its simple and significant scriptural formularies, its government—especially its itinerancy, because of its efficiency in spreading the gospel among the poor and destitute: for these eminent qualities, and lastly, for his unchallenged purity, he ought to have been, and was, revered and loved as a father.

The Conference was impressed with the conviction that the Bishop could not live much longer; for, while his mind seemed clear and vigorous when aroused, yet its tabernacle was evidently falling away. All knew that, while his life had not been marked by any startling events, yet it was very desirable to have the history of it, for the instruction of themselves and the edification of the Church. The following preamble and resolutions were therefore presented by R. Paine and T. L. Douglass, and adopted:

WHEREAS, Our venerable and beloved brother, Bishop McKendree, is now far advanced in the decline of life, and is almost the only remaining minister among us of the early race of Methodist preachers in America; and whereas, he possesses much valuable and interesting information in relation to the organization and government of the Church in these United States, the spread of the work of God, especially in the West and South, the lives and labors of many of his copartners in the ministry, and much other information which may be useful; therefore,

Resolved, That a committee of seven be appointed to wait on Bishop McKendree, and respectfully request him to prepare, or have prepared, for publication so soon as convenient, such a history of his own life, and such information on the various points suggested above, as he may deem proper and expedient.

Whereupon, Thomas L. Douglass, James Gwin, Lewis Garrett, Robert Paine, Alexander L. P. Green, Greenville T. Henderson, and George W. D. Harris, were appointed a committee to carry said resolutions into effect.

The committee appointed to wait on Bishop McKendree, report, that in compliance with the foregoing resolution, they have waited upon him, and acquainted him with the request of the Conference, as directed. In reply, the Bishop states that he belongs to the Methodist Church, that it has a right to claim his services, even to the dregs, and that he will endeavor to comply with the request of the Conference, as he may be able and find it convenient and practicable.

T. L. DOUGLASS, *Ch'n.*

Lebanon, Conference, November 14, 1834.

The following document explains itself; and as it refers to the preceding communication, and is probably the last he ever wrote, it is inserted here. The original very clearly exhibits a marked change in his penmanship; and toward the close, he fails to keep in parallel lines, running them diagonally across the sheet of paper.

At Brother Elliston's, December 1, 1834.

When I set out to preach the gospel, I commenced a regular Journal of my life and ministerial labors. This was continued a number of years, until my papers were consumed in a house that was burned down. By this time I had observed such a sameness in this kind of writings, that its utility was greatly depreciated in my estimation. My lot, too, seemed fixed in an old, settled country, where religious exercises were so familiar as to afford no material of sufficient importance to interest the public mind. My own experience was common among Christians; therefore, though my mind was deeply impressed with many occurrences, they did not appear to be of sufficient importance to interest or profit either the Church or the world. I concluded that my time would be better employed in discharging the various duties assigned me as a Methodist preacher. My field of labor constantly enlarging, I gave up my Journal, and devoted all my time to my regular work. For this omission I had many checks during thirty years, have made some ineffectual attempts to resume it, but have continued my course. Some time before the late Tennessee Conference, I was earnestly addressed upon this subject by individuals. I objected the want of strength of body and mind for the work, but was met with assurances of such assistance as would need only the outlines of the plan, with suitable items, and the work would be done without burdening me. This, it was thought, I could do. I approved of the plan, and consented to do what I could. But, instead of meeting my expectations, they contented themselves with telling me what to do. I therefore abandoned the hope of help from them. Yet, as I have come under obligation by promise, I shall do what I can, which will be little—*very little.* Since the Tennessee Conference, one or two have proffered to assist me, on condition that I would wait on them at suitable times. I shall neither seek nor go one mile out of my way for assistance, but will do what I can, and dispose of it as may seem best.

W. McKENDREE.

Like old men generally, he miscalculated his strength. "*Will do what I can*"—alas! he could do no more. That hitherto indomitable will, which had impelled a body emaciated and enfeebled by age and sufferings, to continue to travel and preach when it should have been resting, could no longer drive the physical machinery; and even that mind, once so elastic, so clear, and so vigorous, always planning and working for God and the Church, was wearied, and found it impossible to isolate itself from its frail tabernacle. "*Very little*" indeed could he do in any other thing; and as to writing his history, sketching the lives of his co-laborers, and the wonderful progress of the Church for forty eventful years, he could absolutely do nothing. It would have been an impracticable task for the most competent member of the Conference to collect the material, assort and arrange the chaotic mass of his papers, between the time of the Conference and his death. It ought to have been begun years before. The fact is, it could never have been done by him, unless he had been imprisoned. He *would go, to the last,* and only ceased to go when compelled to stop: then, body and mind both protested, "*Too late!*" And for this neither he nor any one else is to be blamed.

CHAPTER X.

Bishop McKendree leaves all his papers to Bishop Soule and T. L. Douglass—The Lebanon Conference a time of great interest—He visits the Conference for the last time—Bids adieu—Gwin, Page, Douglass, and McGee there—Returns to Nashville—Preaches his last sermon there, November 23—Goes to his brother's—Depressed—His last battle—Victor—His sufferings—Effect of prayer—Family love—The closing scene—"All 's well"—His burial—Should his remains be removed?—Review of his life and character.

BY his "last will and testament," Bishop McKendree left his papers of every kind to Bishop Soule, to be assisted by T. L. Douglass in the use of them. The latter received the little old "hair trunk," and found it full, but a *jumble.* He seems to have done no more than to look over some of them, and write a few lines of advice as to what should *not* be published. Bishop Soule received it with authority to make such use of it as he should see fit. But he never found time to do more than to put most of the letters into packages, and indorse on them the names of their authors and their dates. Not a line from his pen toward a biography has ever been found. Neither of these good and highly competent men could command the necessary leisure for the task. And if *they* could not do it in twenty years, surely the old Bishop could not have done it in two or three months.

It is rather a remarkable incident that the first Conference he attended as Bishop, was at a camp-meeting at Liberty Hill, in 1808, at Colonel Green Hill's, with whom he and Bishop Asbury camped during the session; and at this, his last Conference, his kind hostess was Mr. Hill's granddaughter.

The Lebanon Conference was a very interesting occasion. More than the usual number of the Bishop's old associates were present. He had lately parted in tears from Burke; and here were Gwin, "one of the kindest friends he ever found, who had given him, for his father and sisters, three hundred acres of land"—the place he called home, and where his remains now rest with his father's and sister's; Garrett, who preceded him to the West, and in 1803, as Presiding Elder of Cumberland District, divided the work with him, and lived and died his true and admiring friend; John McGee, who, with his Presbyterian brother, William, was a leader in the beginning of the great revival of 1799 and 1800, the most powerful and extensive work which has occurred in the United States, not only spreading over the whole West and South, but sweeping, like a great ocean-wave, over all the Northern and Eastern States; John Page, a veteran in the cause, and his greatly-loved "Logan Douglass," besides a host of younger preachers, who revered him as a father.

Among those mentioned above as special friends and former fellow-laborers of the Bishop, is John

McGee. He was in several respects a remarkable man. He was admitted on trial in the Virginia Conference in 1788, with Wm. McKendree, Peter Massie, Henry Birchett, and Valentine Cook; all of them, with perhaps an exception of the last, were converted in the revival under Mr. Easter, as was also Enoch George. What a galaxy! How much does Methodism owe to those great, old-fashioned revivals, which, like earthquakes, shake States and continents!

After spending five years in the itinerancy in the Atlantic portion of the work, Mr. McGee located and came to Tennessee; married, and settled in Smith county. His marriage was a fortunate one, and his domestic relations were happy. But worldly prosperity did not diminish his zeal and usefulness. He was known far and near as a bold, zealous, and powerful preacher. Plain in his dress, pointed in rebuking sin, and sometimes almost irresistible in his appeals to the conscience, he was "a terror to evil-doers, and a praise to them that do well." His ministry was "in the demonstration of the Spirit, and with power." The writer first saw him in 1818, and heard him for the last time at the close of the funeral discourse preached on the occasion of the death of the Rev. L. D. Overall, at the Tennessee Conference at Lebanon, in 1835. Such an unction of the Holy Spirit he has scarcely, if ever, witnessed before or since. It was his last interview with his beloved Bishop.

He had an excellent farm, a comfortable and well-furnished home, and abundant pecuniary means;

and, although surrounded by wealthy neighbors, and in the midst of a large slave population, he never would own a slave. He had the moral courage "to work with his own hands," and teach his family the lesson of self-reliance. He considered slavery a misfortune, if not a curse, to the slaveholder, and would not be "*plagued*" with slaves.

Such was the man whom God honored as one of the principal instruments of the great revival in 1799 and 1800. We have already said he was the father-in-law of Thomas L. Douglass.

Bishop McKendree's last, and perhaps his only, appearance in the Conference-room, has often reminded us of General Washington in his last review and final farewell to his army in 1783.

In ancient times, the Roman Senate decreed a triumph to a victorious general, upon his return to Rome after the subjection of a province, or a great decisive victory over a formidable foe; and, as he entered the city, a pompous ceremony was performed in honor of the victor. He came crowned with a wreath of evergreens; a scepter in one hand, and a laurel branch in the other, riding in a splendid open chariot, preceded by a herald, the Senate and chief magistrates, musicians, the spoils of the campaign, and captives in chains, and followed by his veteran officers and victorious army on foot. They advanced through the crowded streets, amidst the enthusiastic shouts of thousands, to the Capitoline Hill, where feasts were prepared, sacrifices offered, and he received the congratulations of the Senate and people of Rome.

How different the scene before us! Here is a man, bowed down with years; his tottering steps scarcely sustained by his long staff; pale, emaciated, and tremulous; yet he, too, is a victor—has fought the *good* fight, and won the field. He, too, has spoils, and captives, and honors. He has conquered himself—ruled "his own spirit" and the hearts of thousands by the power of truth and the spirit of gentleness and love; but his trophies are unstained with blood, while thousands of captives grace his triumphs, not taken in unprovoked and cruel war, in the carnival of death, on bloody battle-fields, but slaves of sin and Satan, rescued by grace, and made to pass under the "easy yoke" of the "meek and lowly Prince of Peace." No manacled wretches, nor weeping widows and orphans swell his train, but "the song of Moses," and the exultant response of Miriam, rise to heaven in gratitude for deliverance from worse than Egyptian bondage. He bears no scepter in his hand; he flaunts no insignia of his high office on his breast; no coronal of laurel decks his head; not even a chaplet of simple wild flowers adorns his brow and binds his few gray hairs; no shouting sycophants hail him welcome, nor venal muse, in sweet, poetic melody, celebrates his deeds; but a great multitude call him a benefactor of his race, and award him the honor due a long life unvaryingly and intensely devoted to the salvation of men and the glory of God; no pompous pageant attends him, but as a weary, earnest, good old man, having served his God and his generation faithfully, he comes in Christian meekness to greet his children for the last time, to bid them "love one another," and then go away to lay him down and die.

The Conference closed on the night of November 14th, and, as usual, the preachers hurried away to their respective fields of labor, except one or two, who lingered with the Bishop to see him safely back to Nashville. Passing the "Hermitage," he reached the city on the 15th, but was too unwell to attend church on Sunday, the 16th. During the week ensuing he rallied a little, and, at the urgent solicitations of the preachers present, and of his old friends, who greatly desired to hear words of counsel and comfort from his lips once more, he consented, and preached his last sermon Nov. 23, 1834. The church was a very large and substantial edifice, recently finished, and, in honor of his memory, had been dedicated as "the McKendree Church."

On that occasion the spacious house was filled to overflowing; and Dr. Green, who had the privilege of hearing him, says: "In my imagination I can see him at this moment, as he last stood on the walls of Zion, with his sickle in his hand; the gray hairs thinly covering his forehead; his pale and withered face; his benignant countenance; his speaking eye; while a deep under-current of thought, scarcely veiled by the external lineaments, took form in words, and fell from his trembling lips, as by the eye of faith he transcended the boundaries of time, and entered the eternal world. But he is drawing to the close of his sermon. Now, for the last time, he bends himself, and reaches his sickle forth, ripe to the harvest. How balmy the name of Christ, as he breathes it forth, standing midway, as it were, between heaven and earth, and pointing to the home of the faithful in the sky! I look again: the sickle sways in his hand; his strength is measured, and he closes his ministerial labors on earth with the words, '*I add no more!*' while imagination hears the response from the invisible glory, '*It is enough!*'"

This sermon was reported *verbatim*, and forms the first number of the "Western Methodist Preacher." His *work* was now done—*well* done; but when he could *do* no more, he could *suffer* more; and as suffering the will of God is as much a part of our duty as doing it, and quite as important to the full development of the higher Christian graces, so our Heavenly Father in mercy suffers him to pass through the crucible of affliction before he realizes "the eternal weight of glory."

About December 22d, he left Nashville for his brother's residence in Sumner county, under a presentiment, as is supposed, that his end was near, and in accordance with a long-cherished wish to die at home, and be buried there. But before he started on his last trip, a little portion of the skin by the side of the nail on the forefinger of his right hand had become loosened; in pulling it off, it reached the quick, and made it sore. Presently it inflamed, and became swollen and very painful. He thought that the ink from his pen had got into it and poisoned it. The inflammation and the pain increased until his rest and sleep were much interrupted, yet he was enabled to reach his brother's before Christmas. And now, having attended his last Conference, preached his valedictory sermon, and bidden farewell to his kind hosts and their families, and his numerous friends in Nashville, like his Master, he is met by the enemy at the portal of the grave for a last encounter. The conviction that he can travel and labor no longer to build up Zion and win souls to Christ, saddens him.

It was not the resignation of his *office*—he had not sought it nor desired it; it was not its emoluments—he had received no more than the youngest and humblest circuit-preacher; and one hundred dollars for a year of such work as he had done, was no compensation; nor was it that he loved power and prerogative, for in his office power and sacrifice are inseparably united. No, it was none of these things; but it was because he could sacrifice and labor no longer in the blessed work of soul-saving. He was depressed, and, for a season, seemed to be in a severe mental trial. Doubtless his physical condition had much to do in this trouble; and the adversary, who always adapts his suggestions to the circumstances of the tempted, endeavored to use those surrounding this holy man to his discomfort, and thus involve his mind in clouds. But the clouds soon broke—faith and prayer triumphed; the disconcerted tempter fled, and the sunshine of his Heavenly Father's face again shone upon him. It was his last battle with Satan. "He now boldly stepped beyond the valley of dejection, and over the enchanted ground, quite into the celestial land of 'Beulah,' where heavenly voices are heard, and ministering spirits from the better world are not few and far between."

The "incorrigible tumor" on his finger, however, continued to give him excruciating pain, in despite of all medical aid, until his finger wasted away, while the agony seemed to involve, by sympathy, his back and head. It is affecting to learn the aid to which he resorted while in pain. Such was his faith in a prayer-answering God, that while he would be in the greatest agony, he would call on any Christian present to pray, saying to one on a certain occasion, "Pray with me on account of my pain; not as you pray in your family, but in *faith*, with direct reference to my pain." After prayer, he smiled, raised his head, and said, "It is easy now!" Indeed, it invariably happened that after prayer, and sometimes before its close, he would be in a slumber as calm as an infant.

God designed the family as the training-school for this and the future world; and domestic love is the purest instinctive feeling on earth. And if a sister ever loved a brother with a deep and holy affection, it was the case with Nancy McKendree toward her noble, loving brother William. They both lived and died unmarried; and she seemed to live for God and her brother. She waited upon him, and watched by his bedside unceasingly. Once awaking from slumber in the night, he looked at her and his nieces, who were sitting by his bed, and said, with a smile, "You are like a lamp, burning while I sleep, to cheer me when I wake."

On Sunday, four days previous to his death, his brother, the doctor, said to him, "Bishop, you are sinking fast. We shall, in all probability, soon be separated." He replied, "Yes, I know it; but all is well." To questions in regard to his last wishes as to his funeral arrangements, when both of them (having been similarly afflicted with asthma) were seized with a fit of coughing, no reply could be given. Soon after, the Bishop made a signal that he wished to speak. To his nephew, Dudley McKendree, leaning over him to receive his communication, he said, "All is well for time or for eternity. I live by faith in the Son of God." In his most emphatic manner, he repeated. "*I wish that matter to be perfectly understood, that all is well with me, whether I live or die.* For two months I have not had a cloud to darken my sky. I have had uninterrupted confidence in my Saviour's love." He began to repeat a part of a stanza of one of Charles Wesley's beautiful hymns:

"Not a cloud can arise to darken my skies,
Or hide for a moment my Lord from mine eyes;"

but not being able to finish the couplet, it was finished for him. As to his interment, he said, "I wish to be buried in the ancient Methodist style, like an old Christian minister." Being asked if he had any choice as to the text of his funeral-sermon, the hymns, etc., he replied that he had none. When subsequently asked if he had a choice as to the preacher, his answer was, "Not particularly; Logan Douglass as well as any one."

The Bishop now seemed to summon all the powers of his soul to pass the cold stream of death. He ordered the bedstead on which his venerable father had died, years ago, to be brought in, and, if we mistake not, the same bed and bedding to be placed upon it, as he wished to die where his father died; and upon this couch he waited the coming of death. From this time he suffered but little pain, but was calm and composed, like one whose work is done, waiting the coming of his Lord.

Many were the gracious words which fell from his lips to the friends around him. To one he said, "Follow me, as I have followed Christ—*only closer to Christ.*" He was remarkably fond of the phrase, "*All is well.*" To almost all inquiries as to the state of his soul, this was his invariable reply. This was, indeed, his last connected expression, although the last word was "Yes," in answer to the question asked him while dying, "Is all well *now?*" Being interrogated again, on the day of his death, as to his funeral arrangements, he said, "I leave it all to my friends—only preserve the *plainness:* my friends know my wishes." After this, his kind and tender sister asked if he was in pain. He answered, "No." He had long been subject to coughing-fits, and was obliged to be raised up, to avoid suffocation. While in this position, with one of his kind nurses sitting behind him and supporting his head, the question was asked for the last time, "Is all well?" and again he answered, "Yes." Just then, by a sudden, spasmodic contraction, he seemed to have a darting pain in his right side. The muscles in the left cheek seemed to suffer a corresponding spasm, and knotted up with a deep wrinkle, which remained after the pain in the side had passed off. The Bishop, sensible of this muscular contraction, made two energetic efforts to smooth down his countenance. The second effort succeeded, and a dying smile came over the brow and descended upon the lower features of his face. Then the senior Bishop of our Episcopacy surrendered the parchment which he had held since 1808. He returned it as stainless as the mountain snow. The struggle was over. He had fought the good fight, he had finished his course, he had kept the faith. The chariot had gone over the everlasting hills.

After death, the Bishop's features were calm and beautiful. The wars of earth had all passed away. No trace of agony remained. There was a noble sublimity in the inanimate clay, connected with the circumstances of his long and useful life, that made the gazer linger over it, as if he were looking upon features he would see again in radiant scenes over which the curtain of futurity yet hangs its folds.

In conformity with the wishes of the deceased, he was shrouded in a grave-robe of black silk, inclosed in a plain but substantial walnut coffin; and on Saturday he was interred, at the left hand of his father, about forty yards from the old family mansion, where he died.*

His epitaph, by an unknown hand, is as follows:

Sacred
TO THE MEMORY OF THE REV WILLIAM MCKENDREE
Bishop of the Methodist Episcopal Church In the
United States of America
Born King William County Virginia July 6th 1757
Died at his Brothers Dr James McKendrees
In Sumner County Ten. March 5th 1835
He was elected and ordained Bishop
In the city of Baltimore. May 1808
He labored in the ministry of the gospel 47 years
With uncommon zeal ability and usefulness.
And for near 27 years discharged the duties
Of the episcopal office with such wisdom
Rectitude fidelity as to secure the
Confidence respect and esteem of the
Ministers and people of his official
Oversight in travels and labors for
The advancement of the Redeemers
Kingdom and the salvation of the
Souls of men. He occupied an elevated
Position among the most eminent ministers
Of Christ and has furnished an illustrious
Example for christian pastors and Bishops
He finished his course in peace and triumph
Proclaiming in his last moments
'All is well'

The *personnel* of Bishop McKendree was a true index of the man. He was nearly six feet high,

* Many of the Bishop's friends were very desirous he should be interred in Nashville, but his relations, who occupied the old homestead and its vicinity, were understood to be unwilling; and, as his father, brother, and sister were buried there, and he had

and finely proportioned. His forehead was high and broad, his eyes dark, large, and somewhat protruding—their predominant expression, under ordinary circumstances, was benignity, but they were capable of sparkling with vivacity or of expressing severe rebuke. All his features taken together, were in harmony; and when he was excited, it was the most speaking face I ever looked upon His skin, even in the decline of life, was

---

intimated a wish to rest by the side of his father, the subject was dropped; and it has recently been proposed to erect a church-edifice there, which shall be a memorial to his character and a convenience to the community who might worship in it. One or two Conferences, I believe, have proposed to aid the attempt. The writer is strongly impressed now, although formerly opposed to it, that (as the old house and premises have passed into the hands of strangers—all the immediate relatives moved away, leaving scarcely even a distant kinsman in the county; the locality of the grave—secluded from any town, village, or thoroughfare of travel, surrounded by a sparse population, with churches sufficiently convenient—and the grave without inclosure, evincing utter neglect) it would be far better to remove his remains to the Nashville Cemetery, and place them by the side of his noble colleague and old friend, Bishop Soule. This conviction has been deepened by the perusal of a letter from the Rev. Joseph F. Redford, published lately in the Nashville Christian Advocate, in which he describes the condition of the tomb and the general aspect of the place. The brick walls of the tomb, it seems, were taken down by Federal soldiers, during the late war, and the slab engraved with his epitaph was thrown on the ground, where it still lies; and the whole scenery is desolate and dreary, without one redeeming circumstance. It is, moreover, understood that his relations now interpose no objections to the transfer. *Let it be done,* and *quickly;* and let the congregation of the McKendree Church do it, and let Dr. Green see to it.

almost pearly white, and reminded one of a fine mezzotint engraving. The writer first saw him in 1817, and, although he was falling into "the sear and yellow leaf" of life, his appearance was very prepossessing and expressive. In dress he was very neat. A black, round-breasted coat, white necktie, short breeches, with knee-buckles and shoe-buckles, and a white, broad-brimmed hat, was a costume that gave to his fine form a venerable and commanding appearance. In his later years, he exchanged the short clothes and buckles for pantaloons—except on special occasions—but retained the other items of dress. He must have been an active and vigorous man in his prime, and more than ordinarily fine-looking, not to say handsome. His voice was soft and yet penetrating, and was wonderfully persuasive and melodious.

His early educational advantages were not great; but with his quick and observant mind, which he was daily improving, he became a correct and effective speaker. He had fine taste in selecting the best words to express his ideas. He thought, read, and studied much, especially on moral and religious subjects. In the department of biblical doctrines and Church-history and government, he had few equals.

His mind was logical. He excelled in what is called practical or common sense. The Holy Scriptures were read regularly, and studied attentively. He believed them implicitly, and devoted his whole soul to their teachings.

His preaching was spiritual. All merely speculative questions he avoided in the pulpit. Christ crucified for the world, the manner and means of receiving him, and the evidences of having done so, as well as the duties arising from our obligations, were his favorite themes. He was an attractive and instructive preacher, and sometimes a powerful one. Splendid displays of imagination, culled in the field of fancy and carefully stored in the memory, to be used for gaining admiration, were distasteful to him. He was solemn and deeply in earnest in delivering his message. His first and only aim was to be understood by all, and to draw his hearers to Christ; and he would as soon have put on gorgeous apparel as to have dressed his sermons in an ornate, oratorical style. He preferred, in this respect, to imitate Christ, his apostles, and Wesley.

His piety was profound. Conscientiousness was a prominent trait in his character, and one more truthful in word and deed I never saw. He prayed much and regularly—took all his cares and wants to God in prayer. His standard of religion, experimental and practical, was a high one. He watched, prayed, fasted, and labored in earnestness. He was a holy man, loving God with all his heart, and his neighbor as himself. No one ever was known to doubt his purity of character: in this he was a bright exemplar. In his social intercourse there was nothing light or frivolous. A simple gravity was characteristic of his manner; and yet there was in it nothing repulsive. It seemed impossible to associate with him and not to respect and venerate him; and in an ingenuous mind, these feelings soon warmed into love of the most enduring kind.

He loved the Church. It is doubted whether any man since St. Paul—not even excepting Asbury—loved it more. Such was his anxious concern for its welfare, that his very soul was burdened with care. The difference, in this respect, between men equally good and great, has often been seen. Some physicians are so constituted that every case of serious illness among their patients harasses them—they cannot dismiss it from their minds. They enter into the sympathies of their patients and their families; they become nurses, as well as doctors. And such are apt to wear themselves out, and sink into premature graves. Yet others can perform, and faithfully too, their professional duties, and soon banish anxiety from their hearts. It is so with preachers. I have imagined St. Paul was one of the former class—was always oppressed by "the care of all the Churches;" while St. Peter was probably of the latter class. It is so now, and has ever been so, among preachers and Bishops; and they are neither better nor worse for it, if restrained within reasonable bounds, and arising from purely constitutional tendencies. Now, Bishop McKendree, in this respect, belonged to the former class. He could not divest himself of anxiety about any interest of the Church when it was in the least imperiled. From 1820 to 1828, he was greatly troubled. He regarded the efficiency of the Episcopacy and the itinerant system as in peril, in the Reform and Radical movements of that period.

The prosperity and safety of the Church, he firmly believed, were identified with the strict observance of the chartered rights of the constitution. Innovations on this instrument he regarded with alarm. In other things, not tending to lower the scriptural and Wesleyan standard of experimental and practical piety of the Church, he was liberal: so that while he opposed changes, the utility of which he doubted, and was therefore a *conservative*, in other things he was a *progressionist*. Yet he stood openly opposed to sudden and great changes, and his motto might have been "*Festina lente.*"

Like Asbury, Lee, Bruce, and a good many of the Methodist itinerant preachers of their day, Bishop McKendree never married; nor have we any reason to believe he ever attempted to do so. At that time their salary was so small, their appointments so often changed, and their work so arduous, that, as a general rule, to marry was to locate. Indeed, preachers and people disapproved of it; and to marry under eight or ten years of itinerant service, was regarded with general disfavor, almost amounting to proof positive of backsliding, as an itinerant preacher. To be changed every three or six months, to drag a family from the Atlantic seaboard to the Holston or to Cumberland, was a very serious matter. A preacher might love a lady too much to seek her hand; so thought many who could "receive" St. Paul's advice to the preachers of his day. Some of this early class did marry in advanced life, perhaps upon the principle which an old itinerant once gave as his apology for so doing, that he could no longer travel and preach, and was fit for nothing else; he had, therefore, got married and located. Now, the writer thinks that the Church and the world are better off on account of this habit of our fathers. Bishop McKendree was probably far more useful as a single man than he could have been otherwise. The condition of the work at that time seemed to require it of him; and it is very questionable whether the habit of the present day of assuming the care of a family while quite young in the ministry, is the "better" way. The Bishop, while he thought it lawful, did not think it was expedient for *him* to marry: "he never found time to get married."

He was a model Bishop, combining every qualification for this high and holy office—wise, prudent, vigilant, industrious, unselfish, unblamable, and holy—he presided with dignity and gentleness, and preached with power and success. By no act or word did he dishonor his office. He was the first native American Bishop in the Methodist Episcopal Church, and inferior in the aggregate of those qualities which the office requires to no one before or since his day. No man can *ever* fill the niche of Asbury—he was, under God, the father of American Methodism—he was superior to McKendree only in priority of time, length of life, and services. Both of them did what they could—all they could. The mantle of the elder fell on his shoulders, and both unreservedly consecrated their *all* to God and his Church. Wesley drew from the Bible the plan of the spiritual edifice, Asbury began to build it up in America, and McKendree carried forward the work "as a wise master-builder."

It would be unjust to the memory of Bishop McKendree not to notice the fact that he felt the liveliest interest in all the religious and intellectual enterprises of his time. He was the first President of our Bible and Missionary Societies, and when it was proposed to merge the former in the "American Bible Society," he gave it his concurrence, and was ever its ardent friend. His devotion to the Missionary Society needs not to be repeated; so also as to Sunday-schools. He was, moreover, deeply impressed with the importance and necessity of education. He had seen the unfortunate attempt of Bishops Coke and Asbury to build up Cokesbury into a literary institution of high grade. He had been mortified by a similar failure in Kentucky to found Bethel Academy, and he wisely thought that our resources were then inadequate and the country too new to justify costly attempts; but for many years before his death he was exceedingly desirous to see our people unite in erecting a few first-class colleges. The last letter the writer ever received from him, and not long previous to his death, contained fifty dollars for La Grange College, signed, "Nobody." The handwriting detected the giver. No appeal had been made to him; yet, out of his annual pittance, he was prompted by his interest in the cause of education to make the donation, and tried to conceal the donor. His special object was that the money should be applied to place in the College-library the standard religious literature of the Church, for the religious instruction and benefit of the students. Of course it was done.

Was Bishop McKendree a *great* man? In reply, it must be said the answer depends upon the meaning of the question. We readily admit he was not preëminent as a scholar, an orator, a writer, or a preacher; still he was more than respectable in all these particulars, and yet many, doubtless, excelled him in each of these departments—some in one, and some in another. In all that constitutes genius and intellectual preëminence, we admit at once he had many superiors; yet his mind was richly stored with varied and useful knowledge. He had a fine fancy, without a brilliant imagination; his apprehensions were very quick and correct; his judgment was excellent; his language simple, chaste, and appropriate; his manner grave and graceful. He was a sound theologian, a good expositor—always methodical and clear—and in his palmy days a deeply impressive and powerful preacher. In his official deportment, as well as in piety toward God and absorbing devotion to the eternal interests of men, he had no superior: so that while he was in every respect highly reputable, yea, eminent in many things, without claiming preëminence in any one endowment, yet take him in the aggregate—mind, heart, life, labors, and results—*he was a great man;* and we doubt not the judgment of the last day will so decide.

APPENDIX.

AMONG the various documents which have fallen into the hands of the author, it has been judged best to present in an *Appendix* to his "Life and Times," some of those which could not be conveniently introduced in the chronological order of the work, yet serve to illustrate his character and his sentiments, as well as the history of his coadjutors. In pursuance of this object, we first present the admirable Sermon of Bishop Soule on the Death of Bishop McKendree, delivered at the request of the General Conference, in the city of Cincinnati, May 11, 1836, and published by order of that body. We insert it in this place, the more readily because it has frequently been called for, and is now nearly or entirely out of print, and notwithstanding the liberal use made of it in the preceding pages of this work.

SERMON

ON THE DEATH OF THE REV. WILLIAM M'KENDREE.

"Remember them who have the rule over you, who have spoken unto you the word of God; whose faith follow, considering the end of their conversation: Jesus Christ the same yesterday, and to-day, and for ever." Heb. xiii. 7, 8.

WHEN in the providence of God, great and good men are removed from the world, and from those relations they have sustained to their fellow-men, to their eternal rewards, it is highly proper that suitable respect should be paid to their memory, and that their names and their virtues should be handed down to posterity, as examples for the instruction and improvement of succeeding generations. The practice of all civilized nations, from the commencement of the organization of society down to the present period, is in accordance with this sentiment. Nor is it easy to calculate the influence which the opinions and the examples of men of generations, and of ages long since passed away, continue to exert over the habits of *thinking* and *action* of the present race, and which they will not cease to exert through the successive periods of future time. The Jews were distinguished for their sacred monuments, designed to perpetuate the memory of their patriarchs, their kings, and their prophets. But the light of the Christian era affords the purest and most perfect examples of all which, in regard either to *sentiment* or *action*, is worthy to be perpetuated, in fadeless records, to the end of time. One of the peculiar excellences of the New Testament Scriptures is the moral portraiture of the most pure, illustrious, and benevolent characters which ever enlightened and adorned our world. And these characters were everywhere exhibited as patterns for our imitation, as examples both of our faith and practice. But when the mind surveys the simplicity and beauty of truth, and the uncompromising virtue and unsullied integrity of the ministers and followers of Jesus of Nazareth, as portrayed in the records of the apostolic age, and having perceived the majesty and grandeur of the admirable picture, passes onward through a succession of following ages, the contrast becomes a matter of melancholy and painful reflection.

Scarcely had the apostles of Jesus Christ, who had received their commission and their instructions from the lips of their adorable Master, and their immediate successors in the grand work of evangelizing the world, "finished their course," and entered upon their eternal rewards, before the *system* of truth which they had published, and the *plan* of its promulgation by which they had been guided, were subject to innovations in the hands of those who came after them. A single century, from the day of Pentecost, had not passed away before the Gnostic heresy had invaded the infant Church, and corrupted the pure fountains of gospel truth. So early did the "wisdom of men," in the form of a subtle, intricate, and superstitious philosophy, mingle with the sublime doctrines of the Christian revelation the absurd dogmas of "Oriental science." Doctors soon appear, not to preach to their congregations the pure, unadulterated "word of God," but to "teach for doctrine" the unmeaning jargon of their respective schools. In the progress of these corruptions of primitive Christianity, other evils sprung up, and mingled their influence in demolishing that simple and beautiful structure which had been modeled by infinite wisdom, and reared up under the immediate superintendence of Jesus and his apostles.

This work of *earthly wisdom and policy* had not continued long before the relations established by the Christian institutes between pastors and their flocks—between ministers of the gospel and those converted to the faith of Christ through their ministry—assumed a character widely different from that which was formed by the original charter. The superior clergy, giddy with the metaphysical speculations of their favorite philosophy, and corrupted by the "love of the world," soon set up claims to power and rule unauthorized by their "holy vocation;" seeking rather the authority of the civil rulers, to lord it over God's heritage, than that moral influence which was founded in the principles and obligations of a "kingdom which was not of this world." A dark age ensued, in which the light of evangelical truth was well-nigh extinguished; and if it shone at all, was confined almost exclusively to the humble and obscure, both of the clergy and laity. In such a state of things, it is not surprising that homage should be paid to men, which was due only to God; and that the simplicity of the apostolic direction to the Church at Jerusalem to engrave the virtues and labors of their pastors upon the table of their memory, and to regard them in their fidelity as patterns for their imitation, should give place to pompous titles, splendid temples, gorgeous pictures, sculptured marble, and idolatrous festivals. To cap this climax of usurpation and impiety, the professed heralds of a Saviour born in a manger, and crucified upon a cross, claimed the prerogative of deposing civil princes and setting their feet upon the necks of kings; and not contented with the proud pretension to the right of universal dictation in matters belonging to the civil empire, they proclaimed themselves God's vicegerents upon earth and intercessors for men before the throne of heaven.

In casting our eye over this succession of gloomy ages, distinguished chiefly by such melancholy corruptions of the purest system of religion and morals which the world ever saw, it affords us peculiar satisfaction to perceive, at different periods, some rays of heavenly light penetrating the gloom of that spiritual darkness which had covered the face of the earth. Here and there a luminous spot appears upon the dark and dismal abyss. Here and there a daring spirit, a bold defender of the faith of Jesus, rose up *by the inspiration* of the Almighty, and gave "lucid proof" that the "wisdom of the world was foolishness with God."

The morning of the sixteenth century was a day-spring from on high to the Church in the wilderness, and an era full of hope and of promise to the benighted nations. Who can doubt that Luther was raised up by the special agency of God to counteract the corruptions and blasphemies of the Church of Rome?

But the work of this great and distinguished Saxon Reformer was but in part a restoration of what had been lost in the lapse of those ages of apostasy from the doctrines and morals of Christianity which had preceded. Many of the abominations of the papal hierarchy were brought to light—the blasphemous claims of the sovereign pontiff to grant indulgences, remove penalties, and remit sins of all sorts, were exposed and denounced with a clearness of argument and zeal of moral courage worthy of the cause of truth and of the illustrious agents who were engaged in its promotion. Learning and philosophy, always favorable to the progress of the gospel, when guided by the light of the revelation of God, were directed into pure channels, and rendered efficient auxiliaries in the advancement of the Reformation. Universities became the seats of theological discussion, which seldom, if ever, closed without obvious advantage to the cause of the Reformers. Princes long subject to the papal domination, wakened up by the uncompromising Saxon, began to think and speak with freedom on matters of faith and practice. In the progress of the Reformation, numerous persons of distinction and influence were employed by the Divine Providence, as instruments in removing the "works of darkness," and repairing the ruins of the beautiful temple of Christianity. But while this work was in progress, there were more *outside* than *inside* workmen; and the master-builders were not always agreed with regard to the *plan* which should be pursued, the materials which should be used, or the *workmen* who should be employed in completing the noble superstructure. In such a state of things, it should not be considered marvelous that a portion of "wood, hay, stubble," should be mixed with the "gold, silver, precious stones;" and that more regard should be paid to the exterior form, scaffolding, and *outworks* of the building, than to the perfection and beauty of the interior workmanship.

Although this and the succeeding century was a glorious era in the history of the Church, presenting a grand constellation of "burning and shining lights" in the cause of truth, yet it is to be regretted that the Church and State were so incorporated as to produce an unhappy effect on the religious state of the clergy, and consequently to hinder, in some measure, the progress of Christian piety. Prelates of the Reformed Church, while they held in just abhorrence the claims and pretensions of the papal see, saw nothing inconsistent with the religion of a crucified Saviour, or with their calling as his ministers, in being themselves "lords temporal" as well as spiritual. Whatever might have been the external state of the different branches of the Church at the commencement of the eighteenth century, it is very obvious that there was a great deficiency on the part of the ministry. While the prescribed forms of religion were regarded with scrupulous observance, the distinguishing doctrines of the gospel were too seldom proclaimed and too feebly enforced. The result was a general defect in vital godliness and a corresponding laxity in moral discipline. It was in the midst of such a state of things that the great and blessed revival of religion commenced at Oxford early in this century.

The Rev. John Wesley was the chief instrument in the rise and early progress of this revival. The extraordinary acuteness and strength of his mental powers, the variety and depth of his learning, his moral courage, his persevering zeal, and the strict purity of his life, all combined, qualified him, in an eminent degree, for this great work.

And here it should be remembered that it was not the

articles of faith, or the liturgy of the English Church, with which Mr. Wesley contended, or which he desired to change or reform; but he was rather the firm defender of both. And why should we who acknowledge him, under God, as the founder of that religious body of which we are members, place ourselves in opposition to either? But while this great and good man was well satisfied with the doctrine and government of the Establishment, he clearly saw the extensive defect of experimental and practical religion both with the clergy and laity. To remove this defect, and restore the principles and blessings of primitive Christianity to the Church, were the great objects of his studies and his labors. But the era of which we now speak, embracing the history of Wesley, and those who were "workers together with him," is distinctly marked by several very important points.

Mr. Wesley, notwithstanding the prejudices of his education, became fully convinced that bishops and presbyters were the same order in the primitive Church; and consequently that the doctrine of succession and exclusive right of ordination, existing in the bishop, as maintained by many of the prelates of the English hierarchy, were not founded in the Constitution of the Christian Church, or warranted by any practice in the uncorrupted period of her history. In addition to this conviction, the providence of God, in an extraordinary manner, led Mr. Wesley to perceive that a divine call to the work of preaching the gospel, and the qualifications for this holy vocation, were not confined to those who were "regularly educated for the sacred office;" but that in the wisdom of Him who "seeth not as man seeth," the "foolish things of the world were frequently chosen to confound the wise." Hence his admirable and truly scriptural test of those who think they are moved by the Holy Ghost to preach.

The employment of "lay preachers"—that is, persons who were neither educated for the ministry, nor in the clerical orders in the Established Church—forms a very prominent and important feature of the Wesleyan system, which, by the blessing of God, has been productive of the most extensive and happy results in the four quarters of the globe. Another characteristic of this system is the organization and establishment of an *efficient itinerant ministry*, in conformity to that command, "Go ye into all the world, and preach the gospel to every creature," and in accordance with the practice of the apostles and their immediate successors in the work of evangelizing the earth. As the commencement of this era in the history of the Reformed Churches was distinguished by the revival of the pure doctrines and moral discipline of the gospel, so its extension, and almost unparalleled progress, have been attended by the powerful influences of the Holy Spirit. To turn men from "darkness to light, and from the power of Satan unto God," and to build them up in that "holiness without which no man shall see the Lord," is the grand design of the preaching of the gospel. And to accomplish this design, Christ must be preached in all his offices. The whole system of his religion must be proclaimed. Its doctrines, precepts, promises, and threatenings, must be clearly set forth and enforced. The whole must be brought home to the hearts and consciences of the hearers. Sinners must be made to feel their sinfulness and guilt, and to know that salvation is by "grace through faith" alone.

These are, and have been from the beginning, the leading features of the Wesleyan revival. In its rise and progress it has enlisted the influence of a considerable number of men, distinguished as much for their extraordinary talents, and their profound learning, as for the depth of their piety, the purity of their lives, and the extent and usefulness of their labors. But by far the greater part of those ministers who have been honored of God, as instruments in the advancement of this great and extensive revival of primitive Christianity, have been men who made no pretensions to talents of a superior order, or to the peculiar advantages of learning and science. They have been called, in the wisdom of the divine counsels, from almost every profession and occupation in life. Thus has it been shown in this latter day, as well as at the beginning of the gospel dispensation, that the proud pretensions of reason and philosophy, however they may be viewed by men, are of little account with God; and that the success of the "preaching of the cross" essentially depends upon the doctrine of that promise, "Lo I am with you alway, even unto the end of the world." Among the instruments thus called and qualified by the great Head of the Church, in the progress of this work, William McKendree, that beloved minister of Jesus Christ, whose Christian and ministerial character this discourse is designed to exhibit as an example for those who shall come after, occupies an elevated and distinguished station.

In my attempt to accomplish this object, I shall endeavor, first, to point out the character which the apostle has given of a Christian pastor, or minister; and secondly, show wherein this character has been sustained and exemplified in the Christian life, ministerial labors, and official oversight of the late lamented senior Bishop of the Methodist Episcopal Church.

I. The words of our text lead us back in our meditations and researches to the original fountains of gospel truth. They point us to the origin of a system which claims to be of divine appointment, and designed to be perpetuated to the end of time. They direct our attention to the first

Church, or assembly, ever organized on the principles of the Christian institutes—the Church at Jerusalem. In this city prophets had pointed to the Messiah, and proclaimed the laws and the conquests of his kingdom. Here Jesus Christ, the author of our salvation, *in his own person,* had taught the doctrines of that kingdom. Here he was persecuted, arrested, crucified. Here he slept in the tomb, and here he rose triumphant from the dominion of death and the grave. At this city he directed his chosen apostles to remain "until they were endued with power from on high," as an essential qualification for the work he had appointed them to do. Here they received that power in the promised descent of the Holy Ghost, on the day of Pentecost. Here the fountain was opened, and from here the "law went forth," and the word of the Lord flowed out. In this city the apostles of Jesus, who had received their instructions from the lips of their divine Master, planted the *first Christian Church.* Probably we have in the organization of this Church as perfect a model as the world has ever seen. The relation and reciprocal duties of the pastor and his flock, of the minister and "those over whom he was appointed minister," are set forth in the view given of this Church with a simplicity and beauty strikingly characteristic of the purest age of Christianity.

It is not pretended that the *precise formula* observed in the Church at Jerusalem is essential to the existence of every Christian community. Indeed, it appears highly probable that such internal regulations and external forms as were not essential to the doctrines, order, and moral discipline of the "household of faith," as laid down by Christ and his inspired apostles, were varied in the primitive Churches, as change of place or circumstances might require. But as the Church is the "body of Christ," and "the temple of the living God," the preservation of an order of ministers appointed by Christ, holding steadfastly the fundamental doctrines of the Christian revelation, the preaching of the pure word of God, and the administration of the discipline and ordinances of the gospel institution, are essential to its very existence. Without these there can be no living Church, no assembly or community pleasing and acceptable to God. All associations professedly Christian, in which all, or any, of these points are totally wanting, or materially defective, have either never been formed "according to the will of our Lord Jesus Christ," or they have fallen and become apostate. In view of these prerequisites as the essential constituents of a Christian Church, we observe—

1. *That the ministers of the gospel, in the apostolic age, were distinguished by their special calling to the work of the ministry.* No one can have carefully examined the history of the divine Saviour, as furnished in the holy evangelists, without having perceived that the "preaching of the gospel" has been ordained as the means of faith and salvation, and as the chief instrument by which the Christian cause is to extend, and finally cover the whole earth. It is equally plain from the same records, that the appointment of the agents by whom this work is to be carried on and finally completed, is the exclusive prerogative of Jesus Christ—a prerogative which he has never delegated, which he now holds in his own hands, and will continue to hold till the end of time. He commenced the exercise of this authority in the selection of his first disciples to attend his person and receive his instructions, preparatory to the work which was afterward assigned them. He continued the exercise of it by sending out these disciples at different times on errands of mercy while he continued upon earth. But the most signal exhibition of that authority was made after his resurrection, and immediately before he ascended up

into heaven, to take possession of the mediatorial government at the right hand of the Father. This was a period in the history of human salvation pregnant with interests of the deepest concern to man. It was a point in time when the "Prince of life, Immanuel, God with us," gave his last and fullest instructions in regard to the means and manner of the promulgation of his kingdom upon earth. His right of legislation and government was asserted: "All power is given unto me, both in heaven and in earth." The commission given to the apostles, who were present on the occasion, and to all the true ministers of the gospel salvation, is declared to be by virtue of this right: "Go ye, *therefore*, and teach all nations," etc. "And lo, I am with you alway, even unto the end of the world." Who can doubt that both the right of appointment, and the annexed promise of perpetual aid from the continual presence of Christ, embrace the succession of the Christian ministry through all future time?

The principles which the great Head of the Church had established at this memorable period, and which were to remain unchanged through all the succeeding ages of the world, were strikingly illustrated and confirmed shortly afterward on the day of Pentecost. To the commission, and special instructions with regard to its execution, was now added the gift of the Holy Ghost, as the fulfillment of the promise of the Father. By his agency the chosen apostles were "endued with power from on high," and were thus qualified to go forth in their Master's employment, with zeal and authority which their adversaries were not able to gainsay or resist. It was the zeal of conviction; it was the authority of truth; it was the power of God. As the work advanced, others were called to participate in the blessed employment; but in no instance was any one admitted to labor in this vineyard without proof of his being specially called and chosen of God. It is worthy of our particular attention, that when the apostles and disciples were assembled at Jerusalem, after the ascension of their divine Master, and before the descent of the Holy Ghost, in filling the vacancy in the apostolic college occasioned by the apostasy of Judas, they made no pretensions to any *right* or *authority* to determine on the person who should fill that holy office. They were fully persuaded of the exclusive *right* of Him who had chosen them at first, and who had so recently assured them that all authority in heaven and earth was in his hands. And in this persuasion, having selected two from their little company, "they prayed, and said, Thou Lord, which knowest the hearts of all men, show whether of these two thou hast chosen."

The answer was given by lot, and he whom God had chosen "was numbered with the eleven apostles." This is the last instance of the use of the lot recorded in the Holy Scriptures. A different method by which God's election of men for the work of the ministry might be known, was introduced on the day of Pentecost, and will remain in the Church till the "consummation of all things." All true ministers of Jesus Christ have been "moved by the Holy Ghost" to preach the everlasting gospel. By his influence they have been enlightened and persuaded of their holy vocation; and by his agency success has attended their labors, and support and comfort administered to their souls in all their tribulations. It is therefore very meet and right that the Church should continually pray that the Lord would pour upon all the ministers of his sanctuary the Holy Ghost for the office and work to which he has called them.

The beautiful climax of the apostle in the 14th and 15th verses of the 10th chapter of the Epistle to the Romans, is an inimitable illustration of this doctrine. Salvation is

God's free gift both to Jews and Gentiles; and this grace God has richly provided in the gospel of his dear Son. And whomsoever will call on the name of the Lord, shall receive this salvation. "But how shall they call on him in whom they have not believed? and how shall they believe in him of whom they have not heard? and how shall they hear without a preacher? and how shall they preach except they be sent?" The message to be published is the gospel of peace, the word of reconciliation; glad tidings of good things; and he who publishes it must be *sent* by its Author. A great man has the following admirable remark with reference to this message: "None can effectually preach this, unless he have a *divine mission.* The *matter* must come from God; and the *person* who proclaims it must have both *authority* and unction from on high." Hence it will appear who are truly in that "order of succession" appointed according to the will of our Lord Jesus Christ. Whatever may be the vain pretensions of men, those, and *those only,* who are sent of God, who are moved by the Holy Spirit to preach the gospel of the kingdom of heaven, are in this succession.

2. Being thus called and qualified, the first ministers of the gospel went forth "preaching the word of God." The word of God here means the whole system of the gospel revelation, embracing the doctrines, precepts, and sanctions therein contained; especially what appertained to the character, office, and work of Jesus Christ as our Mediator and Saviour.

One of the peculiar features of the primitive preaching of the gospel word was the *purity* in which the doctrines of Christ were maintained and taught to the people. The Jewish teachers were exceedingly zealous of the traditions of their fathers, and, corrupting the oracles of God, "taught for doctrines the commandments of men." The schools of learning and philosophy became the authors and patrons of theories as absurd and conflicting in their principles as immoral and destructive in their tendency. But while "darkness covered the earth, and gross darkness the people," the servants of Jesus were holding out the lamp of life, and pointing the nations to the "Lamb of God who taketh away the sin of the world." While the "Jews required a sign, and the Greeks sought after wisdom;" while a corrupt and superstitious religion, in alliance with "science falsely so called," was enslaving the minds of men with the most dangerous errors, and leading them from God and from happiness, these unassuming messengers of truth were preaching "Christ crucified—Christ the power of God and the wisdom of God." They were publishing the narrative of the incarnation, crucifixion, and resurrection of Jesus of Nazareth, and proclaiming salvation as God's gracious gift, through faith in his name. While, after all the speculations of reason and philosophy, the nations were veiled in uncertainty and doubt with regard to God, the immortality of the soul, and a future state of existence, these "unlearned" men declared the nature, and attributes, and counsels of Jehovah, and showed that "life and immortality were brought to light in the gospel." But while they preached "the unsearchable riches of Christ," the whole system of doctrine was applied to the experimental and practical purposes of life, to renew the hearts and regulate the conduct of men. They had received the records of the truth of God, and out of those records they did not travel. Christ had specially instructed them to teach the nations to *observe* all things whatsoever he had commanded them. In strict conformity to these instructions, their ministry was always practical. They "preached" a faith which was unto justification—a faith which confided in all the promises of God--a faith which worked by love and purified the heart.

3. The ministers of the apostolic age were distinguished as well by the extent of their travels and labors as by the purity and simplicity of their doctrines. Their plan of "preaching the word of God" was strictly itinerant. In this they had taken the example of their Master as their pattern, his authority as their commission, and his command as their obligation. Nor does it anywhere appear that they had any other view but to continue the operation of this plan, till all the nations of the earth should be discipled to Christ, and the knowledge of God be as extensive as the influence of the natural sun. It was not the apostles only who were thus employed in the extensive promulgation of the gospel. The disciples who were dispersed from Jerusalem by the persecution which raged at the time of the martyrdom of Stephen, went "everywhere preaching the word." Among these were, doubtless, many of the "devout men, dwellers at Jerusalem, out of every nation under heaven," who heard the apostles, on the day of Pentecost, "speak, in their own tongues in which they were born, the wonderful works of God." These, having been converted to the faith of Christ by the preaching of the apostles, traveled into their native countries, testifying and preaching the things which they had seen and heard. In this event the Divine Providence was obviously employed in preparing the way for the universal spread of the gospel. And it is a very remarkable and interesting truth, that before the twelve chosen apostles had finished their course and entered into the joy of their Lord, the "word of God had been preached over a great part of the known world." Had the purity and simplicity of the Christian doctrine and discipline been preserved, and the same plan of diffusing its heavenly truths perpetuated till the present time, is it not highly probable that the whole earth would have been subdued to the dominion of Messiah, and the songs of salvation to

God and the Lamb been heard from every nation, and kindred, and people, and tongue?

4. The first Christian ministers were dead to the world, and intent only on promoting the cause of their divine Master, and the salvation of the souls of the people.

In the administration of the word, they preached not themselves. To be the servants and messengers of Christ, and as such the servants of all for his sake, were the great objects of their pursuit. They uniformly spoke of themselves with humility and self-distrust, and pursued their arduous employment "in weakness, and fear, and much trembling." And, whatever God had committed to them or wrought by them, they proclaimed themselves to be "earthen vessels," and ascribed the "excellency of the power" of their ministry to God alone. Jesus Christ was the end of their public preaching as well as of their private "conversation." In all their words and deeds they aimed to promote his glory and advance and establish his kingdom. The divinity of his nature, his participation in the essential attributes of the everlasting Father, his unity and equality in the Godhead, and his eternal Sonship, were themes on which they dwelt with peculiar clearness, interest, and delight. Animated with an ardent and unconquerable desire for the salvation of the souls of men, which had been begotten in their hearts by the Holy Spirit, they set forth, both in their private intercourse and in all their ministerial labors, the deep humiliation to which the Lord Jesus submitted for the redemption and salvation of the world. They continually published his atoning sacrifice, the blood of the cross, as possessing saving efficacy for the removal of guilt and pollution, and the greatness and the tenderness of his compassion for a world of miserable sinners. They declared his veracity in all his great and precious promises, by which the confidence and hope of his people were to be encouraged and supported. In all these respects—in his nature, in his relation to the Father, in the sufficiency of his merits, in his loving kindness and tender compassion, and in the validity of his promises—the primitive Christian ministers represented Jesus Christ to be the same yesterday, to-day, and for ever, and as such pointed all men to him as an almighty and immutable Saviour. This was with them the all-absorbing subject. The pleasures, the riches, and the honors of the world were not the matters of their conversation or their pursuit, but "Christ was all and in all."

5. The primitive ministers had authority to rule, or govern, in the Church. "Remember them that have [or had] the rule over you," and "obey them that have the rule over you."

It was obviously the end of the dispensation of Christ to form a universal Church, or community, of believers, collected out of all the nations of the earth, and to perpetuate this society to the end of time. The fundamental principles on which this association should be founded, and the moral rules by which it should be governed, were clearly laid down in the doctrines, and precepts, and examples of the adorable Saviour.

It is equally clear that an order of officers charged with the organization of this community, with the due administration of the holy ordinances, and with the enforcement of wholesome discipline, is of divine appointment. While we consider these points as manifestly set forth in the Christian institutes, we are free to acknowledge that "neither Christ himself nor his holy apostles have commanded any thing clearly or expressly concerning the external form of the Church, and the precise method according to which it should be governed." What I have here noticed as being of divine appointment is, I apprehend, fully embraced in the commission which Christ gave to his apostles—"Go ye and disciple all nations," convert them to the faith of the gospel, and make them my *followers*. This being accomplished, "baptize them in the name of the Father, and of the Son, and of the Holy Ghost." Formally initiate them as members of the great Christian community, and as belonging to the heavenly household. And being thus formed into a body with the same faith, interest, and affection "teach them to observe all things whatsoever I have commanded you." Make them to understand the precepts which you have received from me, and enforce the obligations to obedience.

In these three points, if we include the ordination of their successors in the sacred office, consisted the *rule*, or *government*, which the ministers of Christ, by virtue of their office, were authorized to exercise. And the end of this government was the "perfecting of the saints, and the edifying of the body of Christ." It was wisely appointed for the prevention or cure of all disorders in the Church, and for the building up of believers in their most holy faith, and preserving the whole body in "the unity of the Spirit and in the bonds of peace." Although the word which the apostle uses in the text, and also in the 17th verse, to express the authority of Christian pastors and bishops, properly signifies a ruler, or one having command, it is not a legitimate inference that this authority was of the same character with that of civil rulers. It certainly never was the design of Christ, or the practice of his apostles, to enforce the discipline of the gospel by such pains and penalties as properly belong to the civil magistrate. Indeed, the authority and influence of the primitive rulers in the Church—and the same may be said of the true Christian ministers in every age—"was founded, not on force, but in the fidelity with which they discharged the duties of their function, and in the esteem and affection of their flocks." How these ecclesiastical rulers were to exercise the authority with which they were invested, is very clearly shown in the Epistles of St. Paul to Timothy and Titus, and in the First Epistle of St. Peter. It was to be done by the influence of a godly life—by examples of patience and charity, illustrative of the excellency of the Christian system, and worthy of all imitation. "But be thou an example of the believers, in word, in conversation, in charity, in *spirit*, in faith, in purity. Feed the flock of God which is with you, taking the oversight—not as being lords [temporal or spiritual] over God's heritage; but being ensamples, or patterns, to the flock. In all things show thyself a pattern of good works: in doctrine, uncorruptness, gravity, sincerity." Entreaty, reproof, and rebuke, with exhortation, complete the panoply with which the ministers of Christ execute their office as rulers in the Church of God. "Rebuke not an elder, but *entreat* him as a father; the younger men, as brethren; the elder women, as mothers; the younger, as sisters, with all purity. Reprove, rebuke, exhort, with all long-suffering and doctrine." Public censure, and excommunication from the communion of the Church, were the highest punishments which the ecclesiastical rulers were authorized to inflict; and these only when, in the judgment of the Church, the offenders were guilty of such misdemeanors as merited these punishments. The terrors of the papal excommunication are not to be found in the records of the primitive Church; and it appears very certain that the administration of the discipline of the gospel was never designed to inflict any other temporal penalty than such as might result from the separation of the unworthy person from the fellowship of the Christian community.

If the preceding observations afford a correct view of

the office and work of the ministers of the gospel of Christ, it will not be difficult to perceive that there is a corresponding obligation on the part of those among whom they labor in word and doctrine. It is the duty of the flock to esteem their pastors highly in love, for their work's sake; to cherish for them sentiments of affection and respect; to seek counsel and consolation from them, in all their tribulations and conflicts; to submit to their godly admonitions, and to imitate their godly examples. And when it pleases God to remove them from their militant charge to his eternal kingdom and glory, those among whom they have exercised their holy function should remember them with affection, gratitude, and esteem. Without any apology for the length of the foregoing observations, I proceed—

II. To show wherein the character of a primitive Christian pastor, or minister, has been sustained and exemplified in the life, ministerial labors, and official oversight of the late senior Bishop of the Methodist Episcopal Church.

1. Bishop McKendree was born in King William county, State of Virginia, on the 6th day of July, 1757. His parents, John and Mary McKendree, were both natives of the same State. His father was a respectable planter, and his son William was brought up in the same occupation, and early taught the arts of husbandry and the habits of industry and economy. The McKendree family had received their religious instructions in the Church of England, which at that time was the prevailing religion of the southern colonies. The history of the Church at that day affords us a melancholy picture of the state of Christian morals. The clergy were more fond of ease, and wealth, and worldly pleasure and gratification, than of the sacred duties of their holy function. The religious instruction of youth was much neglected, and very defective; and attendance on balls, horse-races, card-tables, and other places of amuse-

ment, was generally considered not only consistent with a profession of religion and membership in the Church, but also with the character and calling of those to whom was committed the "cure of souls." This was truly a day of spiritual darkness. But notwithstanding this lamentable condition of religion and morals, young McKendree was restrained from gross immoralities, and preserved a character free from reproach, even among the most religious of the day. At a very early period he was convinced of the depravity of his nature; his conscience became tender, and he formed resolutions to live according to the light which he had received. The following is his own description of his state at the period of which we now speak: "I do not recollect to have sworn more than one profane oath in my life; yet, as far back as memory serves, I am conscious of the prevalence of evil propensities, of a heart disposed to wickedness, so that, notwithstanding the restraints by which I was kept within the bounds of a respectable morality, my heart was far from being right with God; it was deceitful and desperately wicked. Of this deplorable state of things I became exquisitely sensible by reading the Holy Scriptures at school, when I was but a small boy. For want of proper instruction, my apprehension of God, the Redeemer, and the Holy Scriptures, was very superficial. I literally 'understood as a child;' and with the simplicity of a child, I yielded to the dictates of conscience, refrained from what appeared to be wrong, and, as a child, endeavored to imitate the examples of those holy men of God, as set forth in the Scriptures." Had these impressions been cherished by pious instructors, and by parents who had the power as well as the form of godliness, there can be little doubt that this amiable youth, like young Timothy, would have, from a child, known the Holy Scriptures in such a manner as to have made him wise unto salvation, through faith which is in Christ Jesus, and thereby prepared the way for his entering the arduous work of the gospel ministry at a much earlier period of his life than he did. But, for the want of such helps, and in consequence of opposition and discouragements from those who should have taught him the way of righteousness and aided him to walk therein at this tender age, his impressions were weakened, conscience became more inclined to slumber, and his religious resolutions were shaken. But still the fear of God did not forsake him. It was about the time of the commencement of the revolutionary struggle, by which the colonies were finally separated from the British government, that the Methodist preachers—then under the direction of the Rev. John Wesley—first visited that section of Virginia in which the McKendree family resided. William at this time was about nineteen years of age, possessed with an exquisite sensibility, and a heart all buoyant with anticipation. The ministry of the word was attended by the power of the Spirit, and many were convinced that "these men were the servants of the most high God." Those convictions which had in a great measure become extinguished by the amusements of the world, were now revived and strengthened in the mind of this interesting young man. He says of himself, "I yielded to conviction, and resolved to lead a new life." In conformity to this resolution, he proposed to unite with the Methodist Society as a seeker of religion, and was received on trial. But here again his resolution was shaken, and, halting by the way, he failed to obtain the prize. His undisguised representation of his case clearly shows the danger of awakened persons associating with those companions, however civil they may be, who neither love nor fear God—especially before age and experience have fortified the heart.

Having noticed his connection with the Society, he adds,

"But my attachment to worldly associates, who were civil and respectful in their deportment, had grown with my growth, and my conviction was not accompanied with sufficient firmness to dissolve the connection; and their future conduct being accommodated to my reformed manners, I continued to enjoy the friendship both of the Society and of the world, but in a very imperfect degree. They continued to counteract and impair each other, until the love of the world prevailed, and my relish for genuine piety departed. I peaceably retired from Society, while my conduct continued to secure their friendship." In this situation, with no material change in his religious state, except a gradual decline of his concern for the salvation of his soul, he continued for several years. But his abiding conviction of the importance and necessity of religion, and his exquisite sensibility to consistency of character, preserved him from gross immoralities, and prevented a rapid progress in the way of sin. In the year 1787, he being about thirty years of age, a powerful and extensive revival of religion commenced in the Brunswick Circuit, in which he lived, under the ministry of that devoted servant of Christ, the Rev. John Easter. In the course of this year, Mr. Easter added about twelve hundred members to the Church. This was a year of the deepest interest to McKendree—it was the year of his conversion to God—the year in which he experienced that inward and spiritual revelation of the Son of God, which was an indispensable qualification for preaching his unsearchable riches. He records this eventful change in the following expressive terms: "My convictions were renewed. They were deep and pungent. The great deep of the heart was broken up. Its deceit and desperately wicked nature were disclosed. And the awful, the eternally ruinous consequences clearly appeared. My repentance was sincere. I was desirous, and became willing, to be saved on any terms. And after a sore and sorrowful travail of three days, which were employed in hearing Mr. Easter, and in fasting and prayer, while the man of God was showing a large congregation the way of salvation by faith, with a clearness which at once astonished and encouraged me, I ventured my all on Christ. In a moment my soul was relieved of a burden too heavy to be borne, and joy instantly succeeded sorrow! For a short space I was fixed in silent adoration, giving glory to God for his unspeakable goodness to such an unworthy creature." Although his evidence of acceptance with God was so clear as to remove all doubt from his mind, and enable him in humble confidence to cry, "Abba, Father!" it was but a short time before he was perplexed with doubts and fears relative to the reality of the change. In this state of uncertainty he continued for six weeks. But notwithstanding his exercise was deep and sorrowful, he was graciously supported, and received many encouraging manifestations. "But," to use his own words, "instead of receiving in faith, and giving glory to God, I reasoned all into uncertainty, and had multiplied perplexity and sorrow for my reward." At the close of this severe conflict, he received a new and full assurance of his adoption into the heavenly family, in regard to which blessed event he says: "But thanks be to God, who, by a manifestation of truth, accompanied by its own evidence, removed all my doubts, I was confirmed in the faith of the gospel, and of my personal acceptance, in which I have remained steadfast to the present day. Many have been my imperfections and failures, and I have had convictions and repentance for them; but nothing of the kind has shaken my confidence in the reality of the change wrought in me by the Spirit of God at my conversion." Soon after this, he heard the doctrine of "Christian perfection set forth in its native simplicity," and such were its peculiar beauties and divine excellences in his estimation, that he immediately resolved, by God's grace, to seek and obtain the blessing. This resolution he carried into practice; and the result, which he gives in the following words, should be matter of encouragement to all who desire this blessed state. "Eventually," he says, "I obtained deliverance from unholy passions, and found myself possessed of ability to resist temptation, take up and bear the cross, and to exercise faith and patience, and all the graces of the Spirit, in a manner before unknown." Soon after he had experienced the witness of his acceptance with God, he began to feel a deep concern for the salvation of his fellow-creatures, especially those who had been his particular friends and associates. With these he conversed in private on their eternal interest, and exhorted them with tears to flee from the wrath to come, and to embrace Christ as their Saviour. His soul was frequently drawn out in secret prayer, with ardent desires for their conversion to God. He soon began to exercise in the public prayer-meetings. The fruits of these early labors were obvious. Numbers were convicted, converted, or comforted, through his instrumentality. It was but a few months from the time of his conversion till his mind became deeply exercised in regard to the work of the ministry. And these exercises were greatly increased by the fact that many of the experienced and pious members of the Society, as well as the preachers, were deeply impressed with a conviction that it was his duty to preach the gospel. But this did not satisfy him. He wanted for himself a full proof of Christ speaking in him, and was fearful of preaching before he was sent. The Rev. Mr. Easter, who was his spiritual father, and who was of the opinion that God had called him to the work, proposed to him to travel with him round the circuit. He yielded to this proposal with fear and trembling. On the one hand he feared that the course pursued with him by those in whose piety and judgment he had great confidence, and who consequently had much influence with him, might lead him to a premature attempt, which was liable to eventuate in the injury of a cause which he most ardently desired to promote; and on the other, having strong conviction of duty in his own mind, he was tremblingly alive to the consequences of refusing to obey. His deficiency in literary acquirements—having had only a common English education—his conscious want of experience in the knowledge of men and things, and especially his apprehension of his superficial acquaintance with the Holy Scriptures, presented to his mind so many formidable difficulties in the way of a successful prosecution of the work, as to produce the most severe conflict. In this fiery trial he left Mr. Easter and returned home, but was unable to attend to business in consequence of the deep struggle and anguish of his spirit. In this way, to use his own words, "he was tossed to and fro" until the sitting of the Conference, which took place in Petersburg, Virginia. Here he was recommended by the preacher, received on trial, and appointed by the Bishop to Mecklenburg Circuit. This was in less than nine months from the time of his conversion. He was never licensed as a local preacher before he commenced traveling, and never located afterward. So that he never sustained the character of a local preacher, either before or after he was admitted into the Conference.

The state of his mind, with reference to his call to the ministry, at the time he joined the Conference, and for more than a year after, and the manner in which he became fully satisfied of his duty in this respect, I prefer to give in his own words, which are as follows: "I went immediately to the circuit to which I was appointed, relying more on the judgment of experienced ministers, in whom I confided, than on any clear conviction of my call to the work; and when I yielded to their judgment, I firmly resolved not to deceive them, and to retire as soon as I should be convinced that I was not called of God, and to conduct myself in such a manner that if I failed, my friends might be satisfied it was not for want of effort on my part, but that their judgment was not well founded. This resolution supported me under many doubts and fears, for entering into the work of a traveling preacher neither removed my doubts nor the difficulties that attended my labors. Sustained by a determination to make a full trial, I resorted to fasting and prayer, and waited for those kind friends who had the charge and government over me to dismiss me from the work. But I waited in vain. In this state of suspense, my reasoning might have terminated in discouraging and ruinous conclusions, had I not been comforted and supported by the kind and encouraging manner in which I was received by aged and experienced brethren, by the manifest presence of God in our meetings, which were frequently lively and profitable; and sometimes souls were convicted and converted, which afforded considerable encouragement, and by the union and communion of my Saviour in private devotion, which he graciously afforded me in the intervals of my very imperfect attempts to preach his gospel. In this way I became satisfied of my call to the ministry, and that I was moving in the line of my duty."

In taking a summary view of the dealings of God with his servant, as previously noticed, the following particulars are worthy of our special attention: 1. He had a STRONG *conviction* in his own mind that it was his duty to preach the gospel, and call sinners to repentance. 2. This conviction was strengthened by the knowledge he had that pious and devoted Christians and experienced ministers were of the same opinion. 3. The consciousness of his deficiency in those qualifications which are requisite for a minister of Christ, filled him with many doubts relative to his call to the work. 4. He feared the consequences, and trembled to take the responsibility of disobedience. 5. In this state of solicitude and suspense he entered upon the work, waiting for providential events to decide the doubtful point. 6. But he waited with fasting and prayer. 7. The kindness with which he was received by the friends of the Redeemer, greatly encouraged him in his efforts. 8. He saw the fruits of his labors; the presence of God was with him in the congregations, and sinners were awakened and converted. 9. He had sweet communion with his Saviour in his private devotions. 10. By these means he was fully persuaded that he was moved by the Holy Ghost to preach. It is not difficult to trace in these points the experience of primitive ministers of the gospel. The calling is by the same divine agency in every age. The promise of the presence of Christ extends to the end of time; and the same fruits are to result from the preaching of the word now as at the beginning. The gospel is now, and will continue to be, the power of God unto salvation. And all true converts to the faith of Christ are still as they ever have been, seals of the ministry of those through whose instrumentality they have been brought out of darkness into God's marvelous light. We cannot speak minutely of Mr. McKendree during the first years of his ministry. It would swell this discourse beyond its prescribed limits. Suffice it to say, that he traveled with great acceptability and usefulness as a circuit-preacher for seven years, in which time he filled some of the most important circuits in Virginia, and one year he was stationed in the city of Norfolk. Some of these were years of great affliction in that part of the work where he chiefly labored. The schism which commenced in the Church in that quarter in 1791, and which was matured the following year, threatened an extensive and ruinous division. At the commencement of these difficulties, his mind was greatly exercised in regard to the course he ought to pursue. And at one time, fearing the measures adopted by the Conference would be injurious to the Church, he declined taking a regular appointment; but he soon became convinced of his error, and a few days after the close of the Conference, met the Bishop, and took a regular station in the city of Norfolk. From this time he devoted himself more diligently to a critical examination of the system of government recommended by Mr. Wesley, and adopted by the General Conference in 1784. This examination resulted in a full conviction that the system was not only well adapted to the ends proposed—that is, "to reform the continent, and spread scriptural holiness over these lands"—but that it was agreeable to the primitive order and government of the Christian Church. Confirmed in his judgment of the fitness of the government, and of the importance of preserving a general itinerant superintendency, guarded by suitable checks and responsibilities, he used the influence of his talents and personal character, in the most prudent and judicious manner, to counteract the effects, and prevent the progress of schismatical measures. And there is good evidence that his labors, in this respect, were not in vain. With reference to the early years of his ministry, he says: "The object of my pursuit was the glory of God, the salvation of my own soul, and to be useful as a Methodist preacher. For these ends I sincerely sought to understand the will of God in his gracious plan of redemption—*his* terms of saving sinners—the duties required of men both before and after conversion, and conscientiously walk by and enforce them as I was able. And I deeply regretted that my performances fell so far short of what I conceived to be the measure of so good a cause.

In the discharge of my duties as a traveling preacher, the rules of the Church, and especially of a 'Methodist preacher,' were my directory. I therefore conscientiously endeavored not to break those rules, but to keep them. That the legitimate law should govern, is a principle from which I have not knowingly departed. By strictly attending to this rule, I have had some trouble and affliction, but I have been supported by a good conscience."

These are sentiments worthy to be written in the heart and preserved in the memory of those who succeed him in the sacred office. They are strikingly descriptive of the true character of the excellent man who wrote them. May his sons in the gospel imitate his sincerity, zeal, and fidelity!

He was ordained Deacon in 1790, and Elder in December, 1791. At the close of eight years as a regular circuit-preacher, in 1798, he was appointed Presiding Elder of a District in the Virginia Conference. Here his sphere of useful labor was greatly enlarged. This District extended from the Chesapeake Bay over the Blue Ridge and Alleghany Mountains, and embraced a large tract of country on the western waters. The rides were long, and the charge required of the Elder constant preaching, and much attention and care in the management of the various and important business of the District. He records with gratitude to Heaven the blessings he received during the three years he continued in this charge. His ministry was attended by a divine unction. Sinners were awakened and converted to God, believers were comforted and built up in their most holy faith, many were added to the Church, and the field of labor was considerably enlarged. In those days it was in accordance with the spirit and views of Methodist preachers, whether on circuits or Districts, to seek the enlargement of the bounds of their work, and pray earnestly to the Lord of the harvest to send forth laborers to cultivate the field. The oversight of the District, in the administration of the discipline, was conducted with great wisdom and prudence, and to the satisfaction of the preachers and members. The spirit of schism, which had previously prevailed in some parts of the District, greatly subsided, and the love of union, peace, and order was revived. Our venerable departed friend comprehensively records the events of the time he employed on this charge in the following sententious manner: "On this station I was blessed with many friends, abundant in kind offices, and some of them able counselors. We were blessed with a revival of religion. Many professed to obtain regenerating grace, and joined the Church. The members provoked one another to love and good works, and their advancement in the divine life was evident. The abundant labors and care which the charge imposed were too great for my strength; my studies were therefore partially prevented by attention to other branches of duty, and my nervous system was somewhat impaired. But I was abundantly compensated, in having intimate union and communion with the adorable Saviour; and the increasing prosperity of the Church at once invigorated my zeal and increased my joy in the Lord." Thus he closed his extensive and arduous labors on the District.

In 1799, he was appointed to a District in the Baltimore Conference, contiguous to that on which he had traveled the three preceding years. This District was little less in extent of territory than the former. It extended from the Chesapeake Bay over the Blue Ridge, and terminated at the foot of the Alleghany Mountains. This was to him a year of labor and trials; but he says, "They were forgotten in overwhelming communion with God and reviving and encouraging interviews with my followers. Here," he adds, "I found fathers and mothers in Israel, by whose example I was edified and comforted."

In the spring of 1800, he was returned to the District from which he had been taken the year before, and in the fall of the same year Bishops Asbury and Whatcoat passed through the District, and took him with them to the Western Conference, which met at Bethel, in October. Here he was appointed to the oversight of the whole Conference, in the character of a District, which embraced the State of Kentucky and that part of Virginia west of the Great Kanawha River, East and West Tennessee, and all the settled territory west of the Ohio River, including what is now the State of Ohio, and an extensive mission in the Illinois. The Natchez Mission was also connected with his charge. He had now to travel about fifteen hundred miles to compass his District; and the whole extent of it, with the exception of East Tennessee and that part of Virginia which it included, was a new and rapidly populating country. This was a field of labor and enterprise well suited to the enlightened views and ardent devotion of this excellent minister of Christ. It was a work worthy of apostles, and one which required the zeal of apostles to accomplish it. He entered into it with a deep sense of his dependence upon divine aid, and with that vigorous and persevering action which, by the blessing of God, was attended with abundant success. It must be recollected that a very large portion of the country embraced in his new charge was just settling with emigrants from the old States, who were subject to all the inconveniences and privations common to the first settlers in all new countries. Small companies of these emigrants would locate themselves in neighborhoods many miles from each other, without any other method of intercourse than the pocket-compass, or trees marked with the ax, or the tops of underbrush bent down and half-broken.

These were the *landmarks* and *highways* of our McKendree through a large part of the vast Valley of the Mississippi. It was his wise and benevolent plan, with the handful of preachers in his charge, to advance with the increasing population of the country, and to plant the standard of the cross and preach Jesus and the resurrection in the most frontier settlements. Pursuing this judicious course, the field of labor continued to enlarge in proportion to the rapid advance of emigration. In the prosecution of this plan, he and his fellow-laborers (of precious memory) had necessarily to encounter and overcome many formidable difficulties. They were frequently ministers of gospel consolation to the people in their camps or cabins in the woods or canebrakes, before their fields were sufficiently opened to raise a comfortable support for their families. In getting to them, for want of roads or paths, they were conducted through the trackless woods. And for want of bridges or boats, they swam creeks and rivers. They carried their provisions, for man and beast, on their horses, cooked their simple meals in the wilderness, slept at night on their blankets, (frequently interrupted by the company and howling of wolves,) and in the morning went on their way rejoicing The following is the description of these western scenes drawn by our venerable friend, whose experience had qualified him to give a striking picture. He says, "While on the way through these frontier settlements, if we came to a creek or a river without a boat, or canoe, or log, we had the privilege of swimming the stream; and when safely landed on the other bank, it was a consolation to reflect on having left that obstruction behind, and that the way to the next lay open and plain before us. If night overtook us before we could reach a house, it was our privilege to gather wood where we could find it, make a fire, eat our morsel, and supplicate a throne of grace with as free access as in a palace or a church. Being weary, we rested sweetly and securely under divine protection. And when we arrived at our intended place, if the accommodations were of the humblest kind, we had the inexpressible satisfaction of being received with a *hearty* welcome, and accommodated with the best the family could afford; and though very inferior in the estimation of the delicate and those accustomed to sumptuous fare, yet all the real wants of nature were supplied. We eat heartily, slept sweetly, and rejoiced with the pious and affectionate people, who received and treated the ministers of the gospel as angels of God. And above all, when the time arrived for us to deliver our message, the people flocked together and seemed to wait to hear what God the Lord would say. The prayers of the pious ascended the hill of the Lord, divine energy attended the word preached, sinners were convicted of their sins, many were converted to God, and the Church enlarged and built up in the faith once delivered to the saints." In this vast western work he continued to labor as a Presiding Elder from the fall of 1800 till the spring of 1808. In view of the whole, he says, "My appointments required much riding. I preached often, and sustained a great charge; and yet I esteem those among the happiest days of my life. Strange as it may seem, there, in the midst of privations and many exposures, my impaired constitution was restored and my health greatly improved. I enjoyed peace and consolation through faith, and was enabled to walk with God." During the eight years of his labor in this Western Valley, the work was greatly enlarged, and a number of regular Districts were formed.

In the spring of 1808, he was elected by the Western Conference to attend the General Conference, in the city of Baltimore. Here he was appointed on the committee to form a constitution for the organization and government of a delegated General Conference. But before the committee had fully matured that important system and prepared it to lay before the body, he was elected by the General Conference to the office of General Superintendent, or Bishop, of the Methodist Episcopal Church. He was ordained on the 18th day of May, 1808, by the imposition of the hands of Bishop Asbury, assisted by the following Elders, viz., Jesse Lee, Freeborn Garrettson, Thomas Ware, and Philip Bruce. I cannot follow Bishop McKendree in his almost unparalleled travels and labors, from the time of his election to the Episcopal office till death removed him from the militant Church, even with that degree of minuteness which would be necessary to give a tolerable view of the extent and usefulness of the exercise of his ministerial functions. However desirable such a narrative might be, in a discourse occasioned by the removal of such a man as Bishop McKendree, it would require a volume to accomplish it. We must therefore satisfy ourselves, for the present, with a few brief sketches of this very important epoch of his history, in hope that an enlarged biography of his long, laborious, and useful life will at no very distant period be given to the Church in which he has exercised the oversight for so many years. His field of labor was now changed from a District in the Western Valley to the United States and Territories, and the provinces of Upper and Lower Canada; and instead of presiding in quarterly-meetings, chiefly in thinly-settled circuits, he was now called to the joint superintendence of the temporal and spiritual interests of the whole Church, embracing the preachers and members of seven Annual Conferences. In the prosecution of this arduous work, for many years, he traveled annually from four to six thousand miles, and a great part of the time preached nearly every day. Nor would he yield to the use of a carriage, but performed his extensive journeys on horseback, till the infirmities of age and the greatness and variety of his labors had enfeebled his constitution and greatly impaired his health. While he retained his physical strength and action, he was always ready to advance in the face of difficulties and dangers. Diligence and perseverance were stamped upon his whole character; and if he failed to meet an appointment, (which was very seldom the case,) it was apprehended that some extraordinary dispensation of Providence had delayed him. He left the city of Baltimore about the first of June, shortly after the close of the General Conference at which he was constituted Bishop, and traveled through Virginia, Tennessee, Kentucky, and the Territories west of the Ohio River, and penetrated the "western wilds" one hundred miles up the Missouri. Here he attended a camp-meeting in the true "backwoods" style, with that excellent man of God, the Rev. Jesse Walker. His house, at this meeting, was the preachers' saddle-blankets, sewed together and spread over a pole, supported by forks placed in the ground, after the manner of soldiers' tents. One end of this house was made of green brush; the other was left open, and in front of it the fire was made. His food was bread, and flesh broiled on sticks by the fire. He returned through the Territories to meet Bishop Asbury and the Western Conference, on the 1st of October, at Liberty Hill, in Tennessee. Thus, in four months, he accomplished a tour of about fifteen hundred miles on horseback—a considerable part of it without roads, bridges, or boats — frequently swimming creeks and rivers, and sleeping many nights in the woods, with heaven for his covering and earth for his bed. This first extensive frontier visit of a Methodist Bishop was attended with happy results. Many people had conceived of the Superintendents, or Bishops, of the Methodist Episcopal Church, as being men clothed with power dangerous to society. They had considered them as ecclesiastical dignitaries, inaccessible to the common classes of people, surrounded with pomp and wealth, and ruling with almost absolute authority. And there were not wanting Protestant teachers of religion who were forward in producing and cherishing such sentiments in the minds of the people. Bishop McKendree's appearance and manners were well calculated to correct such views, and remove the prejudices of those who had formed their opinions under the influence of misrepresentation. Thousands flocked to see and hear the "Methodist Bishop." But how were they disappointed! Instead of costly and fashionable costume, his dress was of the plainest mode, and of common materials. Instead of austerity of manners, and the signs of ecclesiastical power, they found him affable, familiar, and persuasive, gentle to all men, ready to participate with ease and sweetness of temper in the circumstances of the poor and afflicted, and ever intent upon diffusing happiness in every circle of society in which he moved.

In this Western tour he met a number of quarterly and camp-meetings, and preached in the demonstration of the Spirit and with power to listening thousands; and the blessed fruits of those labors remain to this day.

His administration in the first Conference, at which he presided conjointly with Bishop Asbury, which has been named before, was every way satisfactory to the preachers and people.

Here he commenced his regular annual visits to the Conferences, traveling sometimes with his venerable colleague, Bishop Asbury, and sometimes alone, as was found most convenient, in view of visiting the Churches and preaching to the congregations in the most profitable manner in the intervals of the Conferences.

His manner of conducting the business of the Conferences was almost universally approved, and his administration of the government was uniformly sustained by the General Conference. In this laborious, extensive, and difficult oversight, he continued, traveling about six thousand miles a year, till 1816, during which time the work had been greatly enlarged, and several new Conferences were organized. From 1812 till 1816, Bishop McKendree's labors were considerably increased in consequence of Bishop Asbury's inability, through age and severe affliction, to sustain the charge as he had before done. In the fall of 1815, these two venerable and laborious men met for the last time at the Tennessee Conference. Bishop Asbury preached, although unable to stand on his feet, and ordained with feeble and trembling hands a few preachers. Here they separated, taking different routes, intending to meet at the South Carolina Conference, in Charleston. But Bishop Asbury failed to reach the place, and they met no more. In March, 1816, Bishop Asbury was removed from his labors and sufferings to his eternal rest, and Bishop McKendree was left alone in the General Superintendency of the Church. For some time previous to the sitting of the General Conference in May of this year, Bishop McKendree was severely afflicted. He was confined to his bed on his way from the Baltimore to the Philadelphia Conference, and was not able to attend the latter. He was brought to the dwelling of his old friend Dr. Wilkins, in the vicinity of Baltimore, where he remained till the sitting of the General Conference. Here it was very evident that his arduous labors, extensive travels, and the infirmities of age, had greatly impaired his constitution and enfeebled his physical energies. It was obvious to all that it was indispensably necessary to afford him aid in his superintending oversight. For this purpose two aged and experienced brethren were elected and ordained as his joint colleagues in this vast field of labor; but notwithstanding his feeble state of health and the appointment of two additional Superintendents at this General Conference, he continued to discharge the duties of his office with untiring perseverance, and his travels and labors were rather increased than diminished.

In the winter of 1817–18, he attended the South Carolina Conference in Georgia, and went on to the Virginia Conference at Norfolk. At the close of this Conference he set out on an extensive Western tour, and traveled by the way of Lynchburg, through the Western parts of Virginia, and East and West Tennessee. After resting a few days at his brother's, in Sumner county, he continued his journey through the Southern parts of Kentucky, crossed the Ohio River, and visited the lower parts of the State of Illinois; crossed the Mississippi at Cape Girardeau, and visited the frontier settlements about the old Lead Mines, and from thence to the Missouri River; and crossing it, attended a camp-meeting on the north side. After attending this meeting, he returned through Illinois, Indiana, and Kentucky, visiting the Churches by the way of St. Louis, Vincennes, Louisville, Shelbyville, and Maysville; and attended the Ohio Conference at Steubenville in the fall of 1818. His affliction was such at this Conference as to excite the deep sympathy of his friends, who advised and even entreated him to relinquish his design of visiting the South Carolina Conference the ensuing winter by way of Mississippi, and through the extensive nations of Indians; but his work was before him, and his trust was in God. He commenced the intended journey in circumstances which would have deterred most men from the attempt. He could neither mount nor dismount his horse without help, and when mounted, one misstep or irregular motion of the horse produced exquisite pain. But feeble as he was, he pursued his course through the States of Ohio and Indiana, and attended the Conference on the White River, and from thence to the Tennessee Conference in Nashville. Here he took two young men for the work in Mississippi, prepared a pack-horse to carry their provisions through the Indian Nations, and set out for the Mississippi Conference, which was to meet on the Pearl River. Long rides, irregular living, and great exposure, added to the care of the Churches, proved to be too great for his declining strength; and three days before he reached the seat of Conference, he sunk under the fatigue, and was very near falling from his horse. The balance of his journey was pursued in great weakness. He commenced the business of the Conference, but was unable to proceed. A brother was called to the chair, and a bed was placed in the room on which the Bishop lay, and afforded such counsel and aid as his feeble state would admit. On the Sabbath, the congregation met on the camp-ground. The Bishop was taken in a carriage, and laid on a bed near the stand during the sermon. At the close of the preaching, he was taken from the bed, and being supported by two preachers, performed the ordination service, in the presence of a large, attentive, and deeply-affected congregation. This work being accomplished, he was put into the carriage and conveyed to his lodgings, where he remained, with the kindest treatment and in the hands of a skillful physician, through a long and painful affliction. His recovery from this illness was very slow, so that it was judged unsafe for him to attempt to travel, except on a visit to the mission at New Orleans on a steam-boat, till about the middle of April, 1819. At this time, his physicians and friends considering it not safe for him to remain in the low country during the warm season, advised his return to a more northern latitude to spend the summer. Accordingly he set out, accompanied by two preachers, although in a very weak and delicate state of health. His feebleness of body prevented him from reaching the public stands on the road, in consequence of which he was under the necessity of lying in the woods eight or ten nights in passing through the Choctaw and Chickasaw Nations on his way to West Tennessee. After resting a few weeks at his brother's, in Sumner county, he *visited* the Harrodsburg Springs, in Kentucky, where he continued a considerable part of the summer, visiting and preaching in the neighborhood as he was able. In August he attended the Ohio Conference in Cincinnati. From this Conference he moved slowly, as his feeble health would permit, through Kentucky, Tennessee, and Virginia, and arrived in Georgetown during the session of the Baltimore Conference in that place. Here he was received with a sincere and ardent affection, and with lively expressions of gratitude to God for the preservation of his life. On the first day of May, 1820, he opened the session of the General Conference in Baltimore, but was seldom able to preside, or even to attend the sittings of the Conference. During this eventful session, Bishop McKendree was deeply afflicted, both in body and mind. With the interests and prosperity of the Church no man was ever more perfectly identified. Whatever tended to disturb her peace, or weaken the bands of confidence and fellowship within her pales, was with him a matter of painful sensibility. He was always watchful of those ancient landmarks, set up by the wisdom of age and experience, and tested by extraordinary proofs of divine approbation, in a genuine, extensive, and continued revival of evangelical religion over this continent. He contemplated with admiration the peculiar adaptation of the doctrines, government, and discipline of the Church of his choice to the proposed ends. He had thoroughly examined the grand itinerant system, and was fully persuaded of its agreement with the primitive order of the Church. He had witnessed its mighty and efficient operations in turning thousands and tens of thousands from darkness to light, and from the power of Satan unto God. And he had studied men and things too well not to perceive that a *general itinerant superintendency* was essential to the efficiency, and even to the preservation, of this system. Under all these considerations, Bishop McKendree was deeply affected with any measures which, in his judgment, had a tendency to weaken the energies or change the plan of the government. Such measures he apprehended to be in a train of operation at the General Conference of 1820. With these measures he was afflicted, but his earnest and constant prayer was, that God would so direct and overrule the deliberations and acts of that body as to promote the peace and harmony of the Church, and advance the general interests of religion. In consideration of Bishop McKendree's extreme debility, and in hope that his health might be restored, the General Conference passed a resolution releasing him from the discharge of his official duties, and advising him to pursue that course which would best suit his personal comfort and convenience, and be most likely to improve his health, and at the same time requesting him to resume the functions of his office as soon as his strength would admit.

He ever afterward spoke of this act of the Conference with expressions of affection and gratitude. From this period till the sitting of the General Conference in 1824, he passed through the deep waters of affliction. Unable through bodily infirmity to travel and meet the Conferences, and jointly with his colleagues superintend the important business of the Church, while efforts were making at different points to produce schism in the body, and his character assailed with a severity which savored but little of the spirit of the gospel, the refined and exquisite sensibility of his nature was wounded, and his deep solicitude for the harmony of the preachers and people was frequently expressed in fervent prayers and many tears.

In reviewing the scenes of these four years, the Bishop speaks with deep humility and lively gratitude. He says, "The last four years I have been afflicted in body and in mind. In some measure my anxiety and zeal for the Church appeared to have been the effect of a deficiency in faith and trust in God. In these deep exercises I saw more clearly the depravity of my own heart, and have cause to regret that I failed so to exercise patience and faith as to grow in grace as heretofore; but the Lord mercifully sustained and graciously saved me from sinking in the deep waters. I remember with gratitude being rescued from sinking under the trial by timely encouragement and support from brethren in the ministry and in the membership." At the Conference of 1824, the Bishop's health was considerably improved, and the conflicting elements of disunion and schism appeared to be subsiding. The prospect of a better state of things produced a happy effect in his mind. When the Conference closed, he set out on a tour through the Western States, preaching every Sabbath, and sometimes on the week-days. In this journey he traveled from Baltimore to Wheeling in Virginia, to Columbus in Ohio, to the Wyandotte Mission at Upper Sandusky, returning to the Ohio Conference at Zanesville; from thence by the way of Lancaster, Chillicothe, Maysville, and Frankfort, to Shelbyville, the seat of the Kentucky Conference. After attending the Conference, he continued the journey to Louisville, crossed the Ohio River, and proceeded through the State of Indiana to Vincennes, crossed the Wabash, and traveled through Illinois to Padfields, twenty-five miles from the Mississippi; attended the Missouri Conference in

November, and proceeded through the South part of Illinois; recrossed the Ohio River into Kentucky, and visited Hopkinsville and Russellville, and passed into Tennessee; preached at Fountain Head, Gallatin, Nashville, and Franklin, and attended the Tennessee Conference the 1st of December at Columbia. During this long and laborious journey, Bishop McKendree was a great part of the time so feeble as to require the assistance of friends to get in and out of his carriage. The roads were exceedingly bad, and sometimes almost impassable. The waters were high, bridges and boats gone, and for the last month the weather extremely cold and unpleasant. Several times the horses and carriage were near swimming, and once in crossing a deep and dangerous river on a very cold day, the ferry-boat having been sunk in the stream, the water swept over the horses' backs, and the carriage sunk so deep that the water came in so as to wet the Bishop above the knees. His clothes were soon frozen, and in this condition he had to ride three or four miles to reach a house.

He remained with his friends in Tennessee through the winter of 1824–5, visiting the Churches, and preaching frequently. He spent the ensuing summer in the West, and in the fall crossed the Cumberland Mountains and attended the Holston Conference, and traveled extensively through Virginia. In the spring of 1826, he visited the Baltimore, Philadelphia, and New York Conferences, and returned to the South in the fall; spent the winter in the bounds of the South Carolina and Virginia Conferences, and returned to the Baltimore and Philadelphia Conferences in the spring of 1827. After the close of the Philadelphia Conference, he returned to Baltimore, and set out on a journey to the West in May. He crossed the Alleghany Mountains by the way of Cumberland, visiting and preaching in the principal societies. He traveled through the State of Ohio by way of Zanesville, Lancaster, and Columbus, and visited the third time the Wyandotte Mission; returning, he passed through Urbana, and visited many of the towns in the South part of the State, and attended the Kentucky Conference in Versailles in October; from thence he went to Tennessee, and spent the winter with his friends, visiting the neighboring societies, and preaching frequently as he was able. In March, 1828, he set out in company with two of the delegates from the Tennessee Conference for Pittsburgh, the seat of the General Conference, and arrived a few days before its commencement. Although he was unable to preside, his presence and counsel were highly appreciated by the Conference, especially in regard to some very important transactions. At this Conference, although trembling on his staff, and pressed beneath the weight of more than seventy years, and the cares inseparable from his office, his mind was peculiarly peaceful and tranquil, and his spirit was greatly comforted in prospect of the establishment of the harmony and the increasing prosperity of the Church.

After the close of the Conference, he went down the Ohio River to Maysville, and visited Lexington and Frankfort, and attended the Kentucky Conference at Shelbyville. From thence he proceeded to Tennessee, and prepared to go to the South. After visiting and preaching in a number of towns, and attending six or seven camp and quarterly-meetings, he set out for Georgia, through the Cherokee Nation. This was a difficult, laborious, and dangerous route. He passed the Lookout Mountain in the Nation under circumstances of trial and peril. He preached a number of times to the Indians, attended the Grand Council of the Chiefs, and proceeded by way of Athens, Lexington, and Greensboro, to Milledgeville; thence to Sparta and Petersburg, and crossing the Savannah River at Rembert's, visited several Districts in South Carolina, and recrossed the

Savannah to Augusta; preached a number of times both to the whites and the colored, and proceeded to Savannah. From this city he passed into South Carolina, visited several plantations, instructed the slaves, and attended the Conference in Charleston. He continued his route through South Carolina, North Carolina, and Virginia, attended the Conference at Lynchburg, and after spending some time in visiting the Churches in the lower parts of Virginia, attended the Baltimore and Philadelphia Conferences, and returned by the District of Columbia; again crossed the Alleghany Mountains, and attended the Ohio Conference at Urbana, and the Kentucky at Lexington, and spent the winter in Nashville and its vicinity.

During the spring and summer of 1830, he was unable to travel very extensively, but visited the Churches and attended popular meetings as his strength would admit. In October he attended the Kentucky Conference, and notwithstanding his age and infirmities, he had it in contemplation to visit South Carolina, and meet all the Atlantic and Northern Conferences as far as the Genesee, before the sitting of the General Conference in Philadelphia in the spring of 1832. In the judgment of those friends who were best acquainted with his delicate state of health, this project appeared to be rather the result of unabated zeal in the great and blessed work in which he was engaged, than any deliberate calculation with regard to his physical powers to accomplish it. His whole soul was absorbed in the enterprise, and, in view of it, he seemed to have lost sight of himself.

He was advised, as he would have effective aid, to visit the Holston Conference, as an experiment of his ability to accomplish his contemplated tour. To this he yielded with readiness and apparent pleasure. The distance was between three and four hundred miles, over the Cumberland Mountains, and the greater part of the way a very rough road. However, the journey was commenced; but before he arrived at Knoxville, it became very obvious that he was sinking, and many fears were entertained for the result. But the journey was continued under such weakness and general prostration as required that he should be lifted into and out of his carriage, and this frequently eight or ten times in the course of the day. But all was patient suffering; not a murmur, not a complaint escaped his lips. And although his traveling companion, in removing him from his carriage, and replacing him in it, could not refrain from shedding tears of affection and sympathy over this aged, venerable, and persevering minister of Jesus Christ, those tears would be met with a smile of heavenly resignation, and with expressions of gratitude for the attention paid him in his afflictions. He reached the seat of the Conference a day or two after the commencement of the session, but was unable to attend to any business, and only visited the Conference-room once, and then remained but a few moments to give the preachers a kind of apostolic valedictory. He was confined to his bed the greater part of the time during the session, and at its close was able to sit up but little. Under these circumstances, he consulted some of his old and well-tried friends in regard to his future course. He was assured that in their judgment it was impracticable for him to prosecute his contemplated continental tour, and consequently they advised him to return by slow and easy stages, as his feeble state would admit, and spend the ensuing winter in Nashville and its vicinity, without farther exposure. His reply was prompt and emphatical, "I approve your judgment and submit." But it was obvious that, although his mind was fully convinced of the fitness of this course, his heart was in the great work which he viewed with so much interest, and which he ardently desired to accomplish before his departure. It was observed that when he relinquished this enterprise, the tears flowed freely from his eyes. But to recross the range of the Cumberland Mountains, a distance of more than three hundred and fifty miles, through a mountainous country, in rocky and dangerous roads, and the season far advanced, was both a difficult and hazardous undertaking in his delicate and almost helpless condition. But the most formidable difficulties must yield to circumstances so imperious. The journey was commenced the next day after the Conference closed, and continued with patient perseverance till he was safely lodged at his brother's, in Sumner county. This journey was a mingled scene of suffering, patience, and comfort. On the way he traveled through heavy falls of rain, and sleet, and snow; and although every motion of the carriage over rough places, rocks, or roots, gave him severe pain, his mind was tranquil and cheerful. As soon as the roads became comfortable in the spring of 1831, he left his winter retreat, and traveled slowly through Kentucky and Ohio, attending quarterly and camp-meetings, and visiting the societies, and preaching frequently. In the fall he crossed the Alleghany Mountains, and passed the winter in Baltimore and its vicinity. In May, 1832, he attended the General Conference in Philadelphia. He lodged with his old and long-tried friend, Dr. Sargent, where unremitting, cordial, and affectionate attention was shown him by the kind and amiable family. He was very feeble, frequently unable to reach the Conference-room; and when he did, was seldom able to remain but a short time. On these occasions he went in and out before this body of ministers like an ancient patriarch, silvered over with age, and leaning upon his staff, leaving a kind of presentiment in the mind of the preachers that this would be his last visit on such an occasion. His discourse on the death of Bishop George, and the ordination of two brethren elected by the General Conference to succeed him in that sacred office, will never be forgotten while those who heard it live.

At the close of the Conference he took an affectionate leave of his friends, and especially the preachers, as though he expected to see them no more till he met them in the heavenly city. He returned to Baltimore, and after resting a few weeks, and enjoying the society and conversation of many to whom he had been long united in the bonds of Christian love and friendship, he set out for the West, and crossed the Alleghany Mountains, which he had so often crossed in weariness and affliction before, for the last time. He passed through the western part of Pennsylvania, the north of Virginia, the States of Ohio and Kentucky, to Tennessee. In the latter part of this journey it became necessary to fix a bed in his carriage, on which he might lie down, being too feeble to support himself on the seat. The following year he spent chiefly in West Tennessee, visiting various parts of the work, attending popular meetings, and preaching in the power and demonstration of the Spirit. In January, 1834, he visited Natchez, New Orleans, and Woodville, passing down the Cumberland, Ohio, and Mississippi Rivers by steam-boat. He preached on board the boat, and in the several places he visited, with an energy and effect truly astonishing. In the spring of 1834 he returned to Nashville, visited and preached in different places through the summer, and in the fall attended the Tennessee Conference. He preached for the last time in the new church in Nashville, on Sabbath, Nov. 23, 1834. Here ended the pulpit labors of this venerable minister of the gospel of Jesus Christ, who had traveled and preached for almost half a century. Here that penetrating, yet pleasant voice, which had been heard with delight by listening thousands in almost all the populous cities in these United States, and which had sounded forth the glad tidings of salvation in the cabins of the poor on the remote frontiers, or to numerous multitudes gathered together in the forests of the Western Territories, and which savage tribes had heard proclaiming to them the unsearchable riches of Christ, died away to be heard no more. Here he finished the ministration of the words of eternal life, and closed his public testimony for the truth of the revelation of God. In the latter part of December he removed from Nashville to his brother's, which was his last travel. From this time it was obvious that he was gradually sinking to the repose of the tomb. But he had one more conflict before the warfare was accomplished. From the time that Bishop McKendree became unable to perform the entire effective work of a General Superintendent of the Methodist Episcopal Church, his mind was frequently deeply exercised with the apprehensions that he might become unprofitable in the vineyard of his Lord. And it would seem as if he sometimes thought nothing was done unless he could compass the whole work, as he had been accustomed to do in the days of his strength and vigor. He had for many years moved with the foremost in activity and perseverance, and the idea of following in the rear, and being left behind, was painful to him, and frequently drew tears from his eyes. And this sentiment often led him to exertions and labors far beyond his strength. This fear that he should outlive his usefulness in the Church of God, and become unprofitable to his fellow-creatures, was the last afflicting exercise of mind through which he passed; and from this he was speedily and happily delivered by the prayer of faith. He sunk patiently and sweetly into all his Heavenly Father's will, and waited in lively hope and abiding peace for the hour of its departure. The inward conflict had ceased; his confidence in God was unshaken; faith, strong and unwavering, stretched across the Jordan of death, and surveyed the heavenly country. With such sentiments, and in such a peaceful and happy frame of mind, the dying McKendree proclaimed in his last hours, "All is well!" In this emphatical sentence he comprehended what St. Paul expressed in view of his departure from the world and exaltation to an eternal inheritance: "For I am now ready to be offered, and the time of my departure is at hand. I have fought a good fight; I have finished my course; I have kept the faith. Henceforth there is laid up for me a crown of righteousness, which the Lord, the righteous Judge, shall give me at that day." The last connected sentences which ever dropped from the lips of this aged and devoted servant of God, who for almost half a century had made Jesus Christ the same yesterday, and to-day, and for ever, the *end* of his conversation, were: "All is well for time or for eternity; I live by faith in the Son of God; for me to live is Christ, to die is gain.

"'Not a cloud doth arise to darken my skies,
Or hide for a moment my Lord from mine eyes.'"

In this calm and triumphant state of mind he continued till he sweetly "slept in Jesus" at five o'clock P.M, March 5, 1835, in the seventy-eighth year of his age. "Let me die the death of the righteous, and let my last end be like his."

After the notices which have been taken of our beloved and lamented Bishop in the foregoing sketches of his life, it might seem unnecessary to add any thing farther; but I cannot feel fully satisfied of having discharged my obligation in this solemn and interesting subject, without a brief and more summary view of his character; but to do this in a suitable manner—to say neither too much nor too little—

is not an easy task. It will be *difficult*, nay, it will be impossible, to satisfy all. Some will think too much, others too little, is said; but without undue regard to either, I will endeavor according to my ability to speak the truth, and nothing but the truth, without fear or flattery. That Bishop McKendree had faults, is certain; it is equally true that he was deeply sensible of them. Of him it might be said, with the strictest propriety,

> "He felt an idle thought, an actual wickedness,
> And mourned for the minutest fault with exquisite distress."

But his faults, or rather his infirmities, were always on virtue's side, and scarcely deserve to be named in view of the excellences which adorned and dignified his moral, Christian, and ministerial character.

If clearness of conception, richness and variety of sentiment, judicious arrangement and association, strength of argument, zeal as the effect of conviction of the *truth* and *importance* of the subject, simplicity and purity of language, powerful application, and above all, the unction of the *Holy Spirit*, constitute a great and good preacher of the gospel of Jesus Christ, Bishop McKendree has a just title to that character. His personal appearance in the pulpit was always dignified, and his action chaste and unostentatious. His voice was clear, harmonious, and pleasant, possessing not unfrequently peculiar strength and energy.

His preaching was always heard by the attentive and candid with pleasure and profit, and frequently with applause, by every class of the community. His discourses were full of sentiment, and he never employed words only as the representatives of ideas. It was very obvious to the attentive hearer that much *close thinking* had been bestowed on his subjects, but he used no elaborate method of communication; no quaint sentences or phrases beyond the comprehension of his hearers escaped from his lips, but his style was chaste and frequently nervous.

Bishop McKendree very justly considered the Divine Oracles to contain the *subject-matter* of the Christian ministry, and to be the best directory with respect to the *manner* of teaching, as well as the matter to be taught. Out of these sacred records he was not known to travel in his public ministration of the word. In them he was deep-read, and always at home. Few men have ever entertained clearer or more just views of the leading and fundamental doctrines of the Christian revelation, and few men have ever exhibited, illustrated, and applied them with greater effect. He had a talent peculiar to himself for illustrating the doctrines and obligations of religion by the most appropriate figures drawn from nature or art. In these illustrations he seldom failed to produce the most happy effect. He was an accurate and admiring observer of nature, and he drew from her exhaustless depositories abundant means of setting forth the admirable analogy and perfection of the gospel. Nor was he inattentive to the different occupations and pursuits of men, or even to the incidents of civilized or savage life, so far as he could use them for the purpose of giving efficiency to religious instructions, either to the believer or unbeliever. As a striking example of this happy talent, it may be remarked that the short but comprehensive sentence by which he expressed his complete victory over the fear of death, and his confident assurance of a heavenly inheritance, was first taken from a sentinel at a post where danger might be apprehended, and consequently where a watch was needful. From this station the sentinel was heard to cry at measured periods, "All is well!" I need not say how happily and how appropriately this expression of security and triumph was employed by this veteran soldier of the cross of Jesus, who had for so many years remained a faithful sentinel on the walls of Zion. He did not preach the doctrines of the gospel as subjects of *abstract science* or theoretical speculation, but brought them home to the hearts and consciences of the hearers. If he spoke of the natural depravity of the human heart, he made the audience feel that they were depraved; if he reasoned of righteousness and of judgment to come, his hearers trembled, while their consciences joined in with the revelation of God. And so clear and powerful were his appeals on the subject of future accountability and retribution, that it would almost seem to the listening assembly that the judgment was set and the books open. The divinity of Christ, the extent and fullness of the divine atonement, the riches, and plenitude, and freeness of the gracious provisions of the gospel, the perfect suitableness of the system of salvation in all its requirements, and helps, and promises, to the condition of depraved, sinful, and guilty creatures, the blessed effects of a voluntary submission to the proposed terms—to be saved by grace through faith—and the fearful consequence of rejecting Christ and his salvation, were subjects on which he dwelt with a clearness of conception, strength of argument, and power of conviction, of which there are not many examples among his contemporaries in the Christian ministry.

Who has ever heard Bishop McKendree preach a sermon in which experimental and practical godliness were not distinctly presented and strongly enforced? I never did, although I have heard him many times. Conviction, conversion, sanctification, or perfect love, producing a sincere and joyful obedience to all the commands of God, were interwoven with all his public as well as his private ministrations; but above all, there was an unction from the *Holy One*, a *divine energy*, attending his ministry. His preaching was in the "demonstration of the Spirit and of power."

Few preachers since the days of the apostles have had more fruits of their labors. Who can reckon up the number that will appear in the morning of the resurrection, clothed with white robes, and decked with crowns of glory, who were brought to the knowledge of salvation through his instrumentality!

But while we remember Bishop McKendree as an excellent and useful preacher in the gospel, we must not forget him as a wise and judicious ruler in the Church of God. For twelve years he filled the responsible office of a Presiding Elder, and for nearly twenty-seven years he sustained the office of a General Superintendent of the Methodist Episcopal Church. During this long period of official services, many cases of great importance and of no ordinary difficulty occurred in the course of the administration of the government; but he traveled through these cases with such patience of investigation and rectitude of design, and arrived at a decision with such clearness, as seldom failed to give universal satisfaction. And it is a remarkable fact, that during the whole period of his official oversight, he never was accused, before any tribunal having jurisdiction in the case, of having departed from the principles of the constitution, or the rules of the Church; or of having used the authority which had been committed to him for the administration of the government for any other purpose, or to any other end, than what what was originally designed. It is true, this venerable man was charged by individuals, and in inflammatory publications, with the "love of power," and with the "abuse of the Episcopal prerogative;" *but never were charges more groundless*—never were charges more feebly sustained. No man whom I have ever known possessed a more just apprehension of the nature, extent, and uses of the authority with which he was invested than Bishop McKendree; and no man ever exercised that authority with more perfect subjection to constitutional guards, and with a more sincere and conscientious design to employ it, not for personal emolument, but for the specific purposes for which it was given. Men in every age of the world who have been restless under the legitimate administration of laws, and indisposed to be "subject to the powers that be," have been accustomed to exclaim against the love and the abuse of power; and in cases where they have succeeded in transferring authority from other hands to their own, history will give information of the manner in which they have used it.

Bishop McKendree's course in the administration was governed by an enlightened and extensive view of the whole system. He distinctly apprehended the relation which the several departments of the government sustained to each other, and the constitutional powers which belonged to each. And it was his constant aim to preserve those powers in such a balance, and subject to such checks and restrictions, as would secure the right of all, establish the union and peace of the Church, and preserve the uniform and judicious administration of wholesome discipline. It is certain that this groat man possessed a strong and ardent attachment to the system of Methodism. But this attachment was the result of conviction, consequent upon the thorough examination of the principles and designs which the system embraces, and the suitableness of the principles to the accomplishment of the ends. He was firmly persuaded that a "general itinerant Superintendency," as secured by the constitution of the Church, with sufficient powers to administer the government, and responsible to the General Conference for the use of those powers, was of vital importance to the preservation of the itinerant system, to a uniform administration of the Discipline, and to the internal union and harmony of the body. With such views, he uniformly deplored the existence of measures which had a tendency either to deprive the Superintendency of those prerogatives which were essential to its very existence, or so to restrict its power as to render it inefficient, and consequently to bring it into contempt.

Bishop McKendree was never satisfied with a superficial view of any important proposition. He was accustomed to trace principles, either in doctrine or government, in their practical operation, and either to sustain or disprove them, by pointing out, with a clearness peculiar to himself, the certain results. In this way he aimed to give a permanency to the principles of the government, and to the executive administration.

Upon the most careful examination, after an intimate acquaintance for many years, I know of no essential qualification of an ecclesiastical ruler which our dear departed Bishop did not possess in an eminent degree. He was well acquainted with men. He had read human nature in all its diversified character. He well understood the principles and ends of Church-government. He was calm and deliberate in all his official acts. His mind was too pure and elevated to admit of partiality in the exercise of the functions of his office. While his heart was susceptible of the tenderest friendships, and alive to the purest and most exquisite sympathies of which human nature is capable, he was firm and unyielding in his adherence to those principles which he had established for the government of his administration. In fixing the stations of the preachers, at the Annual Conferences, it was his uniform practice to obtain all the information in his power, from the various sources to which he had access, relative to the state of the whole field of labor, and the qualifications and circumstances of the preachers who were to cultivate it. This information being obtained, he was always disposed to seek the aid of the views and counsels of those whose experience and office qualified them to be useful helpers in this highly responsible work; and, conscious of the imperfection of all human knowledge, and of the insufficiency of human agency, and of his liability to err, the whole was submitted in humble prayer for divine direction, for the forgiveness of faults, and for success to attend the well-meant endeavors to advance the interests of the Redeemer's kingdom. In the performance of this important branch of his official oversight, Bishop McKendree deeply sympathized with the preachers of his charge and their families in their labors, privations, and sufferings. With him it was a sacred principle to yield to individual accommodation, in consideration of age, afflictions, or family circumstances, as far as it could be done consistently with the good of the whole. But if, after the most careful and impartial examination, such individual convenience appeared to him to be detrimental to the general interest, there was neither hesitating nor compromise with regard to his course. Individual accommodation must always submit to the public good. But he never bound heavy burdens and laid them on men's shoulders, which he himself was unwilling to bear. Who has known any man more ready and willing to endure all the labors, and sacrifices, and sufferings of a Methodist preacher? By such a course, Bishop McKendree established and retained the *affectionate and respectful* confidence of the preachers and people over whom he presided, and whose interests he had deeply at heart. And in his *prudent, mild, and firm* administration of the government, he has left a worthy and illustrious example for the imitation of those who may succeed him.

In his Christian character, our beloved Bishop was eminently a "pattern of good works." He had a deep and abiding sense of his dependence upon the grace of God, through Christ, both for wisdom and ability to perform his duties in such a manner as to be approved of God and profitable to men. Under the influence of this conviction, and fully apprised of his liability to err, he was "clothed with humility" and "prayed without ceasing." He was a man of *daily*, habitual, and *fervent* prayer. He "lived by faith," and "walked closely with God."

He was a zealous and uniform friend of those institutions, both literary and religious, which were established and patronized by the Church, and which had for their objects the improvement of society, the glory of God, and the salvation of souls. These institutions he supported by his personal visits, by his prudent and encouraging advice, by suitable representations of their characters and claims, and by liberal contributions of money, to the full extent of his means. He took a very deep interest particularly in the Missionary and Sabbath-school Societies. He considered those associations as most efficient auxiliaries to the preaching of the gospel, in "reforming the continent, and spreading scriptural holiness over these lands." He neglected no opportunity of visiting the Sunday-schools and meeting the societies, and encouraging all concerned in them to zealous perseverance. He had thoroughly examined the principles of the General Book Concern, and regarded it as one of the most important institutions for the promotion of Christian knowledge and piety. He viewed it in the light of a noble and extensive Christian charity, diffusing the blessings of moral and religious truth, and at the same time supplying the means to feed the hungry, clothe the naked, and relieve the wants of the widow and fatherless. As such, it had his cordial support. His liberality in the use of the limited means he possessed, was strikingly expressive of that principle of love to God and his neighbor which influenced all his actions. This liberality was divided, with a strict and conscientious regard to economy and utility, between benevolent institutions, houses of public worship, and needy individuals. Of the last, the widows and orphans of those preachers who had labored, and suffered, and died in the itinerant ministry, were special objects of his kind attention.

Bishop McKendree was grave, yet generally mild and cheerful in his conversation and manners. Who ever heard from the lips of this devoted servant of Christ, vain, trifling, or unprofitable conversation? Who ever saw him unemployed, or employed to no valuable purpose? In this respect, he has left an example worthy of the imitation of all Christian ministers. In a word, he exercised all the Christian virtues in an eminent degree, and for the most valuable purposes. With him patience was the *power of suffering*, faith was a divine conviction of things not seen—a living and abiding confidence in God, through Christ, effecting a personal interest in all the great and precious promises, and producing, as its fruit, a humble, and willing, and joyful obedience to the commands of God. The hope of the gospel was the anchor of his soul; the love of God was shed abroad in his heart by the Holy Ghost—even that love which "suffereth long and is kind, doth not behave itself unseemly, seeketh not her own, is not easily provoked, thinketh no evil, beareth all things, hopeth all things, endureth all things, and which never faileth." This was the ground of his zeal for God, and for the salvation of the souls of men. It was the constraining principle which inspired and governed his actions, and gave life and vigor to all his religious duties.

As a man, as well as a Christian and Christian minister, our venerable friend had a refined and exalted sense of propriety and consistency of character.

He had examined the relations and obligations of man

in a state of society with great carefulness and accuracy, and his views of the relative duties were clear and elevated; and in his intercourse with his fellow-men, he was strictly governed by these enlightened views.

He rendered honor to whom honor was due—was gentle to all men; yet he would reprove offenses as occasions and circumstances required, without undue respect of persons.

In conversation he was chaste, unassuming, and respectful—always interesting and profitable, and sometimes peculiarly animated.

He was unembarrassed in the presence of those who move in the scientific and elevated walks of life; and his condescension, kindness, and affability, inspired the humble poor with confidence and esteem. To the servant and his master he was, on all suitable occasions, equally accessible. He was exquisitely sensible of any departure from the principles of purity and propriety, either in conversation or actions. And in every class of society in which he moved, he aimed, as far as it could be done, "to please his neighbor for his good to edification."

To sum up all in a few words: in the character of Bishop McKendree, now with God in the heavenly place, beyond the breath of human praise or blame, were combined the essential qualifications of a great, and good, and amiable man; a sensible, pious, and devoted Christian; a prudent and conscientious ruler in the Church of God, and an able, zealous, and useful minister of the gospel of Christ.

Finally, brethren, let us remember our dear departed pastor and Bishop, who has had the rule over us, and who now rests from the labors and sufferings of his militant charge. We ask not for him any pompous titles engraved on perishable marble; we ask not for him the external badges of mourning; we ask not that our pulpits be hung with drapery of sorrow, or that the ministers of the sanctuary of our God should be clothed with the habiliments of woe; we ask for him a purer, a more hallowed, and a more durable monument.

O let the picture of his heavenly virtues be deeply engraved on our hearts! O let him long live in the memory, and affection, and esteem of the ministers and people of his pastoral care and official oversight! Though our beloved McKendree be dead, he speaks to us from the mansion of the tomb. He speaks to us in the silent but expressive language of a pure and illustrious example. Hark, my brethren, as if you heard from the sacred repository which now contains all that is mortal of our venerable friend, that charming voice so often raised to plead the cause of truth, and direct perishing multitudes to the "Lamb of God who taketh away the sin of the world." What language does he hold? What instructions will he impart? Does he not say, "Brethren, be ye followers of me, even as I also have been of Christ—be men of one vocation and one work; be humble, steadfast, and zealous in your holy calling; be faithful to God and to the souls of the people committed to your charge; be men of prayer, and diligence, and punctuality"?

But while we regard him as an example for our imitation, let us remember him in his abundant labors, with gratitude to the Father of all mercies for so great a blessing bestowed upon us. Let us remember him with humble and fervent prayer, that God would raise up and preserve in his Church men of like minds, who shall, like him, count all things but loss for the excellence of the knowledge of Christ Jesus their Lord, and glory only in the Redeemer's cross. Let us imitate him in that zeal and fidelity with which he exercised the peculiar functions of his holy office. And while we press forward in our Heavenly Master's work, encouraged by the light, and comfort, and triumph of his illustrious example, let us trust in God, through our Lord Jesus Christ, waiting in earnest expectation and lively hope of the resurrection of the body and life everlasting.

God grant, my dear brethren, that like our venerable McKendree, in the hour that closes the scenes of earth, and dissolves our relations to our militant charges, we may be able, in view of the past, and in prospect of the future, to proclaim, "ALL IS WELL!" Amen.

LETTER FROM BISHOP ASBURY TO THE REV. JOSEPH BENSON.

The following communication from Bishop Asbury to the Rev. Joseph Benson, of England, merits special attention. It bears date a short time before his death, was indited by him while confined to his bed, and was written and certified to in the copy before the author by the Rev. Thomas Mason. He and Bishop McKendree had parted in Tennessee to pursue different routes to the South Carolina Conference. They met no more. Bishop McKendree, as already related, made the trip in time, and presided at the Conference in Charleston; but the feeble senior broke down, after a desperate and exhausting struggle, before he could reach the city, and was taken dangerously ill when not far from it. At the earliest period of his partial convalescence—for he never fully recovered—and while propped up in his bed, with closed eyes and death-like pallor, he slowly indited this letter. The long and well-fought battle of his extraordinary life was nearly over; but he seemed determined, before he should yield to the rider of the pale horse, to do two things—to reach Baltimore in time to attend the General Conference

May 1st, and to vindicate himself from the suspicions which "Diotrephes" had instilled into the mind of the aged Wesley against him and his colleagues, but which were dissipated by his humility and untiring labors, and at the same time commend his beloved American Methodism to the confidence and affection of their brethren in his "fatherland." The first he failed to accomplish, having died in Virginia on his way to the General Conference, March 24, 1816, but the latter was effected, leaving not a shade upon his fame in the mind of any one on either side of the Atlantic. Indeed, this had long since been done.

It is said that when the hour of death approaches the exile, his native land and early associates loom up to his imagination, and he yearns for them: so of our self-expatriated Asbury. He had left his country and his brethren to plant Methodism in the wild Western Hemisphere, and nobly had he fulfilled his mission; and though often looking and longing for a little leisure to revisit his native land, yet had he looked and longed in vain. Stern duty demanded unceasing labor; and now, when hope had fled of reünion on earth, his heart and thoughts turn thither, and he sends this, his last affectionate greeting, through his friend Mr. Benson, and seeks his influence in behalf of the Church which his own death is soon to leave in orphanage. 'Tis the language of a dying father commending the younger children of the family to the love and kindness of their elder brethren. Mr. Benson was three years the junior of Mr. Asbury, and died five years later.

Since they had parted in England, both of them had become eminent—beloved and venerated by a whole community—the latter as Bishop, the former as a preacher, commentator, President of the Conference, and who then, as Editor of the Wesleyan Methodist Magazine, was at the head of the Church-literature of the British Connection. The reader will see, in the beginning of this letter, that Mr. Asbury's memory was at fault as to their comparative ages—sad evidence of old age, which generally first shows itself as to the recollection of dates and names.

Repeated allusions occur in this letter to a person under the name of "Diotrephes," who, it is evident, Bishop Asbury suspected to have prejudiced Mr. Wesley against him. The probability is that he meant Thos. Rankin. He was sent by Mr. Wesley to America in 1773, as his General Assistant, returned to England in 1777 on account of the Revolutionary War, and never came back. He spent the greater part of his time in London, seems always to have had the confidence of Mr. Wesley, and no doubt at one time expected to occupy the position in America which Mr. Asbury attained. It was, perhaps, natural he should feel disappointed at the result, and be tempted to criticise with undue severity the man who, without wishing to do so, had superseded him. He may have been honest in his opinions as to the expediency of the course taken by Mr. Asbury and his associates in the premises, and it is to be hoped he was unconscious of the blinding influence of a disappointed expectation. Charity would trust that it was so; but in any event, he subjected his motives to a severe and just imputation in bringing about a temporary alienation of Mr. Wesley from the pure and faithful Bishop. "Diotrephes" loved "the preëminence," and "received not" St. John. It is feared that Mr. Asbury found his "Diotrephes" in Mr. Rankin.

There is a sentiment in this letter to which attention is invited, and against which we enter our decided protest: it is, that no man who attains the age of seventy, however qualified in every other respect, should continue to "hold a highly responsible office in the Church of God." We are sorry to see the name of Mr. Asbury attached to this opinion, as we were to hear it a few years since from the lips of one of his worthy successors: in both cases the authorities for the opinion are of high respectability, but by a strange coincidence they were superannuated Bishops. Yet it matters not by whom uttered, it is unsustained by historical facts. If its application is made exclusively to Methodist Bishops, and the itinerant labors of Mr. Asbury's day, we have nothing to say; but if the disqualification assumed be not physical, but psychical, we dissent most emphatically; and, moreover, if it is intended to embrace only high officials in the Church as an exceptional and proscribed class, neither the propriety nor the justness of the rule is apparent. We admit that a man of seventy, whether a Bishop or not, cannot ride on horseback, nor in a "thirty-dollar chaise" as Messrs. Asbury and McKendree did once, and thus traverse from five to eight thousand miles a year, as well as can a man of twenty; but surely the Church should not, and does not, and never did, impose such tasks upon her chief pastors. A good deal of this work was self-imposed—imposed from anxiety for the welfare of the cause and the most honorable motives, yet in many instances not really necessary—and no wonder that such habits of restlessness and perpetual motion wore down lymphatic constitutions at seventy years of age. Indeed, Bishop Asbury here confesses that at sixty-three he had become unfit to take the chair; and the writer distinctly recollects that Bishop McKendree told him that Bishop Asbury's last advice to him was to travel on wheels, adding, "If I had done so, I might have added ten years to my life." It is always unsafe to deduce a universal proposition from a special case. "In the Church of God" there have always been men "in high responsibility" after reaching their seventieth year.

We freely admit that, with the decay of the physical, the mental powers must sympathize to some extent, and in certain respects; but we assert that, as a general rule, the higher faculties do not suffer proportionally to the bodily senses. The fact is, the decadence of the mind at that period of life is ordinarily the result of its inaction, or of confining its action to a few subjects. Men cease to explore new realms of thought, they add but little to their mental treasure, and are constantly losing their stock on hand without replenishing: thus the mind becomes torpid and effortless. Their friends call them old—treat them as such—they accept the epithet and its privileges, and settle down into an imbecility which they think inevitable; while, in fact, the "green old age" of seventy, to a man of fair health, good constitution, and cultivated mind, is the very season for assorting and harvesting the fruits of his active summer's toils. Then the prejudices and passions of the hot blood of youth may be held in abeyance, conscience, reason, and judgment assert their superiority, and mind, "immortal as its Sire," assumes its imperial sway. Suppose the great men who have attained a world-wide eminince in the arts and sciences, the jurists, statesmen, and divines, had all been stricken from the roll as imbeciles—John, the divine apostle, Wesley, Humboldt, Newton, Marshall, Wm. Pitt, Dr. Franklin, Sir Matthew Hale, Lord Brougham, Madison, Jefferson, Adams, and the like—all of them living over seventy, and some beyond ninety years! Why, in Europe men are scarcely thought to be competent to occupy the highest positions as *savants* in literature or the bench of the jurist before that period. Because Mr. Asbury and Bishop McKendree wore and tore out their physical frames by that time, are we to assume that this is the terminus of mental life? A man who, under ordinary circumstances, keeps his mind awake and active, and while doing reasonable service takes due care of his earthly tabernacle, may, by God's blessing, be in the prime and vigor of his intellectual energies; and let not the suspicion arise that this is the sinister plea of one near the verge of the black line beyond which lie the gloomy shades of intellectual death. On the contrary, it is an impression drawn from many years' observation, and is a deliberate and settled conviction. It is a conclusion which carries comfort and hope to the hoary head crowned with glory.

My venerable and elder brother in the kingdom and patience of Jesus Christ, and the glorious ministry of the gospel of the grace of God, all hail!

We have lived to see better days than our predecessors and ancient contemporaries. I recollect not to have seen your face, to have known you, or to have the least passing interview with you; but when I was a youth between fifteen and sixteen years of age, you were a man, and President of Kingswood School, which must be, in my calculation, between fifty and fifty-five years past. Though I was active some years, and frequently called upon to act as a supply for the traveling connection, and traveled the first year nine or ten months (though less or more, I cannot say correctly) in the Staffordshire Circuit—the circuit in which I lived—in the place of William Orpe, the four Conference-years that I traveled were in Bedford and Salisbury alternately. From thence I came to America, and am now in the forty-fifth year of my mission, which will close the 20th of next October.

I have been broken, breach upon breach, by affliction, so that I am at present completely superannuated, having passed, August 21st, the first period of the life of man. And it has been for some years past a permanent sentiment with me, that in such a case, no man high in office, however great in qualifications, should stand in high responsibility in the Church of God, but rather retire and give place to younger and stronger men in body and mind, such as our junior Superintendent, to whom I have ceded the presiden tial chair of every Annual Conference for these seven years past. It was also my pleasure, when present, always to give Dr. Coke the president's chair. Glory to God, our houses are set in order! Our order of things is such that we have about fifty-five Presiding Elders, that by turns of four years at farthest, yet movable at any time when the Episcopacy judge of the importance of the case. These Presiding Elders serve a probation of seven or fourteen years in large and very consequential Districts, and have their Quarterly-meeting Conferences of the official departments of the local ministry, possibly in some large circuit of long standing, that compose from sixty to eighty, or near one hundred members, and examine characters, try cases, admit and give authority to exhorters and local preachers, examine local preachers and local deacons for election and ordination to Deacons' and Elders' office in the Annual Conference. These Presiding Elders, in the absence of the Bishop, and that rule well, are counted worthy of double honor. In the absence of a Bishop appointed by him, if not appointed, to be elected by the Conference, to preside in and do the business of the Annual Conference. And we have the pleasure to believe that such is their age and improvement, that we have not only half a dozen, but a dozen, if called to preside in an Annual Conference, would do it with ease, dignity, and correctness, assisted by their brethren, the Presiding Elders.

If a Bishop, at any distance where a mail can go, has consequential business to the whole Conference, he has only to communicate to *one* man; he to write to the other Presiding Elders; they to communicate to the men who have charge of stations and circuits—the work is done.

Bishops in Greece or Rome—what have they been in frightful forms? What have they been, men or fiends? Bishops in our age, among the Presbyterians and Independent Churches, the Baptists and the commonality of the people, are ready to suppose that a Bishop is a tyrant—the same as a Pope—dreadful, dangerous creatures. Possibly some very wise men, with all their Hebrew, Greek, and Latin, have not found out the pure derivation of that word. It is very near to a perfect German word, in both consonants and vowels; admitting the German pronunciation and the English pronunciation to differ—Bi-schoft, the chief minister. With us, a Bishop is a plain man, altogether like his brethren, wearing no marks of distinction, advanced in age, and by virtue of his office can sit as president in all the solemn assemblies of the ministers of the gospel; and many times, if he is able, called upon to labor and suffer more than any of his brethren; no negative or positive in forming Church-rules; raised to a small degree of constituted and elective authority above all his brethren; and in the executive department, power to say, "Brother, that must not be—that cannot be;" having full power to put a negative or a positive in his high charge of administration; and even in the Annual Conference, to correct the body or any individual that may have transgressed or would transgress, and go over the printed rules by which they are to be governed, and bring up every man and every thing to the printed rules of order established in the Form of Discipline of the Methodist Episcopal Church in America.

It is an established maxim with us, that if a man is not well taught and practiced in obedience to know how to serve, he will never know how to have command or be fit to take any office in the Church of God, and that stubborn, disobedient men must be mended, though it will take much time and more labor.

Several brethren among us have sincerely wished that there could be some mode of communication and union, such as can take place, considering distance, and circumstances, and administration, and order, between us and the parent Society. We have hoped it would be for the best—then again we have feared we should not find safe hands to put our business into the British Conference to conduct, and that misunderstandings and misrepresentations might bring us into trouble, and bring on a greater separation; and I can truly say for one, that the greatest affliction and sorrow of my life was that our dear father, from the time of the Revolution to his death, grew more and more jealous of myself and the whole American Connection; that it appeared we had lost his confidence almost entirely. But he rigidly contended for a special and independent right of governing the chief minister or ministers of our order, which, in our judgment, went not only to put him out of office, but to remove him from the Continent to elsewhere, that our father saw fit; and that, notwithstanding our constitution and the right of electing every Church-officer, and more especially our Superintendent, yet we were told, "Not till after the death of Mr. Wesley" our constitution could have its full operation. For many years before this time we lived in peace, and trusted in the confidence and friendship of each other. But after the Revolution, we were called upon to give a printed obligation, which here follows, and which could not be dispensed with—it must be: "During the life of the Rev. Mr. Wesley, we acknowledge ourselves his sons in the gospel; ready, in matters belonging to Church-government, to obey his commands; and we do engage, after his death, to do every thing that we judge consistent with the cause of religion in America and the political interest of the States, to preserve and promote our union with the Methodists in Europe." Our people and preachers were coming out of their childhood — they thought for themselves. If this obligation was necessary, why not introduce it in former years, in better times? Matters have strangely changed; much blood has been shed; the minds of the citizens of the United States and the United Kingdom must be exceedingly changed and soured against each other, and the state of things will never be as it has been between the two countries. Some said that the citizens of both countries are so much alike that we shall have war again in ten, twenty, or thirty years. Foreigners by thousands coming to our country and crossing their own; pushing themselves into office, and blowing the coals of strife; magnifying small offenses; raising mountains out of mole-hills; a word and a blow; stricken by wicked and impious officers that do n't know their duty; putting to death a most ancient and noble British character; and a grand, and noble, and generous, and affable American character dying swiftly; and yet both sides crying out, "If you cannot lead us, you shall not drive us;" and both sides going to driving as hard as they can with fire and sword.

Mr. Wesley is to this day, and always has been, respected and loved by hundreds and thousands in America as a great apostolic man; and hundreds of children continually named after him—yea, thousands. In America some of our enemies know that, of all the good and holy men, that our dear John the divine of London, and John the divine of Madeley, at the time of the Revolution, had written more on worldly affairs than any gospel men in Europe or America. I spare the dead, and yet I think that a degree of justice is due to the memory of such an apostolic man as John Wesley. I perfectly clear him in my own mind, and lay the whole blame of the whole business upon Diotrephes, of the Tower of London. Little did I think that we had such an enemy that had the continual ear and confidence of Mr. Wesley. This I believe from good testimony—eye and ear-witnesses, who, some years after, when they saw that my mind was so deeply afflicted that I did not get clear of it for some years after Mr. Wesley's death. Dr. Coke and John Harper told me what they had seen, and heard, and known, and felt. Dr. Coke said that as often as Mr. Wesley went to see Diotrephes, he came back with his mind strangely agitated and dissatisfied with the American Connection; that he did not know what to do to put him to rights; and the counsel of Diotrephes, in a full Conference, was in substance this: "If he [Diotrephes] had the power and authority of Mr. Wesley, he would call Frank Asbury home directly." John Harper was the man who was present in the Conference and heard this advice given, and told me several years after in America with his own mouth. Yet I spare the dead, and must write the truth, that he (Diotrephes) wrote to the Messrs. Wesleys for counsel and advice in our critical situation—advice which we thought truly apostolic and worthy of the minister of the gospel of the Son of God—in substance, was to give as little offense as possible either to Jew or Gentile, or to the Church of God; to have nothing to do with the affairs of this world if he could help it, and mind the business of our spiritual calling. Diotrephes made this instruction pretty public among the preachers and the people, and then they charged him with violating every part of it. He was positive beyond all description, that the Americans should be brought back to the old government, and that immediately. It appeared to me that his object was to sweep the Continent of every preacher that Mr. Wesley had sent to it, and of every respectable traveling preacher from Europe who had graduated among us, whether English or Irish. He told us that if we returned to our native country, we should be esteemed as such obedient, loyal subjects, that we should obtain ordination in the grand Episcopal Church of England, and come back to America with high respectability after the war was ended. Francis did not believe it; and he possessed a senior right after the removal of Boardman and Pilmoor, and God had given him souls for his hire, and souls for his charge among the people; and a number of eminent preachers, both traveling and local, wanted nothing but a man to go in and out before them to give them, if we had not books, order and discipline by the word of mouth. Francis thought as he had possession, it was best to hold it, especially when abundance of respectable members said, "Will you leave us? Will you leave us?" And it was the general language of the American people and preachers, that those preachers from Europe, who were dissatisfied with the measures of the country, had better go home.

At the death of Mr. Wesley, one of his European disciples asked another, "Who will preach his funeral-sermon? Who will write his Life?" They corrected themselves by saying, "Mr. Wesley has written his own Life better than any other man can write it." And O that it had been so! or that if any thing had been done, it had been after the model of the Life of the Vicar of Madeley, compiled by Joseph Benson, which has been made an unspeakable blessing to my mind in reading it. It has been impressed with great weight upon my mind for several years, that it was my indispensable duty to write to some person in London or elsewhere, a true and correct account, because I think that Mr. Wesley has been reproached beyond any thing that was thrown upon him before that period, by the London writer of his Life. You will examine, as an early contemporary of the Oxford Methodists, and the last branch of that order: you will see in substance that, with respect to the American ordination, Mr. Wesley is represented as invading and usurping all Church-order. And yet the author grants if Mr. Wesley had been elected and chosen by the American preachers and people, it would have been in gospel order and proper. Did that author know, or was he ignorant? Why did he write in the dark? The people of Mr. Wesley's charge in America—many thousands—were under total privation of the ordinances of God, and most of the Episcopalians had deserted their stations and Churches from almost every part of the Continent. The Presbyterians held no open communion. The Methodists could not become Presbyterians in sentiment—they would not be Baptists, neither Independents. When the preachers first came to the Continent, with what affection they were received! Multitudes came forward as constant hearers and members of the Society, and immediately the tables of the Lord in their former Churches were closed against them. When our brethren would say, "O that you had been ordained to administer the ordinances of God to us!" it was of no account to say the Episcopal Bishops would not ordain us. "Mr. Wesley should have ordained you." And thus for fourteen or fifteen years hundreds and thousands of preachers and people crying continually for the universal election of Mr. Wesley to ordain ministers for America, because he was, as we believe, an apostolic man, admitting upon trial and into Connection the preachers of his charge, governing and stationing every one of them, that he came short only in ordination. Now, sir, I submit it to you, as to Dr. Whitehead's Life of Mr. Wesley, if there is power and authority in any part of your body, in justice to Mr. Wesley, (asking no mercy,) when called upon by hundreds and thousands for so long a time to exercise the third branch of apostolic power in ordination, and that hundreds and thousands of preachers and people have blessed and praised God for the wisdom given to Mr. Wesley and the Baltimore General Conference in 1784, to form upon such pure principles a truly apostolic Church—the success which has attended the labors of its ministers. We must say that Dr. Whitehead's history must be corrected according to this testimony, or suppressed, as containing a defamation of that man of God, Mr. John Wesley, and the whole body of American Methodists. We feel determined to stand in apostolic order and gospel ground. "Separate me, Barnabas and Saul, for the work whereunto I have called them." And with fasting and prayer they laid their hands on them. Acts xiii. 2, 3. A distinct name, office, and order—elders in the Church of God. Acts xiv. 23.

Never since was any man, for so many years, called upon to ordain ministers for America: never since could a people be so overjoyed, and conform so universally as with one heart and mind. This was what we wanted and requested from year to year; and we have obtained it at last. Bless God, and bless Mr. Wesley!

We do not suffer one officer in the Church of God to assume or invade the rights of another: a licensed exhorter to be always attempting to preach; a traveling or local preacher must not baptize without ordination; a deacon, traveling or local, administer the Lord's-supper but under the order of an elder. On no account will we suffer the elders to ordain alone, but to come forward when called upon by the Bishop (in names and numbers) to assist in the ordination of elders. We do not suffer our Presiding Elders to invade any singular right of Episcopacy.

Here is the simple method which we have followed from the beginning, in the management of our temporal affairs. Our stewards are elected in every Conference. They call first on all the preachers belonging to the Conference, to know what they have received for quarterage in the stations and Districts wherein they have labored the year past. By doing this, they come immediately to know what preachers have already received their full demand, and what preachers are deficient, according to our rules of discipline. Then they call for all the collections that have been brought in, with $200 per Conference from the book interest, and $140 from the Chartered Fund—small matters!—and the dividend must be made among twelve Conferences in the year, instead of nine.

We send you our mite-subscription, to let you see what additional wonders we can perform by the blessing of God, —more especially when we hear such acccounts from your side of the water, of all the Churches that have been maintaining the local ministry sending out traveling ministers to the ends of the earth. We wish them success in the name of the Lord. They are coming right at last! But hail Wesley—hail Oxford Methodists—who, seventy years ago, formed an apostolic society, and sent forth their traveling preachers in apostolic order! Blessed be God, that a number of simple men, from the Oxford Methodists, were directed to establish an apostolic Church, and put the government in the hands of traveling preachers! And yet there must be men that cannot continue to travel, and others that sincerely wish, but have it not in their power to travel, who may be useful, and enjoy all their rights and privileges in their local state, and the traveling ministry held sacred and make the very best of all their superior privileges.

And concerning ordination, that it ought to be held sacred, and considered as the helm of good order, we believe. In every age of the Church it has been, and now is, held sacred.

We have heard of a few simple people here and there, hardly worthy of being members of the Church, pleading their right to sit down with each other, if it be every day, and receive and administer the Lord's-supper one to another; therefore, we conclude that Churches and societies ought to examine well what bearing their sayings and doings will lead to—whether they will introduce division and confusion or unity and good order in the house of God, in the body of Christ.

Will you, my dear sir, do what you can, at this late hour of life, as our agent to the British Conference? And, if you please, call a confidential and young man to your assistance. Will you examine well any letters and communications from America, and judge how far it may be proper to print any of them in the United Kingdoms, and where and in what manner any difficulties may be explained, and methods of gospel order be brought into operation? We have planted, we have watered, we have taken a most sacred charge of Upper and Lower Canada, for about twenty-two years. They form two respectable Districts in the Genesee Conference. They lie side by side on the northern banks of the St. Lawrence, and the United States' Districts and circuits on the southern. The souls of our people in Canada are exceedingly precious to us. They are a willing people, prompt to pay their preachers—they say, "Tell us what to do, and we 'll do it." Exclusive of the most ancient, (who came from various parts of Europe,) the additional and increasing inhabitants now, of both provinces, are multitudes of refugees who went from the United States at the time of the Revolution. Many others have preferred the Provinces to the United States; and there are at this time large family connections on both sides of the line, and many preachers that have changed and interchanged. The manner in which Montreal was taken possession of and is now held, will not, cannot, be dispensed with by the General Conference, by the Annual Conference, nor by the Presiding Elder of Lower Canada. Thomas Birch, one of His Majesty's subjects, late from Ireland, was sent to Montreal in the very moment of time, just at the commencement of the war, and was permitted to stay a year longer than our constitution grants, (the state of the case justifying it,) and returned to the United States with an honorable recommendation from the Society. Strange, when Samuel Montgomery had been sent, with the greatest expedition, six hundred miles to supply the place of Thos. Birch, that Samuel (one of His Majesty's subjects, late from Ireland) should be prevented from taking his charge by the British missionary! And who is to examine Mr. Williams's conduct? Mr. Bennett, of the province of Nova Scotia? the British Conference? or the Directors of the Missionary Society? Henry Ryan, Presiding Elder of Lower Canada, made a visit to Montreal, by order of the Bishops and Genesee Conference. He has obtained testimonies which will be handed forward to the Agent of our affairs, presented in their order. We, as ministers of Christ, think it a sin of sins to divide the body of Christ. There was special caution given to Thomas Birch, Samuel Montgomery, and Henry Ryan; and we have good reason to believe that, possibly, two-thirds of the Society in Montreal would put themselves under the government of the American Connection. But we shall bear long, suffer long, and make every explanation, till the charge is given up to us. Whether the thing has been done through ignorance, or through the influence of wicked and designing men, we shall give our fathers and brethren time to inform themselves, and time to correct their conduct; for we are sure that our Episcopacy could never act so out of order as to send a preacher to take possession of a charge so important, under the oversight of the parent Connection. And yet, in this business, we would touch that venerable body, or any authoritative part of it, with the tenderness of a feather dipped in oil.

Respected brother, may our Presiding Elders address

their letters to you, when cases of a singular nature shall occur? At present, Francis, your friend, with *great difficulty*, has dictated this letter.

One thing more. Upon this continent we are crowded with French people—like polite heathens and barbarians to us. We want French Methodist preachers. Despairing of obtaining any from the traveling connection, since we have read your reports, our only hope is that some of our brethren from Jersey and Guernsey will come over and help us. We have employed an accomplished young Frenchman, of an extensive acquaintance with the French Methodists in those islands, to write for us, and see if such a man as we want can be obtained. And can you aid in this matter? It is our wish that such a preacher, that is willing to come to America, be well recommended by our brethren that know him, to our agent, Mr. Benson, on whose recommendation we shall depend.

My love and a thousand thanks to Mr. Blanchard, for the Minutes; to Mr. Marsden, for the Reports—hoping they will continue their goodness from year to year. Let them direct to any part of the United States, to myself or the junior Bishop or Bishops, whose names will be known upon the Minutes of our Conferences. And should our Father and Brother Benson have any special call and communication to make, be sure to make it to one of the Presiding Elders, and the business will be taken up in good order. Instruction will be given by the Bishops to the Presiding Elders, that they may be called to write to the agents of our American affairs, in London or elsewhere, and possibly to be written to from the men of our confidence in Europe.

And now may the God of all grace, with his eternal Son and ever-blessed Spirit, be with us through time and for ever and ever! Amen. FRANCIS ASBURY.

I, Thos. Mason, who wrote this letter, salute my fathers and brethren in the Lord.

South Carolina, January 15, 1816.

P. S. Mr. Wesley could not come himself to America, but he sent one that was well qualified. Dr. Coke and myself were so liberal as to submit ourselves to an election, before Francis was ordained to his office as Bishop and Superintendent, at the first General Conference, in Baltimore, December, 1784. Dr. Coke, notwithstanding his visits were transient, was very useful, both as a divine and as a classical man. He was esteemed by hundreds and thousands in America. His writings will be read with attention; his memory will be precious. The Americans knew his worth, and knew not only his labors and travels, but some of his sufferings, as he was often compelled by necessity to take up with very mean lodgings, through some of the extreme parts of our country and at very early settlements, as Francis (who generally attended him) and many others can witness. Add to this, that every visit he had to cross and recross the Atlantic. It is true, Dr. Coke had his troubles in America, and it is true that Francis Asbury had his troubles. And we heard that Mr. Wesley had his troubles—and no wonder, when he was told (as possibly made to believe) that no sooner had he granted the Americans what they wished, than they declared themselves independent of him! Had we not lived in all good confidence and fellowship for fifteen years? No complaint on our side—no complaint, that we heard of, from Mr. Wesley. Why then should our generous minds be called to enter an obligation which we never had violated, and which I believe there was no intention to violate? And I must believe that the Americans were greater friends than Mr. Wesley had, through Europe or the world. They had read all his books that had come to hand; they heard of all his excellences, his labors, sufferings, and success; and who with them but Mr. Wesley? Almost every large and steady family among the old disciples must have a Wesley among the children. Francis had been charged (and perhaps very properly) with being a man of gloomy mind, and sometimes a prophet of evil tidings, concerning ministerial men; but many of his brethren, after proper trial, have confessed, if they were evil, they were true in the end.

Mr. Wesley wrote concerning Diotrephes, honest George, and Francis, "You three be as one; act by united counsels." But who was to do that with Diotrephes? Francis had a prior right of government, by special order and letter from Mr. Wesley, a few months after he had been in the country; and if he could not exercise it in the cities, where the first missionaries that came over were located by necessity, (having no proper men to change with them,) yet Francis in the country endeavored to do the best he could. Matters did not fit well between Diotrephes and him, and poor Francis was charged with having a gloomy mind, and being very suspicious, etc.

It would be presumed, because Francis was a little heady, that Diotrephes wrote to Mr. Wesley to call Francis home immediately. Be it as it might, Mr. Wesley wrote such a letter to Francis; and Francis wrote in answer, that he would prepare to return as soon as possible, whatever the sacrifice might be. Then Diotrephes said, "You cannot go; your labors are wanted here." Francis said, "Mr. Wesley has written for me; I must obey his order." Diotrephes said, "I will write to Mr. Wesley, and satisfy him." Shortly after came a letter from Mr. Wesley to Francis, in substance thus: "You have done very well to continue in America and help your brethren, when there was such a great call."

And now, my father and brother, I know not a man in

the British Connection to write to. They are the children of forty-five or fifty years; you are the man, and you were the father when they were children. I leave these things with you, to make any use or no use of them. I have confidence in you, that you will not make a bad use of them.

F. A.

DR. WINANS'S LETTER TO BISHOP McKENDREE, GIVING PARTICULARS OF SAMUEL PARKER'S DEATH.

The author and the subject of the accompanying letter were both ministers greatly beloved and respected. William Winans is an honored and household name in the South-west, and not unknown to fame as a true, wise, and gifted preacher throughout the Methodist domain.

He was born in Pennsylvania, November 3, 1788: when about sixteen, his family removed to Ohio. He was admitted in the Western Conference in 1808; in 1809, at the call of the Bishop, volunteered with Sela Paine, and was transferred to the Mississippi Conference; married happily in 1815, and located on account of impaired health. He was readmitted in 1820, and continued to fill important appointments until 1851, when he took a superannuated relation, in which he continued until his death, August 31, 1857, in his 69th year. He was a member of every General Conference held from 1824 to his death, and was inferior as a clear, logical, and powerful debater to no one in any of these assemblies. He was tall, thin, and negligent of dress, always leaving his collar unbuttoned, and although never boorish or repulsive in his manners, yet evidently thinking but little of his appearance. His intellectual faculties were of the first order. No one would sooner detect a sophism, or more quickly and effectively explode it. When excited in debate, his vehemence of manner was terrible—very great; his mind seemed to be aroused to a white heat, the veins in his bare neck and his forehead swelled as if ready to burst, his language electrified his hearers as his thoughts electrified himself, and so clear, so logical, and resistless were his arguments, that his conclusions were felt to be demonstrations. His antagonist was impaled and powerless. He rarely spoke except on important subjects, and whenever he threw himself fully into a discussion, it reminded me of the heaviest ordnance hurling enormous missiles.

He was a great reader; and while he delighted in profound biblical and scientific subjects, he indulged to considerable extent in *Belles-lettres* studies, and not unfrequently in the lighter works of fancy and fiction. Reading was a necessity with him, and no man in the South indulged in it or enjoyed it more. His study was his sanctum, into which he daily entered, not to be disturbed or to leave except for his meals and family worship. It was a forbidden place to loungers and strangers—his own family being permitted to enter but at his permission. There he read, studied, and wrote for many hours together. Books, manuscripts, maps, and newspapers covered his library shelves, his table, and frequently the floor. He lived and worked there.

He was a voluminous writer. As an instance, I have seen pile upon pile of his notes and criticisms upon the whole of Dr. Clarke's Commentary on the Bible. Many of them were deservedly excoriating. Shall we not have the privilege of reading something from his pen? His published sermons constitute a body of divinity, and although too elaborate for the taste of the day, are profound and exhaustive discussions of his topics. His residence was in a retired section of the country, some twenty miles from Natchez, where he had few congenial associates, and hence his seclusion and devotion to literature. And yet no one enjoyed the society of his friends more than he. His manners in social life were so simple, so affectionate, and hearty, that even the young were ever ready to hail "Uncle Winans" welcome. His love of his Church was strong and unwavering, and his attachment to Bishops McKendree, Roberts, and Soule, and his associates in the Mississippi and Louisiana Conferences, was tender and fervent. In all questions of Church-polity, he was the acknowledged leader of the South-west, and yet he never sought that position, nor seemed to be aware of his influence. Ordinarily, he was retired and silent. His private life was simple and pure, and his piety uniform and profound.

Such was the estimate in which his talents, general intelligence, and elevated patriotism was held by the first men in his section of the country, that, on one or two occasions of great public interest, he was nominated for a high political position; but as he had not sought the nomination, and would not canvass the country, of course it came to naught. Demagogism usually carries the day against patriotism. I cannot forbear to add on this point, that it is to be regretted that he suffered himself to be used for any such purpose. The example is not a good one, and it was the only weakness in his history known to the writer.

In closing this imperfect sketch of Dr. Winans, it may be safely said he was a *great man.* We are aware how frequently and improperly this epithet is used. Words are cheap, and to praise and be praised are pleasant. A great preacher, and a learned divine, a paragon in mind, a Cicero in oratory, and a St. Paul in spiritual efficiency, are sometimes manufactured by biographers out of mere boys and sciolists—a mere tyro in learning, a surface-skimmer in biblical knowledge, pedants and plagiarists, become suddenly, and as if by magic, vastly eloquent, and great preachers. It is sometimes humiliating to compare the original with the portrait. Such indiscriminate and unmerited encomiums are not only disgusting to good taste, but they are morally wrong, and work evil to the subject, and by setting up a low standard for the imitation of young preachers, do immense mischief to young ministers. It is sickening to read such works. The truth is, there are very few great men. Boys do not become men in a day, nor rude and ignorant men make ripe scholars and splendid orators at once. There is not only "no royal road to mathematics," but none to eminence as a preacher, without patient and continuous study, and careful and assiduous practice. If we closely scan our imaginary eagle as he soars aloft in mid-heaven, we shall find, not the royal bird, but one of a very different feather. Many of our fathers were great in faith, zeal, devotion, and usefulness, but were neither Solomons nor Ciceros. We may praise them for their piety, usefulness, and power, but our praises lose their force when given for qualities not claimed nor possessed by them. But William Winans *was* truly a great man, and a good and useful minister. No one who knew him intimately will doubt or deny it; and his memory is still precious to thousands all over these lands. His death was the triumph of a simple, strong, and soul-felt confidence in his Master's word and merits, and he therefore died in holy peace.

At the date of this letter, Mr. Winans was teaching school, having located on account of infirm health. In 1820, he reëntered the itinerancy, and continued as he was able to labor in it for many years. For several years previous to his death, he was a superannuated preacher.

He had known Samuel Parker in Ohio, and if not brought into the ministry by him, had been fostered and guided by his care and counsel. He rejoiced at his transfer to the South, and hoped he would be a great blessing to that destitute region; but alas, how often are our brightest hopes disappointed! Sadly he pens the following obituary of his beloved friend to the Bishop, who felt equally the loss of this noble son in the gospel.

Samuel Parker was a native of New Jersey, born in 1772;* removed to Uniontown, Pennsylvania, where he was converted in his fifteenth year; thence he went to Newcastle, Kentucky, and was admitted on trial in the Western Conference in 1804. In 1809, he became a Presiding Elder upon a District which included the entire States of Indiana, Illinois, and Missouri. In 1813, he was appointed to the charge of the Miami District—the year following, to the Kentucky District. In 1819, he was selected and transferred by the Bishops to the Mississippi Conference, as the most suitable man to take charge of that Southern work. The District to which he was appointed embraced all Mississippi and Louisiana; but he was never able to do any effective work on it, and died on Monday, December 20, 1819.

Mr. Parker was a remarkably popular and useful minister. His address was winning. He was a master of music, and his power of song was wonderful, insomuch that he was widely and familiarly known as "The Sweet Singer." He was regarded as destined to great usefulness in the South, and as "the right man in the right place;" but alas, his Master had other views and other use for him, and took him to himself, leaving his family and the Church astonished and almost crushed by their sudden and great loss! This letter narrates the inci-

* The Minutes say about 1774.

dents of his last hours from the pen of his devoted friend and admirer, William Winans, to whom he had been a father in the gospel. But they have met "on the other side of Jordan" long ago.

Bishop McKendree:

Reverend and very dear Sir:—Your two letters bearing date, the one August 20th, the other October 31st, have both been received, and should have been sooner acknowledged had I known where to direct a letter for you. I can now only return you my sincere thanks for your kindness in writing, without pretending to answer your letters, as there are two subjects of a very interesting character on which I must address you. One of them is the much-lamented death of our beloved Brother Parker. His health has never been amended since you left the country. About the first of October, I think, he was confined to his house, from which he was never able to be long absent. At the time of the Conference, and for some weeks previously, he was scarcely able to sit up; yet he thought himself in no danger, especially as there were some favorable symptoms about the commencement of Conference. In this flattering opinion he had but one associate—*i. e.*, the Bishop. He fondly hoped Brother Parker would be able in a few weeks to resume, or rather commence, active service on the District, and therefore continued him in that office. I was then fully persuaded he could not recover, as out of many whom I had known afflicted in the same way, I had never known one restored to health. After my return home, therefore, I wrote, requesting Brother Parker to furnish me the outlines of his history; informing him that, if it should meet his approbation, and I should survive him, I intended to write for the Magazine a short account of his life. His wife asked him if he intended complying with my request. He replied, he would rather, should his life be written, that I should do it than any other, but added, "I have nothing to say, only that I am a sinner saved by grace." Such was the humility and retiring modesty of this eminent saint. He afterward, for my satisfaction alone, I presume, indicated a disposition to comply with my request; but it was now too late. The chilling hand of death had disabled him by its rapid progress either to write or dictate. On Saturday, the 18th instant, he was helpless; on Sunday, all his powers seemed rapidly sinking, and his wife desired I might be sent for to see him die, or, if too late for that, to preach his funeral-sermon. He wished to see me, but manifested some uneasiness at the idea of putting me to the trouble of going so far. Such was always his tenderness toward others. They sent for me on Monday, and on Tuesday night I reached Brother Bryan's in the neighborhood, where I learned he had died on Monday, and that the grave was then shut upon him. On Sunday I preached his funeral-sermon to a large, attentive, and weeping audience, on Rev. xiv. 13; and I trust that he, whose life was so extensively employed for the good of souls, will not have died in vain. To say any thing to you of his general character would be wholly superfluous. It may not be amiss, however, to state that he was patient, resigned, and cheerful throughout his long affliction. In the immediate prospect of death, he enjoyed a sweet peace—a calm tranquillity of soul—which enabled him to cast a smile of triumph on the tomb which now opened to swallow him up. Asked by Brother McLendon, "Is your way clear?" he replied with a smile in the affirmative. Sister Parker bears her loss with Christian fortitude. Their little son is quite sick. Whether his loss to the Connection in this country can be supplied, is not for me to say. We are now without a Presiding Elder, and must be so for some time; and I am sure there is no man among us can fill the place as he could have filled it. In the wisdom of Heaven and the providence of our Superintendent we repose for a remedy to this disaster. In regard to Brother Parker, I will only add that I intend attempting something for the Magazine concerning him.

The other subject on which I think it necessary to say something, is the business of the New Orleans Mission House. The first project failed, I believe, in consequence of the romantic character of Brother Moore and Mr. Ross, and perhaps the duplicity of ——; but especially because there was no system, no concert, no definite understanding among the parties. Brother Moore appeared before the Conference, and accused all the trustees of a dereliction of a solemn contract. He was answered successfully, I believe; and without attaching blame to any one, the Conference resolved to set aside all that had been done, to vest the powers of the trustees in the missionary and two others, and to advise these agents, if possible, to take Mr. Ross's property. Brother Thomson, of New Orleans, and myself, were chosen for that purpose. We have obtained till February to see whether we can obtain the necessary funds to meet the first demand. The prospect appears very gloomy, and unless largely assisted from a distance, or by the city itself, I do not hope to be able to secure the property. We are instructed by the Conference, if we fail in regard to Mr. Ross's property, to make some other attempt. Please afford us all the assistance you can.

We have had the most sickly season ever known in this country. My own family suffered greatly. Ten of us were very sick, and two died—an infant son and the black boy, which you may remember. I was enabled to be entirely resigned. Brother Seaton has been very sick, and is not yet wholly recovered. Brothers Lane and Menefee married before Conference, and Brother McLendon since. Religion is still in a languid condition among us. We want more preachers, and more life, and love, and zeal among those who are already here. Could I bring my temporal concerns to such a state as to justify the measure, I would offer myself to the traveling connection. I did offer myself to the Bishop to take Brother Parker's place for the year, but he was unwilling to remove Brother Parker, though he himself desired it. I am afraid it will be thought I am influenced by ambition to apply for this office, but really there is no other in the traveling connection I could fill without injustice to my family, and I would be glad, if possible, to fill up some place in this critical emergency. Please to continue the favor of your correspondence, and believe me to be your loving though unworthy brother in the gospel,

WILLIAM WINANS.

Wilkinson co., Miss., Dec. 29, 1819.

LETTER FROM WILLIAM WINANS TO BISHOP McKENDREE.

We subjoin another letter, of a later date, from Dr. Winans to the Bishop. The reader will notice the questions of Church-law propounded in this letter. If the Bishop replied, doubtless he answered the first in the negative, and the second in the affirmative. The Quarterly Conference, or the District Conference, as then organized, possessed original jurisdiction of all cases involving the characters of local preachers, and had authority to investigate them, whether previously acted upon by committees or not. Committees of the kind alluded to in the letter were designed to protect the Church and the character of the accused in the intervals of the Conferences. They were courts of inquiry, not of trial; and no action of theirs could supersede the authority of the court of original jurisdiction—the Quarterly-meeting or District Conference.

Dr. Winans would not have asked these questions at a later period of his ministry, for he became one of the most profound judges of ecclesiastical law in the Church.

Rev. William McKendree:

Dear Sir:—We were exceedingly sorry that no Bishop attended our late Conference: first, because we are all comparatively inexperienced in Church-government; secondly, because no one among us has that preëminence in age and standing required of him who would fill the chair *pro tem.* with dignity and authority; and, thirdly, because we view the Bishops as the arterial part of the circulation in our ecclesiastical body, from which to be separated is to experience paralysis, if not death. Several questions of great importance to good government occurred, which none of us were competent to answer. I think it probable that many such will arise at the next Conference, and I entreat we may have the counsel of our Superintendents, or one of them.

Our Conference sat in peace, and harmony, and love, and I do believe every member was disposed to do the thing he ought. More respect was shown to the delegated authority of the chair than could have been expected, considering how all-unworthy I was of that situation. I feel particularly grateful to my brethren for the resignation, and even cheerfulness, with which they took the stations allotted to them. In this delicate and important branch of the duty imposed on me, I did the very best my understanding (assisted by the other Presiding Elders and Brother Griffin) enabled me. There was one instance in which I felt it my indispensable duty to depart from what I believed to be the views of Bishop George—I mean, in the number and description of preachers to be employed on the west side of the Mississippi. It is a fact wholly incontrovertible, that the provision for that country has never been adequate to a rational experiment. This, for the most part, has been owing to a want of preachers. Last year, however, more might have been sent, without leaving any other place so desolate as was that country, with only two preachers, one of whom was an invalid and the other a young man of the second year. This year it was still more practicable to supply that side of the river without serious injury to this, and I felt it my duty to proceed accordingly. Nothing but a sense of duty would have been able to inspire me with hardihood enough to act contrary to what I believed to be the plan of one of the Bishops. I hope my presumption in this matter will be forgiven.

The work has progressed throughout our whole territory, except in the Louisiana District, in a manner very encouraging. The sum of our acquisition the last year was about fifty per cent. Our increase in preachers too is, all things considered, rather flattering than otherwise. Seven were admitted on trial, and two reädmitted. One has died, Nicholas T. Sneed; two have located, Griffin and Booth; and one has been expelled.

Our next Conference is to be held at Natchez, if practicable; if not, (in the discretion of the Presiding Elder and preacher in charge there,) at Washington. The vicinity of the places, and their relative position, will prevent any serious difficulty or confusion from growing out of this uncertainty.

The Conference have made me sole agent of the meeting-house business at New Orleans. The amount of funds placed under my control, and now on interest, is (with the interest) about $1,200; and this is all that remains of what was collected for the purpose of building a meeting-house in that city! Nothing at present, I think, can be done. There is a greater depression of business and a greater consequent scarcity of money, in this country, than has ever been known since the conclusion of the last war. Indeed, so cruelly was public confidence abused in the last effort that was made in that place, that I would be ashamed to ask assistance from distant friends till we could point to a building going up, and say, "There is your security for the faithful performance of our duty; help us to finish the good work."

If you can find leisure and strength, be so good as to furnish an answer to the following queries:

1. Should a local preacher, elder, or deacon, be called before a committee on certain charges and acquitted, though notoriously guilty, would the District Conference be obliged by this acquittal to pass the case over with silence?

2. Should the committee, in the case supposed, convict the party of an offense deserving suspension, and merely reprove him, or the preacher presiding in the committee neglect or refuse to suspend him, could the District Conference legally bring the offender under trial for the same charges which had been before the committee?

An answer to these queries will be of more service to me than merely to satisfy curiosity, inasmuch as I have reason to fear that one or the other of these questions will become of very great practical importance at the next District Conference.

I left my family well when I left home, ten days ago. I need much more piety. I hope you will give me a place in your daily supplications. I am sincerely your affectionate though unworthy son in the gospel of the blessed Jesus,

WILLIAM WINANS.

Natchez, December 31, 1822.

BISHOP McKENDREE'S LETTER TO BISHOP ASBURY.

It is familiar to all who know the course pursued by Bishop Asbury, that for many years he made all the appointments of the preachers without consulting any one. He knew all the work and all the preachers, and, except it might be in rare cases, did not think it necessary to ask for advice.

But Bishop McKendree was unwilling to follow his example, not thinking it impossible to obtain assistance from old and discreet members as to the propriety of appointing certain men to their work. The senior feared the result, and this letter was penned to assure him that, while he was willing to accede to the proposition he made previously—that the senior should make a list of appointments, which was to be revised by the junior and his advisers, and returned with these revisions to the senior for approval or rejection—he could not consent to take the whole responsibility. He was not sufficiently acquainted with the preachers or the work to attempt it alone, and firmly but respectfully declined doing so.

Cincinnati, Oct. 8, 1811.

Brother Asbury:—I am fully convinced of the utility and necessity of the council of the Presiding Elders in stationing the preachers. But you fear individuals will make it difficult, if not impracticable, for you to proceed on this plan. I am willing to assist you in the best way I can, and, as I am in duty bound, so I hold myself in readiness to render the most effectual service to the Church. Consequently, I am still willing to accede to the proposition which you made at the Genesee Conference, if it may be qualified. If it is still your wish, I will take the plan of stations, after you have matured it—call the elders to my assistance, and, after deliberate counsel, report in favor, or dictate such alterations as may be thought necessary. But I still refuse to take the *whole* responsibility upon myself, not that I am afraid of proper accountability, but because I conceive the proposition included one highly improper.

Yours in the bonds of a yoke-fellow,

W. McKendree.

THE REV. ANDREW MONROE'S NOTES OF TRAVEL WITH BISHOP McKENDREE.

WE have elsewhere noted the fact that the Rev. Andrew Monroe had accompanied the Bishop from Tennessee to the General Conference of 1820, and had furnished the writer with an account of the route. We subjoin an extract from it, the remainder having been lost, the delay in bringing it forward having arisen from the hope of recovering the missing portion.

At the Nashville Conference, held in the autumn of 1819, I was appointed to the charge of the Bowling-green Circuit, Kentucky. About the middle of February, I received a note from Bishop McKendree, written from his brother's, Dr. James McKendree, near Fountain Head, Sumner county, Tennessee, where he had for some time made his home. He requested me to make ready and repair to his quarters, to accompany him to the city of Washington. The Bishop had been long in bad health, and was still very feeble; so much so, that his friends remonstrated against his undertaking the journey. The winter was open and wet, making the roads almost impassable; besides this, we were going on horseback, which would have been a severe tour for one in the vigor of life and health; but the

Bishop's heart was set upon meeting the preachers of the Baltimore Conference, which was to meet in Georgetown, District of Columbia, and neither bad health, advanced age, nor intolerable roads, could intimidate that extraordinary man of God. Getting a supply for my place, I made ready, and in a few days met the Bishop, who was buoyant in spirit and full of resolution. He was provided with the necessary fixtures—riding-horse, pack-horse, etc.—for the journey. We spent the first Sabbath together at Salem. The venerable Valentine Cook had come there to have what he supposed would be the last interview with the Bishop. Cook preached and the Bishop exhorted. Our stopping-place was Brother Cryer's. We left Monday morning, Brother Cook accompanying us. We traveled about twenty miles through mud and rain, and stopped for the night at the house of a friend. I found by this time that my position would subject me to much responsibility and toil, and that my duties were of a very delicate character; but still I considered the society of the Bishop to be more than a remuneration. Tuesday morning we parted reluctantly with our venerable friend, Brother C., and proceeded on our journey. Nothing of special note occurred during the week. We averaged about twenty miles per day. At this rate of traveling, the Bishop was often so fatigued as to need help in dismounting; but in the morning he was ready for breakfast by candle-light, and the first to mount his horse. Although he always desired early breakfast, he never failed (whether at a public or private house) to have religious worship. This he made a part of his duty, either for night or at noon for dinner. I remember but one instance in the entire journey of leaving a house without prayers, and that was at a large hotel at Orange Courthouse.

We arrived Saturday evening at an old acquaintance of

the Bishop's, who lived a short distance from Kingston; remained with him overnight; rode into town in the morning, and stopped with Brother Richards, who kept a hotel at the time. I think he was a local preacher.

Here we met the Rev. Benjamin Edge, preacher in charge. The Bishop preached a short sermon at eleven o'clock, from 2 Peter i. 10. The discourse was doctrinal and argumentative. In it he gave predestination no quarters. I tried to preach at night in the hearing of the Bishop, which was a great trial to me. Here I saw his tenacity for rule severely tried. A local preacher had come from a distant part of the circuit, who claimed to have a certificate of election to Deacons' orders; but as he had no expectation of meeting the Bishop, his paper was left at home. Brother E. was present at his election, and joined him in requesting the Bishop to ordain him. At first he positively refused, and repelled every argument until Monday morning, when he reluctantly yielded to their importunity, and ordained him, after which we started on our journey. The weather was warm, and the mud still deep.

In this connection, I will mention an incident which brings out one trait in the Bishop's character. We had been detained far beyond the usual time of starting; he had been worried, and his patience much tried. I was perplexed in getting off, and forgot his canister of bark. After traveling about half a mile, he inquired if I had put it up, when I answered in the negative. He reined in his horse, took the led-horse from me without saying a word, but in any thing but a pleasant manner. I returned immediately, and getting the forgotten medicine, soon overtook him. We traveled for several miles without speaking: *he* finally broke silence by remarking that, from long sickness and fatigue of the journey, he had become impatient;

that he did not know how I bore with him; but if I would forgive him, he would try and do better. That, of course, was an end to the difficulty. He considered it noble to confess a fault; and his manner was so child-like and sincere, that it was a perfect cordial to the wounded spirit. He complained that day more than usual; stopped with an old friend some time before night; suffered much during the night from asthma, but was ready to renew the journey at an early hour the next day.

. . . .

After breakfast, and the payment of a moderate bill, we went on our weary way twenty miles, through the deep mud, to Orange Court-house, where we stopped at Brother McCormick's. Most kindly did they receive the Bishop and his traveling companion—for in this way he always introduced me. We had a pleasant time. A conversation occurred, in the course of the evening, which may interest some of my readers, as it did me at the time. It shows the state of things in Virginia in 1820.

Mr. McCormick was complaining of the want of an adequate supply of preachers. He said, "We have not enough, and then many of the charges are in the hands of young, inexperienced men." He said that other denominations had the advantage of ours. The Bishop listened attentively to his complaint, and then, in a tone and manner of his own, replied, "It is your own fault—I mean, the fault of you Methodists." All seemed surprised, and Brother McCormick inquired, "How so?" "Well," said he, "the preachers marry, as they have a right to do; then you drive them from the field, by withholding a support."

I learned from the conversation that there was great opposition to married preachers, and also, that although the Bishop was an old bachelor, he was a friend of the married preachers and their families.

We remained at Orange until Tuesday, when we went on as far as Fauquier, where the Bishop, at the earnest entreaties of his friends, preached, to a congregation hastily gotten up, a most admirable discourse, holding his delighted hearers spell-bound for about forty minutes. His theme was "God's love and faithfulness to his children." He had recently passed through the crucible, and was prepared to speak from experience. He illustrated the providence and promises of God with remarkable clearness, and applied them with power.

The next morning we continued our journey. The Bishop's health was somewhat improved, and as we approached nearer our destination, he became more buoyant. I think it was Thursday, a little after noon, when we reached the Potomac bridge. Such a bridge, across such a sheet of water, was to me a grand and novel sight. But the scene was characterized by two incidents: the first was the terror that seized our horses—they were so frightened as to give us strong grounds for fear on our part; the second was a sudden snow-storm, which met us with great violence midway on the bridge—we were quite enveloped for some moments, so that we could see no land. While in the midst of danger, I could but ask the question, Have we been preserved in this long journey, to perish in sight of the destined point? But, thanks and praise to Him who "directs the whirlwind and guides the storm," the violence was soon over, and we arrived safe on land. The Bishop knew where the Conference held its sessions, in Georgetown; so we bent our way immediately to the place, and alighting from the carriage, he left the horses to my care, and without notice presented himself in their midst. He was received as one from the dead—many not expecting to see him this side of eternity. After many salutations and much rejoicing, we were conducted to the residence of Mr. Foxhall, one of the Bishop's old and tried friends, where we had our quarters. He met the Conference that evening, and addressed the body in an interesting and affectionate manner. The subjects that principally occupied his mind, and of which he conversed freely with the preachers and prominent members of the Church, were the missionary cause generally and the Indian missions in particular. Another was the principles of Church-law and polity—the power of the ministry and the rights of the membership, as secured by constitutional law. He also deprecated what he considered a tendency to congregational, or local Methodism. He was very cheerful—seemed thankful that he had been preserved through the toils and dangers of his long journey, and addressed himself faithfully to the discharge of his duties, being the promotion of the permanent interests of the great missionary enterprise. The Bishop had come to the city clad in Tennessee jean, not by any means of the finest quality. This, of course, the city folks could not endure; so, in a very short time, he was presented with a full suit of fine black broadcloth. I remember that he seemed slow to make the change, and when in the act of doing it, he remarked to me, "I am afraid of fine things; fine things delude the soul." Many ordinary Christians boast that they are not afraid of finery; yet this great man of God, past his three-score years, was afraid of its influence, because he was acquainted with the deceitfulness of sin and the wiles of the devil. These were points that he had studied most thoroughly, as every minister and Christian ought to do.

Although we had many difficulties, owing to the Bishop's deep-seated infirmities, the weight of care which continually pressed upon his head and heart, the rain, mud, and mire, and the horses' being badly adapted to the service, still we had cause to be thankful for our health and safe arrival.

LETTER FROM BISHOP McKENDREE TO BISHOP SOULE.

THE Address referred to in this letter of the senior Bishop to Joshua Soule—then Bishop elect—is that already given, and which was written to the Annual Conferences explaining his course at the General Conference as to the Suspended Resolutions, and recommending their adoption, if at all, in a constitutional way—*i. e.*, by the vote of the Annual Conferences, and of two-thirds of the General Conference.

His modesty and unselfishness are exhibited in that part relating to the money appropriated as his salary, and remitted to him by Bishop Soule. Money was not his god. He gave away whatever he received which his personal necessities did not require.

We need not stop to show how truly and highly he prized Bishop Soule. No man had his confidence and esteem in a higher degree, and no one more highly deserved it.

Mr. Soule received this letter while in New York:

Lexington, Ky., Sept. 26, 1821.

Dear Friend:—I waited in Baltimore for an answer to one of my letters with anxious care, because I wished to hear from you before I communicated my intended Address to the Conferences, but was disappointed. The expected letter came safe to hand at our Conference in Lebanon, Ohio. I was much encouraged to find your views of the course so perfectly accordant with my own.

The Address has taken its course through the Ohio and Kentucky Conferences. The result is the same, which is as follows:—After the resolutions passed in General Conference are correctly stated, the Kentucky Conference says: "The above resolutions are, in our judgment, an infringement on the Constitution of the Methodist Episcopal Church, and therefore cannot be carried into effect by our representatives without first obtaining the consent of the Annual Conferences; and, whereas, these resolutions were first adopted and then suspended by the General Conference of 1820, and our senior Bishop advises the Annual Conferences to take such measures as may give the above resolutions the force and sanction of Rules in our Discipline—the other Bishops approving the proposed change in our government;

"*Resolved, therefore, by the Kentucky Annual Conference held in Lexington, September* 18, 1821, That we recommend the adoption of the above stated resolutions, and that the next ensuing General Conference (so far as it respects this Conference) are authorized to adopt them, provided it be done by two-thirds of the General Conference, as stated in the sixth article of our constitution."

Your statement of affairs at the New York Conference gave both pleasure and pain. I am glad things are no worse. The African Conference, as it affects the Episcopacy, is mortifying. I have invited information from my colleague on that subject, but received nothing in point.

I received $100 inclosed in your last, appropriated by the Committee, and Brother Ruter informed me of $40 in the hands of the Book Agent subject to my order. I did not expect the $100 would have been forwarded without my order, nor did I intend to draw for it until necessity dictated the measure. As it was sent on without an order, I instructed Brother Ruter to let the $40 remain in the hands of the Agents; but such was the poverty of this Conference, that I drew the $40 and gave it to the poor, and loaned the $100 to a needy brother.

The missionary business in the Ohio Conference promises a reward for our labor and expense. We have sent on a missionary family to carry the school into effective operation.

In this Conference we have had our troubles. One was expelled, and we indulged a hope that their troubles were over, but in this we were disappointed. There are two appeals to the General Conference offered; yet the Lord blesses, and we are prospering. I have paid very little attention to the business of the Conferences, yet *beloved self* whispers consequence to that little.

Such is the effect of labor, bodily or mental, on my feeble frame, connected with a variety of circumstances, that I am now meditating the abandoning of my intention to pursue the Conferences on through the South as far to the North as I should be able, and of taking up winter-quarters in the West after the Tennessee Conference. Should be glad to hear from you. About five weeks from this time I shall be in Nashville, Tennessee, if the Lord will.

I submitted to your stay in the North because you were consenting to the solicitations of the people, which were founded on necessity in behalf of the Church at that time. It is still my opinion that you should come farther to the South. If you can send a letter time enough to meet me in Nashville, let me know your mind on this subject.

Yours in love, W. McKENDREE.

P. S. Bishops George and Roberts were at this and the Ohio Conference. They are in good health. I understand the former is to go to the Mississippi Conference, the latter to attend the others, meet at the South Carolina Conference, and go to the North together. W. McK.

BISHOP McKENDREE'S LIBERALITY.

THE letter below evinces the same spirit exhibited in the foregoing, and in the whole life of Bishop McKendree. He estimated money by the good it could be made to accomplish, and exercised a strict economy over his personal expenditures, that out of his pittance of a salary he might have something left to be used for the cause of God and the relief of the poor. He had long since given himself to this work, and had worn himself out in it. He had deliberately chosen to make all his investments in heaven, and delighted to "lend to the Lord" by giving to the poor. He was always giving, and no one knows how much or how often he did so, as he generally attempted not to let his left hand know what his right hand did.

The copy is before us from his own pen.

To the Editor of the Christian Advocate and Journal:

SIR:—In one of your numbers we have a proposition from an old Methodist, to give $100 to aid our missionary funds, provided you can procure ninety that will do likewise. One of a later date, by way of amendment, offers $100 unconditionally. My annual allowance for support as a traveling preacher, is $100 and my traveling expenses. The success of our missionary efforts is such a manifestation of divine approbation, and of our call to that work, as to induce me to offer one year's allowance toward the support of the cause of missions. The name of the subscriber is withheld, but the money subscribed will be advanced in due time. Yours respectfully,

AN OLD TRAVELING PREACHER.

Kentucky, March 31, 1828.

BISHOP ASBURY'S PAPERS BEQUEATHED TO BISHOP McKENDREE AND DANIEL HITT.

FROM the following letter to Bishop McKendree, it seems that Bishop Asbury left a considerable collection of documents in the hands of Mr. F. Hollingsworth, of Baltimore, which, in his will, he directed should be given over to Bishop McKendree, or Daniel Hitt and Henry Boehm, if the Church should publish his Journal; and as his Journal has been published, it is probable they were placed in his hands. No mention of the fact, however, appears in any of his papers.

Baltimore, Aug. 20, 1827.

REVEREND AND DEAR SIR:—Mrs. Hollingsworth, the widow of the late Francis Hollingsworth, has in her possession a number of letters and documents of the late Bishop Asbury; and several of our preachers and members having expressed a wish to peruse them, she was doubtful of the propriety of granting this privilege to any person without your consent, inasmuch as the will of the Bishop, under date July, 1814, makes a conditional bequest of these letters and documents, which in substance is as follows:

"Should the Conference think proper to publish my Journal, in that case I wish my Manuscript Journal and papers relating to the Church given to Bishop McKendree, or Daniel Hitt and Henry Boehm; but should the Conference not publish my Journal, I hereby bequeath all my manuscripts and papers, both public and private, to Francis Hollingsworth, with a particular request that all private papers not relating to the Church may be by him destroyed."

I know of no will of later date in relation to these papers: should there be none, the papers, letters, etc., now in the possession of Mrs. Hollingsworth, are subject to your direction, (except the private papers, should there be any.) Some of our brethren here think it desirable to ascertain if there are some documents remaining not published among the Bishop's papers, which might be of service to the Church, under her present agitated situation. Their object is to collect all the information that can be obtained to sustain the character of Bishop Asbury, as also the character of our itinerant ministers, which lie bleeding under the pen of the author of "The History and Mystery of Methodist Episcopacy." It is therefore wished that you should express your desire in relation to these documents. Would it not be as well to let the original documents remain where they are, and if it be necessary, appoint a committee of two or three persons in this place to take duplicates of such papers as may appear to be of use? and when you visit this place again, you will then have an opportunity of seeing them all together. Mrs. Hollingsworth, I believe, has determined to let no person see them without your approbation. The brethren who particularly wished to see those papers are the Revs. Brothers Hanson, Waugh, and Yearley.

Waiting the expression of your sentiments and wishes on the above, I remain yours with respect and esteem,

CHAS. A. WARFIELD.

BISHOP McKENDREE TO DR. SARGENT.

DR. THOS. SARGENT, of Philadelphia, to whom these letters were written, was a valued and devoted friend of the Bishop. His house was his home when in the city, and he was his physician in sickness, and his trusted adviser in Church-affairs. The Bishop must have been most heartily welcomed and kindly cared for by the whole family, as is evident from a large package of letters which breathe the most reverential regard on their part, and the most cordial and fatherly affection on his side. These letters, written at different dates, in the Bishop's own handwriting, are two out of many of the same kind. We have already sketched the Doctor.

Sumner co., Tenn., Feb. 4, 1823.

BELOVED BROTHER SARGENT: — Two days ago, yours of the 2d of November came to hand. It was as a cordial to my heart and mind.

My health is restored beyond my most sanguine hope, for which I desire to be most devoutly thankful; but the nerves remain in a state of great debility, so that I can bear but little mental exertion, especially that of an affecting nature; hence I am not able to bear the full weight of our charge. This conclusion is the result of repeated experiments; yet I can do something, and am willing to do all I can. Could the lightest part of the business of the Conferences fall to my lot, I could do a great deal more than I do; but this would be too great a sacrifice for my deserts. And it is so natural to expect the elder to go in front, that by submitting to bear the burdens of difficult cases, I have brought on afflictions, and had to retire, or afflict a friend by refusing to undertake what I thought was improper. Hence I had concluded to continue in the West until next fall, and then go on; but as the season advanced, I was not quite so well satisfied, and was thinking of preparing for the Virginia Conference. Your letter added encouragement. I am now preparing, and expect, if the Lord will, to set out next week. Last summer we lost a preacher in Washington. I was called on to supply his place, and, for want of another, had to give up Brother Hill. Since October I have been alone: in this way I was about setting off for Lynchburg, Virginia, but Providence has provided a pious local preacher who is going on business, and is more than willing to go with me.

I am deeply interested in Brother Summerfield's welfare. I hope the Lord will preserve and return him to us. I shall be very glad to meet him in Baltimore. In my acquaintance with him, nothing appeared that would militate against your good opinion of him. He certainly ranks amongst the most excellent.

I should be highly gratified to see the British Conference in session, with Mr. Wesley at their head, and join with you in saying, "I hope it will be the old Doctor"* that attends our General Conference.

I am glad that your son Thomas has hoisted anchor, and

* He means Dr. Adam Clarke.

is on the way with a favorable wind. It only remains for him to "be faithful until death" to come to anchor, richly laden, in the harbor of eternal repose.

During the winter I have visited some of the Churches through the south of the State of Kentucky, West Tennessee, and intended seeing North Alabama, but the season prevented. We have had a great deal of rain, high water, and spells of hard freezing weather, but very little snow. At eight o'clock this morning, the mercury in Pool's thermometer stood at 9 degrees, and at twelve o'clock at about 20 degrees. Just before this spell of cold weather set in, I returned, and am now comfortably lodged with my brother-in-law in a cabin about sixteen or eighteen feet square, with a puncheon floor, and covered with slabs; but we have a plenty of bacon, and beef, and chickens, and turkeys, cabbage, Irish and sweet potatoes, and milk and butter. We have a little tea and coffee, with sugar extracted from the trees in the woods; corn and fodder for my horse, and a good bed to lie on. All this with peace and harmony, and Jesus besides! And to complete the blessing, I have the rheumatism in my head and teeth. Now, it is given to us not only to believe in Jesus, but to suffer for his sake, who works all things together for good to them that love him. I must be very thankful for all those blessings, or be guilty of *deep* ingratitude.

Dear Doctor, with all my failings and infirmities, which are many, I am striving to improve the mysterious dispensation of Providence that hangs over me for heaven and eternal happiness. There I hope joyfully to meet you, with your kind companion and lovely children. The Lord bless you and them with temporal and spiritual blessings! My respects to my kind and good friends, especially our beloved Thos. Burch. Yours respectfully,

W. McKENDREE.

P. S. I undesignedly omitted assuring you that your good opinion is most cordially reciprocated. I not only esteem but love you. My affection commenced with my acquaintance, and remains undiminished. Differences in opinion on non-essentials do not produce a change in Christian affection. Sincerity and candor will not only command respect, but increase love, when difference of opinion is conducted with due deference to each other, while Christian feelings justly recoil from a different course. W. McK.

The following note was written to Dr. Sargent by the Bishop, during the session of the General Conference of 1828:

Pittsburgh, May 23, 1828.

Dear Friend and Brother:—At the commencement of the Conference, I received your kind letter, and considered its contents. Your friendship and correspondence have been, and still are, a subject of encouragement, comfort, and support to me. I rejoice to have a place among your friends, and shall endeavor ever to deserve it. The business of this Conference has been conducted with more than ordinary good feeling, yet not without some perturbation. I say nothing of business; you will have it from your representatives. My health is pretty good. I have enjoyed peace and tranquillity of mind through the Conference, and received more friendly visits than on some former occasions. I intend to visit you as soon as Divine Providence permits. Conference is now sitting, pressing to a close of the business. My love to Sister Sargent and the children.

Yours in much love, W. McKendree.

BISHOP McKENDREE'S ACCOUNT OF THE UNION OF THE PRESBYTERIANS AND METHODISTS IN 1805—THE ORIGIN OF THE CUMBERLAND PRESBYTERIANS.

As Bishop McKendree was the Presiding Elder on the Cumberland District during the time the events occurred, narrated by him in the statement below, it may be interesting to give it in his own words.

The Cumberland Presbyterian Church arose during the great religious revival in Kentucky and Tennessee in 1801–3, although it was not organized as a distinct and separate Church until 1810. They rejected the doctrine of eternal and unconditional election and reprobation, as taught in the Westminster Confession of Faith. They claim to occupy middle ground between Calvinism and Arminianism, and adopted a modified system of an itinerant ministry. They have been earnest and zealous laborers, and have done great good in the South and West. To what extent they have had similar success in the other sections of the country, the writer knows not. His own observations, and his personal intercourse with individual ministers and members of the Church, has impressed him very strongly and favorably.

In 1800, a revival of religion was making considerable progress, which it seems commenced the year before, of which the Rev. John McGee has published some account.

At that time the charge of the Methodist Circuit was committed to a preacher of moderate talents, but without the spirit of enterprise to conduct the Church of Christ under such circumstances. He was better disposed to obey and labor than to counsel and lead. At the same time there were several pious and zealous Presbyterian ministers, who united to enter into and carry on the work. They had frequent appointments of a popular character, so arranged as for several to be at each appointment.

The Methodist preacher married, and suffered his pecuniary concerns to divert his attention from his ministerial charge. The circuit was neglected. But he attended the Presbyterian appointments, and labored zealously and successfully. The local preachers followed his example, and the regular circuit-preaching was measurably lost in three or four days' meeting for the sacramental-meetings, and were very popular.

The Presbyterian ministers were respectable for learning, and were honored members of society for their services as teachers and preachers. They ranked with the respectable part of society.

The Methodists were reverenced and honored for their piety and usefulness as preachers; so much so, that whatever liberties might be taken on other occasions, when affliction made it necessary to call in praying people, the Methodists were frequently selected, and their counsel on spiritual matters sought.

When these preachers united in public worship, their influence on their respective adherents drew people of different persuasions together in great numbers.

But the preachers were not of one mind. The Presbyterians were Calvinists; the Methodists, Arminians; and they had been publicly at issue on these doctrines. In this contest the Methodists' sentiments had imperceptibly gained the ascendency over the public mind. If any attended on those occasions in expectation of exhibitions on controverted points, they were disappointed. Many—perhaps the generality of the people—heard them as men of the same views of the sacred doctrines.

But this was not all. The preachers were enabled to preach the word with power, and it was attended with the influence of the Holy Spirit. Sinners were convicted and converted; Christians were built up in the most holy faith; and the hearts of the professors were tenderly united in affection and love. They cleaved to each other as children of one family. Class-meetings and love-feasts were refreshing seasons. They were attended with divine influence and the comforts of the Holy Ghost.

The Presbyterians earnestly requested the privilege of participating in those meetings. The Methodists could not grant the request without infringing on their discipline; but inclination prevailed, and they suffered loss, as a consequence of violating a wholesome regulation. The Presbyterians resigned nothing, but were great gainers.

Class-meetings and love-feasts are calculated and designed to instruct, and lead the seeker of religion to the knowledge of sins forgiven, and his acceptance with God through the Lord Jesus Christ; (Rom. viii. 1, 2, 14–16; John v. 24; 1 John iii. 14;) and to conduct the young converts—the babes in Christ—up to Christian perfection—to holiness, without which no man shall see the Lord. Heb. v. 12–14; Prov. iv. 18; Heb. xii. 14.

Such meetings are truly desirable to Christians while they enjoy the comforts of religion, and are pressing "toward the mark for the prize of the high calling of God in Christ Jesus." But when faith fails in whole or in part, the spiritual exercises of those meetings become disagreeable in a proportionable degree.

The Presbyterian discipline knows nothing of such meetings; nor does it require its members to pass such strict examinations on the progress of religion.

Those among them that desired it, enjoyed those meetings among the Methodists by courtesy, and withdrew or neglected them, as they pleased. As the revival subsided, the zeal for meetings and spiritual exercise cooled off. This was the case among the members of both Churches. This called for a prudent exercise of discipline; but Methodist discipline had no control over Presbyterians—they neglected class-meetings with impunity. The members of the Methodist Church whose zeal was paralyzed, were inclined to neglect their class-meetings, after the example of their Presbyterian friends.

The preachers now felt the difficulty of exercising discipline to profit; regretted that it was ever departed from; but under existing circumstances, thought it prudent not to press their members to duty with rigor, but to apply their crippled discipline to the best purpose, and hope for better times.

This state of things continued, with some modifications, until the close of the Conference-year of 1805. The Presiding Elder of the Cumberland District* intending to locate at the approaching Conference, there was some solicitude felt as to the course his successor would take as to the existing union. To guard against possible events, the

* Lewis Garrett.

Presbyterian minister and the Presiding Elder appointed a union-meeting, so called, for the purpose of initiating the next Presiding Elder into the mysteries of the union. A large congregation of people and a number of preachers came together at the appointed time. The new Presiding Elder,* and a Presbyterian minister from Kentucky, attended the meeting.

The conduct of the ministers in Cumberland, in uniting with the Methodists, had become suspicious in the eyes of their brethren elsewhere, and a minister from Kentucky was sent, it seems, to examine into the matter.

The Presiding Elder preached when he was appointed, as other preachers did, but would have nothing to do with the management of the meeting.

On Monday, the managers of the meeting called all the official members and preachers of both Churches together, to consider the origin and state of the union, and the regulations necessary to perpetuate it. After several speeches, in which much had been said on the subject, the new Presiding Elder was requested to give his views; he complied, and observed that much had been said against proselyting; and that to perpetuate the union, there must be no proselyting. If by proselyting, nothing more was intended than improper measures, and personal influence used to induce members to leave their own Church and join the other, he had no objection to it; for in his estimation, such measures were unchristian and contemptible. But proselyting, as he understood the term, comprehended much more—it means the conversion of a sinner from the power of sin and Satan to the living God; from darkness to light; from erroneous opinions, relative to religious doctrines, to truth. For this purpose it is consistent with Christian

* Wm. McKendree was the new Presiding Elder.

civility and religion to use legitimate arguments drawn from the Scriptures, reason, and experience. If this course is pursued with due deference to the feelings and sentiments of others, no cause of offense is given, nor should offense be taken. That wise and pious men have different views of the doctrines of revelation, is a fact; and it is proper for them, as honest men, to labor to convert their fellow-men to receive what they believe to be the truth. They have opposite views of the truth, and one may be as pious and sincere as the other; therefore let them esteem each other as Christians, recommend their own views with Christian respect to the sentiments of others, and let the people judge for themselves.

By the union of which we are speaking, I would understand two separate and distinct Churches, each having a system of doctrine and discipline in active operation, independent of each other; and, though they differ in point of doctrine and discipline, yet, believing that each is accepted and blessed by the great Head of the Church, they are cordially disposed to live in harmony, peace, and love, and mutually encourage and assist each other, as far as they can consistently with their respective rules and regulations of Church-government. If his ideas of Christian union were correct, he thought the Churches had departed from correct principles—that the fellowship then existing among them was not the union, but the amalgamation of the Churches. The Methodist discipline is not exercised conformably to its provisions and genius. If the Presbyterian discipline is correctly attended to, I am not acquainted with it. To depart from an established and wholesome discipline in order to perpetuate the union of Churches, is an adventurous and dangerous experiment. It may preserve the existing friendship, but its tendency is rather to destroy than perpetuate discipline. Therefore, to establish a profitable union, let the ministers preach the doctrines of their respective Churches, simply, plainly, and clearly; but let it be done in the spirit of meekness and love, and with proper respect to the feelings and sentiments of others; and let them mutually assist each other, according to their respective disciplines.

The Elder's view of the subject seemed to obtain general acceptance. The Methodist discipline began to revive from that time. But a murmuring was soon heard among the Presbyterians, that things were not right—that the Methodists did not attend to the principles of the union; and their preachers spoke of it, in several congregations, in a way calculated to injure the Methodist character.

In this state of things, the Methodists had a camp-meeting at E. Douglass's, on the east of the Cumberland River. The Rev. W. McGee, a Presbyterian minister, was at it, and was appointed to preach on Sabbath at eleven o'clock. In the morning the sacrament of the Lord's-supper was attended to in the meeting-house. W. McGee absented himself. The Elder said nothing to him on the subject until after the sermon; he then took him out and requested his reason for absenting himself from the Lord's table. He said the Methodists had broken the union, and therefore he did not commune. He named Miles Harper as the transgressor, and instanced wherein he had broken the union. The Elder wished to know if he would be satisfied with such reparation or acknowledgments as might be dictated, if Harper had done wrong. He said he would. The Elder spoke to Harper, who was willing and wished to meet the charges. For this purpose, the preachers and official members of both Churches were requested to convene in the meeting-house on Monday morning. The appointment was well attended. After prayer, the Elder informed those present of the design of the meeting, and requested Mr. McGee to state the rules of the union, and wherein they were violated. He requested the Elder to do it. He did so, by repeating the terms as suggested and agreed to in the union-meeting, and appealed to Mr. McGee and those members that attended the union-meeting. His statements were admitted to be correct.

Soon after the investigation commenced, it appeared that for want of evidence, it could not be concluded. The meeting was therefore adjourned to the time and place of a quarterly-meeting which was shortly to be commenced, in a neighborhood where the witnesses would attend. The accuser's presence was much desired, but his business prevented him from attending. But he appointed his substitute, and authorized him to act in his place. As well as I remember, Presbyterian Elders sat with Methodists on the trial. The charges and witnesses were deliberately attended to, and Harper was acquitted.

The Elder drew up a statement of the trial, and proposed for the accuser's agent and himself to sign it in behalf of their Churches, and keep it as an official conclusion of the matter. He hesitated; the Elder therefore proposed, as he was going from thence to a camp-meeting at Fountain Head, where he expected to see the accuser and a number of his brethren, to take the papers, officially certified, and submit the whole to the judgment of the preachers and official members of that meeting. This was a gratification to the agent.

At the Fountain Head meeting the papers were presented to Harper's accuser, in the presence of one or two other preachers and several elders of that Church, united with the members of the Methodist Conference. The paper was read, considered, and approved. The accuser professed to be satisfied. All seemed to be pleased.

The Presiding Elder was glad that Harper was exonerated, and the Methodists found innocent, and that the accuser himself was satisfied; but he had to acknowledge that *he* was not satisfied—that he was dissatisfied with the proceedings against Harper, and with the manner in which the Methodists had been treated; and therefore he then demanded satisfaction in behalf of the Methodists. He then stated charges against Harper's accuser, and directed attention to cases wherein the Methodists had been publicly misrepresented, to the wounding of religious feeling and the injury of character.

Harper's accuser attempted to evade an examination, but the Presiding Elder demanded satisfaction for his injured brethren. The former accuser, now the accused, said they had no power to meet the demand—that their discipline made no provision for such a case. He was informed that the Methodist discipline knew as little about them and the union as theirs did; but they had entered a kind of fellowship called a union, talked of rules and regulations to perpetuate the union, and had charged the Methodists with breaking the union; that the Methodists had met the charge, justified their conduct, and given satisfaction to their accuser—not on any provision of their discipline for such a case, but upon principles of propriety and social obligation; and after all this, they are informed there is no redress for them. The Presiding Elder was not disposed to admit such apologies. Satisfaction for his injured brethren he must have, or resort to some other mode of defense. He was not disposed to be severely just, but would take any acknowledgment that was sufficient to secure the injured character of his brethren.

A respectable elder of the Presbyterian Church said the demand was reasonable, and ought to be complied with. The accused begged that it should be deferred till after their Presbytery, which was at hand. The Presiding Elder consented to the suspension of the trial, on condition that they should meet him at a camp-meeting of his, in Cage's Bend, immediately after their Presbytery, but that means should be used to redress the injury already inflicted on the Methodists.

The Presbyterian ministers did not correct the misrepresentations they had publicly made. He therefore wrote to a preacher an account of the state of things, with direction to read it in those congregations wherein the Presbyterian preacher had made the subject public. The preacher was not to comment on the communication or explain it, but to let the author of the letter and him who first made the subject public settle any differences that might arise.

No return was made to the Presiding Elder at the camp-meeting in Cage's Bend. The charges officially brought by him against the Presbyterian preachers of the union were never settled. They remained under censure. The affair was left to suffer, or sleep, or die. At the interviews relative to the charges against Mr. Harper, the terms and regulations of the union, as stated at the union-meeting, were repeated and admitted. Thus many things were brought to light, knowledge increased, Methodist discipline revived, and numbers were greatly increased.

What was the proper signification of the term "Cumberland Presbyterians," as it was used in those days, the writer is not sufficiently acquainted with the regulations of the Presbyterian Church to say; but he thinks it was applied to a part, perhaps a Presbytery, designated the "Cumberland Presbytery" of the Presbyterian Church, as it existed at that day. Of this body there were four ministers who were distinguished for piety, zeal, and usefulness: Messrs. McGee, (whose Brother John was a very zealous, useful

Methodist preacher—these brothers labored much together, with great success,) McGready, Hodge, and Rankin. These four labored harmoniously and successfully. They engaged the Methodist ministers in their meetings to a considerable extent. They advocated union with the Methodists, and preached so much like them, and spoke so freely against Calvin's notion of decrees and in favor of salvation for all men, that many supposed they had renounced their old system of doctrines. These were prominent, popular characters, and probably many restricted the Cumberland Presbyterians to these four men.

Of the Cumberland Presbyterians the Church became suspicious—whether of all the ministers of that body or part of them, or for what or to what extent their conduct was censured, the writer does not know. It was reported that the Cumberland Presbyterians did not attend to the discipline of the Church; that in the examination of candidates for the ministry, they did not sufficiently attend to the candidate's faith in their doctrines, and licensed men who did not possess the literary qualifications required by the discipline. How this may be, the writer does not know. But it is certain that eventually a number of the preachers of the Cumberland department left the Presbyterian Church and constituted a separate and distinct community. I understand they have been useful and successful.

Of the four ministers already mentioned as leading characters of that part of the Presbyterian Church with which the Methodists of the Cumberland Circuit formed a union, I learned that the first-named joined himself to the seceders who formed a Church in the Cumberland District for the Presbyterian Church. The second and third, after saying many things, and some of them very hard, against their old Confession of Faith, adjusted matters with the

Church and received the Confession of Faith. And the fourth, or last-named, joined the Shaking Quakers. Thus the body of ministers with whom the Methodists were in union has become extinct. There is not a vestige of it in their existing form extant.

BISHOP McKENDREE'S ESSAYS ON OUR CHURCH-GOVERNMENT.

AMONG the numerous papers of Bishop McKendree, some are sermons, theological criticisms, and essays upon doctrinal, metaphysical, and literary subjects; but while most of them are unfinished, he prepared others upon Church-government—especially our own—with considerable care, and left them neatly and carefully put up. The general views presented in them are in part set forth in his circular addresses and letters, but in many cases they are so concisely and clearly stated in these brief essays, that it is thought proper to give a few of them a permanent form. We therefore present the following pieces, carefully written by him. The future historiographer of the Church, and the student of our ecclesiastical history, may hereafter be glad to find the views entertained by the wise and venerable man whose history reaches from the organization of our Church to 1835, and whose life was devoted to the study and administration of our economy; and yet, as laws and their construction, as well as usages and opinions, like every thing else of human origin, are liable to be changed and modified by time and taste, so, notwithstanding our high respect for the Bishop, and our agreement with him in many of his views, we do not consider ourselves bound to indorse all his opinions and inferences as set forth: in the main, however, we assent to them.

DEFENSE OF CONSTITUTIONAL EPISCOPACY.

A General Superintendency is essentially necessary to perpetuate itinerancy; therefore no judicious friend to the traveling plan will transfer the power of choosing Presiding Elders and stationing the preachers from the Bishops to the Annual Conferences, because in this the power of oversight principally consists. Take this prerogative from the Superintendents, and there will remain with them no power by which they can oversee the work, or officially manage the administration; and therefore the Conference must in justice release them from their responsibilities as Bishops. This being done, the office of General Superintendent must cease, and the Methodist Episcopal Church would be no longer under the government of Bishops.

But such a change in the government would deprive the General Conference of an important—perhaps an essential—part of their authority, and put it out of their power to enforce and carry our system of rules into effect. This will appear from the peculiar relation between the Bishop and Conference, or the connection between making our rules and enforcing them. The Superintendents are chosen by the General Conference, are the repositories of executive power, and are held responsible as overseers of the whole charge. By calling upon them, the administration in every part of the work may be brought under the inspection and control of the General Conference.

But if the power of superintending the work were taken

from the Bishops, they must be released from the responsibility; and if *they* should be released, there would be no person or persons accountable to the General Conference for the administration; consequently the connection between making rules and enforcing them would be dissolved. The legislative body would then have no control over the executive—no power to enforce their rules or laws.

The several Annual Conferences are under the control of general rules, enforced by responsible Superintendents; so that if a preacher should depart from the discipline or doctrine of the Church, it is the Bishop's duty to correct, remove from office, or bring him to trial, according to discipline.

Should an Annual Conference dissent from the doctrine or discipline of the Church, the Bishop should enter his protest, and bring the case before the ensuing General Conference. Should the Superintendent join with a Conference in such a departure, the next General Conference will call him to account for it; and by this medium the General Conference takes cognizance of the acts of the Annual Conferences: so that while the Superintendents serve as a center of union and harmony among the Annual Conferences, they, *i. e.*, the Annual Conferences, become responsible to, and are brought under, the inspection and control of the General Conference.

Once more: The General Superintendents serve as watchmen to guard the Annual Conferences against attacks on their constitutional rights.

The delegated Conference is composed of two parts: the representatives of the Annual Conferences and the Bishops. These are equally supported by the preachers collectively, who have secured to themselves in this capacity the right of deciding on any alteration of the constitution; therefore that instrument cannot be altered or changed by the General Conference, unless they first obtain the consent of the Annual Conferences. Now, if the representatives should make a premature attack on the constitution, it becomes the Superintendent's duty, arising out of his relation to the preachers collectively, to arrest the procedure on constitutional principles, and thus, and on that ground, the subject may come before the Annual Conferences, whose right it is to judge in all constitutional cases. Were it not for this check, which brings all disputes respecting constitutional rights to a uniform and safe conclusion, the Church might be involved in difficulties of the most serious nature. The General Conference might pass a rule, to which some Conferences might submit, and others pronounce unconstitutional, and thereby destroy its force. The end is left to conjecture.

But if the executive power were transferred from the Bishops to the Annual Conferences, as it would be if they were authorized to elect Presiding Elders, etc., and the Bishops were consequently released from their responsibility to the General Conference, the Annual Conferences would thereby become independent of each other, of the Bishops, (except for ordination,) and of the General Conference. Being invested with executive authority, and amenable to no superior, consequently under no jurisdiction, they might neglect or reject the rules formed by the General Conference with impunity; and for the Conferences in such a situation to dissolve the bonds of fellowship and union, by introducing different administrations, is among possible events.

In the event of such a change in the government, the General Superintendents might patiently endure the toil of annual visits to ordain preachers, hear complaints, feel the distresses of the discontented, and preside in the Conferences, without power to redress grievances, or manage the business; or they might turn their attention to more comfortable and useful situations; and the General Conference may have the honor of assembling together and forming rules and regulations for the government of the Church, and the mortification of seeing those rules neglected or rejected, and lament their loss of power to enforce their wholesome regulations, and thereby save the Church.

ITINERANCY—ITS SUCCESS—STATISTICS.

The itinerant plan of preaching the gospel, which was pursued by the apostles and their immediate successors, is undoubtedly better calculated to supply the poor with the glad tidings of salvation than any other, and indeed, is the only plan adapted to the universal spread of the gospel. But this apostolic system was soon exchanged for a local plan, which is better adapted to human inclinations and temporal interests. In process of time, when experimental religion was extremely low and almost discarded, it pleased the Lord to call forth that venerable man, John Wesley, and through his instrumentality to revive both religion and the itinerant plan of preaching the gospel. By this means a general revival of experimental religion has been carried far and wide.

But it will appear to a careful observer of our Annual Minutes, compared with the rise and progress of Methodism in Europe and America, that our founder and fathers did not intend to organize a separate Church. They had no preärranged system of government: so far from it, they were frequently opposed to those measures which were providentially suggested as proper expedients for particular occasions, and which terminated in a constitution and system of Church-government.

These things considered, it would seem nothing short of an overruling Providence could have produced so excellent an imitation of the apostolic plan.

Our fathers set out with this profession: "We believe that God's design in raising up the preachers called Methodists, in America, was to reform the Continent, and spread scriptural holiness over these lands." Influenced by this persuasion, they went forth proclaiming salvation through the merits of Christ by faith to all people. Increasing numbers crying, "What shall we do?" induced them to resort to church-yards, market-houses, streets, the woods, for houses could not contain the thousands that flocked together to hear the word of life. Rules and regulations were introduced to meet the necessities of an astonishing increase of members, and a rapid extension of the field of ministerial labors.

In 1784, the United Societies in America, contrary to the original intention of our founder and fathers, were formed into an independent Episcopal Church; and the rules which, from time to time, had been introduced for the benefit of the Society, were incorporated into the system of government.

When the societies were formed into a Church, there were 46 circuits, 83 traveling preachers, and 14,988 members. From that time the work of the Lord far exceeded any former years; so much so, that in 1792, there were 18 Districts, 137 circuits and stations, 226 preachers, and 65,980 members. But the increase of numbers was attended with additional difficulties. A few years' experience taught the necessity of revising and perfecting the system of rules. For this purpose a General Conference was called, and met according to appointment, Nov. 1, 1792, and was continued by adjournments, once in four years, until May 6, 1808, which was the last General Conference of this description. At that time there were 35 Districts, 313 circuits and stations, 540 traveling, and about 2,000 local preachers, and 151,995 members. Hitherto the Conferences possessed unlimited powers. The system of government was therefore subject to be changed and modified as the Conference pleased. Sundry alterations and additions were made at those five Conferences; but the principles and constituent parts of the system remained unaltered. The plan of government bore the scrutinizing test of experience and criticism; and the system of government was thereby perfected, settled, and confirmed.

THE DELEGATED SYSTEM — THE CONSTITUTION AND SUPERINTENDENCY.

Such was the confidence which the local preachers and members reposed in the wisdom, goodness, and prudence of the traveling ministry, that the Church enjoyed a good degree of harmony and peace, as well as prosperity; yet many of her friends looked forward to the possible events of every succeeding General Conference with solicitude for the peace and safety of the Church, for the General Conference at that time possessed unrestricted powers; and those traveling preachers who had stood out a certain probation, and met at the appointed time and place, whether many or few, constituted the General Conference; consequently there was no constitutional security that the system of government would be perpetuated, or the terms of communion preserved.

In 1808, there were 540 traveling preachers, and 128 of that number constituted the General Conference. That Conference, being satisfied of the propriety and utility of their system, and fully awake to their situation, resolved to confirm and perpetuate their well-tried plan of government. To this end they constituted a *delegated General Conference*, formed a *constitution*, and so limited and restricted the powers of their representatives as to preserve the system of government inviolate, and secure the rights and privileges of all the members. The Annual Conferences ratified and confirmed the constitution. It was accepted and adopted unanimously, by every Annual Conference electing and sending representatives to act under it.

The General Conference thus constituted, is invested with "full powers to make rules and regulations for the Church, under certain limitations and restrictions," and to enforce those rules by means of the General Superintendents, who are amenable to them for the administration. A General Superintendency is therefore indispensably necessary; neither the General Conference nor the itinerant plan could exist long without it. Hence it is provided in the constitution that the General Conference "shall not change or alter any part or rule of our government so as to do away Episcopacy, or destroy the plan of our itinerant General Superintendency."

Now, as the same power which constituted the delegated Conference thus confirmed and perpetuated the General Superintendency, it must be equally as permanent as the General Conference itself; and to guard against such afflictive and destructive alterations as it was in the power of the former Conference to make, the delegated Conferences are not "to revoke, alter, or change our Articles of Religion, or to establish any new standards or rules of doctrine contrary to our present existing and established standards of doctrine." It was the belief of those doctrines that first united the preachers and people in sentiment and affection; and the cordial belief of them, like silken cords, still binds the whole Connection in harmony and love. The fourth article preserves "the General Rules of the United Societies," and the fifth perpetuates the mutually ageeed to and long-established rules by which disorderly preachers and members are to be dealt with. By these judicious regulations, the General Conference have lost their power to make injurious changes; and the rights of the members being secured, the public mind is happily delivered from fear of ruinous changes: it rests under the protection of those limitations and restrictions; consequently the Church has nothing to fear, from the fact that the government is mainly in the hands of the traveling ministers.

The General Superintendents are constituted the supreme executive, or the deputy of executive power.

It is the duty of a Bishop, or Superintendent, "to preside in the Conferences; to ordain bishops, elders, and deacons; to travel through the Connection at large; to oversee the spiritual and temporal business of the societies." And for the faithful performance of those duties, they are amenable to the General Conference, who have power to expel them for improper conduct, if they see it necessary. But in order to constitute them justly responsible, they should be clothed with sufficient power to discharge the duties enjoined on them. Therefore they are invested with the power of ordination, and full power to superintend the work at large.

The traveling preachers collectively have delegated to them these powers: to fix the appointments of the preachers for the several circuits; in the intervals of the Conferences, to change, receive, and suspend preachers; to form Districts; to choose, station, and change Presiding Elders, etc. But the work extended so rapidly that in a few years it became impossible for the Bishop to superintend in person; therefore Presiding Elders were introduced as assistant superintendents; and, as the Bishops were the only responsible persons for the administration, they were to choose the Presiding Elders, who are fully authorized to superintend the work in the absence of the Bishops. Therefore the office of a Presiding Elder is not separate or distinct from that of a General Superintendent, but is inseparably connected with a part of it, and included in it. They are deputized by the Bishops, who bear the whole responsibility of the administration, as their assistants in the Superintendency. Therefore the Bishops must appoint the Presiding Elders, or be relieved of responsibility for the administration. Hence the Bishops appear to be primarily the overseers of the preachers, as well as of the whole body of the Church. But at the same time that they are acknowledged as the head of the body, they are but *principal servants*, chosen by the preachers, and bound to govern according to rules made by them, and by which they themselves have agreed to be governed. They are thus accountable to the very persons over whom they exercise authority, and "may be expelled by them for improper conduct, if they think it necessary."

Such a General Superintendency may help to carry on the glorious work and increase our joy, but they have no power to oppress.

CHECKS ON GENERAL CONFERENCES AND BISHOPS.

The representatives and the General Superintendents who compose the General Conference, do not act as separate and distinct bodies; and yet such is their respective relations to their constituents, that they form a check on each other in order to preserve the constitutional rights and privileges of the preachers and people.

In the sixth article the mode of altering or amending the constitution is pointed out, and stands thus:

"*Provided, nevertheless,* That upon the joint recommendation of all the Annual Conferences, then a majority of two-thirds of the General Conference succeeding shall suffice to alter any of the above restrictions."

By this proviso our constituents have reserved to themselves the right of judging in constitutional cases, and effectually prohibited every infringement on their sacred rights. The Superintendents have no negative on the General Conference; but if that body should attempt to exceed the bounds of their delegated power, the Superintendents may declare the procedure unconstitutional; and if it should remain a subject of dispute between the Conference and Superintendents, it must be referred to the Annual Conferences as a constitutional question.

In this way the General Superintendency is a safe and easy check on the delegated Conference. But the Bishops are amenable to that body for their administration. The Conference is therefore a powerful check on them in the exercise of their powers. It is the Bishop's prerogative "to form Districts," etc. But this is so connected with the power of choosing, stationing, and changing the Presiding Elders, that if they were deprived of power to choose the Presiding Elders, that of forming Districts should be taken from them. But the Bishop's authority to superintend the work at large consists principally in his power to choose the Presiding Elders, for they act under the Bishop's authority, and are their assistants in the General Superintendency. But if the Presiding Elders were chosen by the Annual Conference, received their executive authority from that body, and were accountable to them, the Bishops would have no power to overrule their administration, and therefore ought to be released from the obligation.

It is the duty of a Bishop, in the intervals of the Conferences, to change, receive, and suspend preachers, as necessity may require, and as the Discipline directs; but this is so closely connected with the power of appointing the preachers for the several stations, that if the Bishops were deprived of the latter, they ought not to retain the former, because such a divided Superintendency might destroy itself. A committee might station the preachers at Conference; and immediately after, the Bishop might make an entirely different arrangement by changing of the same preachers. But a very considerable part of the Bishop's authority to oversee the work is contained in his power to station the preachers; for in the arrangement of the preachers, the Superintendents at once selects the governing preachers, clothes them with executive powers, and supplies the Church with officers, for the exercise of discipline, in every department of the whole work. But if the form of government was altered, as stated above, the Bishops would be completely divested of the powers of an overseer—they would have no authority to overrule or manage the business officially; and therefore, justice requires they should be freed from the duties and responsibilities of overseers. This being done, the remaining duties of a Bishop would stand thus: to preside in our Conferences; to travel through the Connection at large; to ordain bishops, elders, and deacons.

The following questions may deserve a serious thought: Can a man be found who would think his time and talents well employed in that station? If there is, would it be profitable and safe to employ or set one apart to fill such an office? Would the Form of Discipline recognize such a one as the General Superintendent of the Methodist Episcopal Church? Could the constitution recognize such a one as the President of the General Conference? Would he have a legal claim to a seat as a member of the General Conference?

THE DELEGATED GENERAL CONFERENCE CANNOT GIVE THE ANNUAL CONFERENCES THE AUTHORITY TO ELECT PRESIDING ELDERS.

The delegated General Conference have no authority to empower the Annual Conferences to elect Presiding Elders, and invest them with superintending authority; neither have they power to constitute Presiding Elders a committee to station the preachers.

The General Conference possess only a delegated power, which is to be exercised under certain limitations and restrictions; but this power is not transferable, for no representative has a right to transfer his delegated powers to another. Of course, a body composed of such members can have no such right; neither does the constitution authorize the General Conference to transfer their delegated power, or to make such a change in the form of government; therefore it is not within the limits of their delegated powers to effect such a revolution.

Even the body from whom the delegated Conference derived its existence and powers, never elected Presiding Elders, nor stationed the preachers; and there is room to doubt if it ever was the prerogative of the collective body so to do. That the preachers who composed it had a right, as individuals, to make their own appointments, and therefore had an undoubted right to authorize whom they pleased to make appointments for them, is admitted by all; and that the preachers did formally authorize the General Superintendents to choose the Presiding Elders and appoint the preachers for the several stations, will be denied by none; therefore the former General Conference cannot claim the power of appointing Presiding Elders and stationing the preachers, otherwise than the preachers who composed it had power to divest the General Superintendents of that power and confer it on another, or exercise it in their collective capacity, if they had been so minded. But this they have never done. That they did not, and intended that it should not be done, will appear from the following circumstance:

When the report of the Committee which was appointed

to draw up a constitution was before the General Conference, a member moved the postponement of that subject for the express purpose of bringing in a motion to authorize the Annual Conferences to elect the Presiding Elders. It was done; and that body, who had as much right to introduce the proposed alteration as they had to form the constitution, took up the proposition, amply discussed the subject, and *rejected* it.

The friends of the proposed alteration thought the constitution would put it out of the power of the delegated Conference to effect the desired change, and therefore proposed to make the alteration before the constitution was ratified. But the preachers preferred the old plan, and therefore rejected the motion. After twenty years' experience, and with the constitution fully before them, they refused to invest the Annual Conferences with power to elect Presiding Elders, and at the moment of constituting the delegated Conference, deliberately confirmed it, and continued it in the General Superintendents, with whom it had been intrusted from the beginning. The Presiding Elders never were elected by the preachers, either in their Annual or General Conference capacity, but were from their commencement chosen by the General Superintendents, with the consent of the preachers collectively; and this rule was ratified and confirmed by the same authority that constituted the delegated Conference. Now, as the Bishops do not derive this power from the delegated Conference, but from the preachers collectively, the delegated body can have no authority to take it from them. This can be effected by none but that body from whom they received it.

That the delegated Conference is authorized to elect and consecrate a Bishop, and that a Bishop so consecrated is invested with the powers of an overseer, is undoubtedly true; and that the Bishop is authorized to choose the Presiding Elders, is equally so. Now, a Presiding Elder so chosen is thereby clothed with power to oversee the temporal and spiritual business of his District. But it does not follow that the Bishop created the office, and therefore he may abolish it; or that he confers the power, and therefore he may withhold it. The case is fairly thus: The office of Presiding Elder was created, the duties of that office appointed, and power to discharge those duties conferred by the preachers collectively, which the Bishops have no authority to abolish. They may choose and change the officer, but cannot abrogate the office, nor its powers and rights.

In like manner the office of a Bishop was constituted, the duties of that office appointed, and power to discharge those duties conferred by the preachers collectively, over which the delegated Conference has no control. The General Conference is authorized to elect and consecrate a Bishop, and the man so consecrated is invested with the powers of a General Superintendent, and is amenable to that body for the administration, consequently *he* is under their control; but they have no authority to do away the *office*, or to divest the Bishop of power to perform the duties of his office; therefore it is not within the limits of the delegated Conference's power to effect such a change in the system of government.

The same conclusions will follow from a fair construction of the constitution.

Among the limitations and restrictions under which the delegated Conference must act, one says, "They shall not change or alter any part or rule of our government so as to do away Episcopacy, or destroy the plan of our itinerant General Superintendency."

To superintend is to oversee—to overlook or to take care

of others with authority; and superintendency implies superior care—the act of overseeing with authority.

The words, "itinerant General Superintendency," in the constitution, must mean the same thing which is called the "Duties of a Bishop," and pointed out in the 4th section of the Form of Discipline. For the Bishops are "elected by the suffrages of the General Conference to exercise the Episcopal office, and superintend the Methodist Episcopal Church in America." (P. 24.) And a part of the Bishop's duty is to preside in the Conference. But the constitution says one of the General Superintendents shall preside in the General Conference; therefore the Form of Discipline knows no General Superintendents except those who are elected and ordained Bishops according to the Form of Discipline, and thereby authorized and bound to discharge the duties of that office as pointed out in the 4th section of that book. But the authority of Superintendents consists principally in their power to choose Presiding Elders and station the preachers, because the responsibility of the governing preachers directly to the Bishops enables them to overrule the administration. But if the Bishops were deprived of the power of choosing Presiding Elders and stationing the preachers, or of appointing the governors of Districts and circuits, which is the same thing, and those officers were thereby released from their responsibility to the General Superintendents, they would no longer have power to superintend the Methodist Episcopal Church. Then the government by Bishops would be at an end, and our itinerant General Superintendency would be destroyed; therefore the constitution will not admit of such a change in the system of government.

Forasmuch then as the propositions under consideration imply a change in the constitution, and no such change can take place without the consent of the Annual Conferences, in conformity to the provision made for altering any article of the constitution, the Conference may propose the change to the ensuing Annual Conferences for their examination and consent; but farther they cannot go with safety.

LETTERS FROM BISHOP McKENDREE TO JOSHUA SOULE.

If the Resolutions of 1820, making the Presiding Elders elective, and constituting them a council to station the preachers, had not been suspended, Bishop McKendree would have protested and taken an appeal to the Annual Conferences, on the plea of their unconstitutionality, which might have led to serious complications and disagreements between the Conferences themselves and between the preachers and the Bishops, as well as between the Bishops themselves. Much disaffection, and perhaps a serious secession, might have resulted. But the suspension of those resolutions until the next General Conference gave a new turn to the subject, and enabled him to refer the question, in a modified form, to the Annual Conferences, by proposing to grant the wishes of those who voted for the resolutions, by a corresponding change in the constitution—thus avoiding a direct issue upon their constitutionality. The following brief extract from his letter to Bishop Soule fully explains his views and opinions on this matter at that crisis:

Dear Brother:—Bishop George left Raleigh on Thursday at twelve o'clock. Next morning I set out, and preached in Oxford the next Sabbath—forty miles from Raleigh. But the spring has been very wet and cold, which affected my health, and prevented our getting on sooner.

I wrote to you by Bishop George, and requested an answer to be directed to Dr. Wilkins; but I do not think the business (on which I am very desirous to have your judgment) was sufficiently laid before you, therefore I write this before your answer comes to hand.

I think you were informed that I intended to bring the Suspended Resolutions before the Annual Conferences, commencing with the next Ohio Conference. But it is my intention to invite the Annual Conferences to authorize the ensuing General Conference to adopt the Suspended Resolutions. That they are unconstitutional, and, if carried into effect independently of the Annual Conferences, will have a ruinous effect on our system of government, I have no doubt. Nor do I consider it an improvement of our itinerant system; but, as far as I see, it leaves power enough in the Superintendency to carry the rules into effect, if the business can be harmoniously conducted—and without harmony it will be ruined any way. Therefore the resolutions might be admitted, if constitutionally established.

Presuming on the correctness of this statement, I anticipate several important benefits from the intended course.

1. It will bring fully before us the principle on which the controversy turns, and prepare all for the decision. At the last General Conference, after contending for so much more, they professed to be satisfied with the Restrictive Resolutions. If this was the result of conviction, they will be pleased to have their wishes constitutionally established; but should they object to it in this form, all may apprehend danger.

2. It may prevent much evil. When men pass a certain

line, they stand committed, and frequently must go through, however painful and hazardous the consequences. If the resolutions are not for the better, they may be the best that many can bear, and therefore save us from worse things.

3. It will ratify and permanently establish our constitution, and thereby effectually guard against farther encroachments on the Episcopacy, and effectually secure the rights of our preachers and members.

The suspension of the resolutions enables me to take this course; otherwise, it must have been an appeal on their constitutionality. The possibility of conducting this dangerous contention so as to prevent ruinous consequences, and restore peace without making a greater sacrifice, inclines me to think the affair was providentially directed.

Respects to Sister Soule. Yours in love,

W. McKendree.

Dumfries, Virginia, April 17, 1821.

The following letter is a rejoinder to Joshua Soule's reply to the foregoing, and shows that the reply suggested serious objections and apprehensions as to the fate or consequences of the Address of the Bishops to the Annual Conferences on the Suspended Resolutions. They doubtless harmonized as to their views of the character of those resolutions, but we infer from this letter that something in the Bishop's "course" on the question was met by objections—perhaps upon the ground of policy, or as likely to subject him to unpleasant collision with the ardent friends of the resolutions, who denied their unconstitutionality.

But the pure-hearted and far-seeing old Bishop bravely pursued his course, and saved the Church from a measure which must have resulted disastrously to the effectiveness of her Episcopacy and itinerancy, if it had not been prevented.

Dear Brother:—Two days ago I came to Baltimore, and received your letter. The course to which you oppose such weighty considerations proceeds upon a supposition that a ruinous change will take place, if something be not done to prevent it—that probably this is the most favorable opportunity I may ever have. I have no expectation of satisfying the dissatisfied; but if it might save what I esteem such a blessing to mankind, the end will be fully answered.

To induce the Conferences to comply with the request, it should be laid before them so as to preclude contention, and at the same time show the distinctive tendency of the measures pursued, with the propriety and utility of the request. It is presumed the friends of the old system will see and approve. This will change the face of things. All will see that the strongest opponents of the revolution are disposed to accommodate the dissatisfied, as far as they can in accordance with our system of government and the rights of its members. That it will meet with disapprobation, is not doubted; but opposition to it will meet with considerable difficulties. To oppose receiving what they have been so warmly contending for, when offered in a harmonious and constitutional way, would show a design upon the government itself. It is supposed that it will at least bring the subject to issue unmasked, and set it for trial on the principles of our system and our rights. Several Conferences having tacitly decided the change to be unconstitutional, will be a powerful barrier to its passage. But if this cannot prevent its going into effect independently of the Annual Conferences, it will certainly pass if no such measures shall be taken. In that case, we shall have the satisfaction of having done what we could. If it should succeed, the public mind which has rested on the constitutional security of their rights, will more securely and confidently rest on their system.

I shall be in this neighborhood about two weeks. Let me hear from you. I should be glad to know the worst of what I may have to encounter—should be extremely glad to consult you on the draft of a communication that now lies by me. My physician advises me not to visit you this spring. I believe his advice is good, and therefore decline the visit.

I shall wait patiently for information after your Conference, but should be glad to get your strictures on the first part of this letter immediately, if practicable. As yet it is known by two only, and they are at a distance. I am inclined to consult one or two in this quarter.

I expect to send on an important communication from Colonel McKinney on the subject of Indian affairs, directed to the New York Conference. It was my intention to send a letter of direction, and commit the management of that business to you. For these purposes you must attend the New York Conference, if possible.

Yours most respectfully, WM. MCKENDREE.

Dr. Wilkins's, May 12, 1821.

This letter shows the great anxiety of the Bishop as to the action of the Annual Conferences upon his favorite measure, referred to in the two preceding letters, and that, so far as it had been tried, the result had vindicated his wisdom, as the sequel did most conclusively. It also exhibits his indomitable spirit in enduring the hardships and perils of attending the Conferences, when borne down with age and infirmities. Surely his moral heroism and self-sacrificing labors prove him a worthy successor of the confessors and martyrs, who "counted not their lives dear to them." Allusion is made to the transfer of Mr. Soule from the New York to the Baltimore Conference, which occurred shortly afterward.

Dear Friend:—After considerable delay, in order to give the fullest account of my progress under divine protection, I acknowledge the reception of yours of October 17. Your views of my course, and the information on the state of that subject in the North, both comforted and encouraged me. And indeed such aid was highly necessary; for I was very much oppressed with cares and fears, and had to stand alone. Upon discovering what I was about, my colleagues dictated and urged a very effeminate course, which, as I told them, would defeat their own purposes. Of this I think Bishop Roberts is now pretty well satisfied. In the Ohio Conference, one came out in direct opposition to the validity of the constitution, but found no supporter. Mr. Ruter said handsome things in its favor. The younger man was run down. In that and the Kentucky Conference, the existing plan was warmly contended for—the Suspended Resolutions barely admitted.

I did not write to the Missouri Conference, but suffered Bishop Roberts to manage the Address as he pleased. He thinks it would have passed if I had been there. With difficulty he prevailed upon them to lay it over to the next Conference. The Tennessee Conference took up the subject, and without opposition pronounced the Suspended Resolutions an infringement of the constitution, (as did the other Conference that acted on the subject,) and seemed as ready to confirm a second resolution, to which the Bishop objected, saying they might as well do nothing, and received for answer, "We intend to do nothing more than to prevent the resolution from being carried into effect." One interfered, and the subject was laid over, and never concluded until the last day of the Conference. Some of the principal men assured the Conference that they were sincere in what they said on the subject at other times, and that they could now as sincerely vote for its passage. They seemed to be of one mind in their movements, and voted for its adoption on constitutional principles. From what passed, I apprehend the following considerations influenced their minds:

1. If the passage of those resolutions would prevent a division, and harmonize the body, it would be bad policy to prevent their being carried into effect.

2. This course will not compel the General Conference to make the change, but authorize it as the constitution directs, if in its judgment the change should be thought necessary.

3. As Bishop Roberts decided that the representatives, when chosen, would be subject to their instructions, and at full liberty to act according to their best judgment, they thought it would be the most effectual way to prevent carrying the resolutions into effect by a bare majority, in opposition to the constitution, and put an end to the controversy, by establishing and confirming the constitution. A new scene is opening: a little time may show us the way more clearly.

I am strangely preserved, and still know not for what, except to make more thorough preparation for my passage to a better world. I never sustained my relation to the Church with so little encouragement and comfort as at present.

The help afforded was not sufficient for me to bear the burden of managing a carriage through the western country; I therefore left it in Tennessee, resolved to come on horseback, if able—if not, to winter in the West. I bore the toils of more than one hundred miles, to the Tennessee Conference, and from this took courage and came on. I have been graciously supported on the journey through the mountains, and wonderfully preserved from the effect of lying in the woods, traveling nearly thirty miles a day through tremendous rains for three days together, and crossing deep and dangerous streams, where the water ran over several of the horses' backs, but where none were injured. All arrived safe. The horses are afflicted, but the men are in health. O that I could praise God as I ought to do!

At the late Conference, I conversed with the Bishop on your transfer, as intimated, and send the inclosed, that you may appear officially if I should not be there. It is presumed you may wish to attend the New York Conference, to which I have no objection—however, in this you are at liberty. If you move at once, bring a recommendation from your charge.

I have many things to say when we meet.

W. McKendree.

Clark county, Georgia, November 28, 1821.

LETTERS OF BISHOP McKENDREE AND BISHOP GEORGE.

FROM the following letters which passed between Bishops McKendree and George, it appears that Bishop McKendree read his Address to the General Conference of 1820 to his colleagues before he presented it to the Conference, and that while Bishop George approved it, he subsequently favored the resolutions making the Presiding Elders elective according to the compromise plan which was afterward reconsidered and suspended through the influence of Bishop McKendree and the Bishop elect, Joshua Soule. This change in Bishop George's course drew from Bishop McKendree a letter of remonstrance, and a reply. It is due to Bishops George and Roberts to say that the writer has reason to believe that neither of them was in favor of the Suspended Resolutions upon the ground of the intrinsic merits of the plan, but simply as a "*peace-measure,*" and did not at that time take the ground that it involved a constitutional question, as did the other two named above. We hold that Bishops McKendree and Soule were correct, and it is highly probable that before their death the other two agreed with them, both as to the inexpediency and illegality of the measure.

Baltimore, May 19, 1820.

DEAR BISHOP:—Previous to the commencement of the General Conference, at your request I submitted my Address, which you examined and approved, and proposed that it should be changed from a single to a joint Address, and for yourself and Brother Roberts to sign it with me, and have but one, to which I had no objection.

I understood that you professed to be more than ever confirmed in the propriety of the government; but Bishop Roberts's opinion, known to us, prevented him from coming into the measure proposed by yourself; nor did I consider him at all to blame. To obviate the inconvenience, I proposed, as my Address professed to be deficient, and referred to you to supply that deficiency, that you and Bishop Roberts should prepare a joint Address for that purpose, that the two might present to the Conference a complete view of the work. To this proposal I think Bishop Roberts consented, and thought with myself that it might be done with propriety; but you rejected it, because, as I understand, you declared in favor of the sentiments contained in my Address, and supposed that joining with Bishop Roberts would expose you to censure.

Notwithstanding all this, I heard with surprise some time after that you were pursuing measures which were calculated to produce a conviction that you were friendly to an alteration of our government, inviting a private meeting of individuals to confer on a proposition calculated to affect the government, and in other ways using your influence to produce a radical change in our system, which from your profession had an additional claim on your patronage. These things, connected with some others not very dissimilar in appearance, induce me to request an explanation, that I may be delivered from the disagreeable impressions made on my mind by these circumstances.

Yours respectfully, W. McKENDREE.

BISHOP GEORGE'S REPLY.

Baltimore, May 19, 1820.

DEAR BISHOP:—Having attentively examined your communication, my intention is to answer in the integrity of my heart. And first, you think I avowed an opinion in favor of your Address. To this opinion I do without any kind of hesitation agree. If you ask for an explanation of my subsequent conduct, in agreeing to or in any way aiding the compromise that now forms the rules or resolutions by which the government is to be administered, my answer is plainly this: In your Address you say that an effective General Superintendency is essentially necessary to our itinerant preaching of the gospel. To this I do sincerely agree; but you may distinctly understand me when I say, that if the resolutions or rules passed by this General Conference affect the springs of that Superintendency so as to enfeeble its operations, I have not sagacity to comprehend it. On this my mind rests with tranquillity, believing that I have acted up to my judgment, and under the influence of my clearest convictions. Had the resolutions given the power to the Annual Conferences to elect at pleasure, or nominate indefinitely, to this mode of obtaining Presiding Elders, my opinion would have been that such a mode of proceeding would have been an unconstitutional transfer of power. But when the Bishop has the right of nomination, and the Annual Conferences the right to sanction that nomination, I cannot comprehend any radical change in the government. As to my joining Brother Roberts in an Address purporting that my views were in unison with his, (if his are the same they were at the last General Conference, and I know of no change,) viz., that Annual Conferences should elect their Presiding Elders, I could not in conscience do any such a thing. But again: the making out an Address when I considered the subject entirely and completely before the General Conference, would, in my estimation, have been superfluous. I close my remarks on this part of the subject by saying, what I have done, less or more, has been with a sincere desire to close the controversy, and promote peace, harmony, order, and usefulness among us as fellow-laborers in the vineyard of the Lord. If I have erred, as soon as I am convinced I hope my gracious Lord will enable me to make suitable concessions. Permit me to say that I have held your friendship in high estimation: my intention at present is never to do any thing intentionally to forfeit either your confidence or friendship. I still hope you will tell me of my faults, personally or by letter; and when and where I can amend my doings, I shall most certainly do so. Pray for me.

ENOCH GEORGE.

DONATIONS.

The following letter from Dr. Emory to the Bishop, illustrates the high and merited confidence universally reposed in his character as a man of integrity and trustworthiness in every thing. It moreover shows the honorable conduct of the lady, who, although not legally bound to carry out her deceased husband's bequest, yet agrees to do so, provided the Bishop will accept and appropriate the money. Dr. Emory was Assistant Agent of the Book Concern at the time.

DR. EMORY TO BISHOP M'KENDREE.

Murfreesboro, N. C., Jan. 17, 1828.

Reverend and Dear Sir:—Dr. Wm. J. Waller, of this station, informs me that a lady of Virginia, near Suffolk, has in her hands one thousand dollars, which she wishes to present to the Methodist Episcopal Church through you. This information Dr. Waller received from the Rev. O. Bernard, who traveled the circuit within which the lady lives, and received the information directly from the lady herself. The circumstances, as I learn them, are, that her husband, now dead, devised a certain tract of land for the use of the Methodist Episcopal Church, which, either by some informality or inattention, was never received by us. For this land the lady (his widow) has realized the above sum, which she wishes to appropriate agreeably to what she knows to have been her husband's wish. I understand that it is her desire to pay it to you personally, and to place it at your disposal. The particular object of this communication is to inquire if you think it probable that you will visit Virginia within any short period; and if not, whether you would feel free, under the circumstances, to address a letter to the lady, suggesting the propriety of paying it to any other person. Should you think proper to do so, as I calculate to attend the Virginia Conference at Raleigh, North Carolina, I would endeavor to see the lady on my return, and present your letter. It is believed that she would, in all probability, be governed by your advice.

I sent you by mail from New York a copy of the "Defense of our Fathers," etc., which I hope you received.

I am on my way to the South Carolina and Virginia Conferences, and collecting, etc., on the route.

With the best wishes for your health and happiness, I am very respectfully and affectionately yours,

J. EMORY.

MRS. WESSON'S DONATION OF ONE THOUSAND DOLLARS.

If casting two mites into the treasury of the Lord, by a poor Jewish widow, was deemed an act worthy of divine commendation and perpetual remembrance, may we not chronicle the gift of a thousand dollars from a Gentile widow for the same end? As to the pecuniary condition of the donor, we know nothing. All we can say is, that this Christian lady determined to be the almoner of her own bounty while living, and selected

Bishop McKendree as the distributer of her money, thus evincing her confidence in his wisdom and integrity. When this money was received, and how applied, we know not. The probability is that this benevolent lady had the pleasure of knowing that her donation had been faithfully and usefully applied, and that before she died her "mercy was twice blest."

What a pity it is that so few imitate her example, and thus escape the law's delay, with all the expenses and occasional wrangles attending testamentary bequests for charitable and religious purposes!

April 11, 1828.

REVEREND AND DEAR SIR:—Sister Elvira Wesson, who resides in the neighborhood of Moring's Meeting-house, in the county of Surry, and State of Virginia, desired me to say to you that she wished to make a donation of one thousand dollars to the Methodist Episcopal Church; and that it might take its destination, she now wishes, in her lifetime, to place the money in the hands of the senior Bishop, with whom some forty years past she had an acquaintance. It is with pleasure I make this communication, as I feel confident it will be productive of good to that cause which you have so efficiently labored to spread, and which, for nearly forty years, have been my source of comfort. If you can come on, I shall be pleased to see you at my house; and by addressing me by mail to Surry Courthouse, I will make an appointment for you to preach at Moring's. Please to apprise me whether you can come on shortly or not; and if not, whether another Bishop cannot come. Yours, in the bonds of the gospel of Christ,

JOHN COCKES.

FROM BISHOP McKENDREE TO BISHOPS GEORGE AND HEDDING.

New York, May 16, 1826.

DEAR BISHOPS:—I received your joint communication addressed to me, bearing date the 12th inst. Why Bishop Soule, who is as deeply interested and as officially concerned in its contents as either of us, should be unnoticed, may appear somewhat extraordinary; but it is hoped that it was not designed to treat him disrespectfully in his official character.

Your letter contains an inquiry concerning several important points relative to our official interviews in Philadelphia, and as it is presumed that my reply is desired as a ground of your justification, I am willing to answer according to the best of my recollection.

The facts embraced in your communication are substantially correct, but are so associated with other facts and circumstances as to require them to be noticed in this connection. Having been disappointed in not meeting the Bishops in Baltimore on the 8th of March, as had been agreed on by a majority of them, I proceeded on, attended by Bishop Soule, to meet you in Philadelphia.

I arrived on the 12th of April, and the next morning addressed a note to Bishop George, requesting an interview as soon as practicable, and proposing to wait on him at such time and place as might suit his convenience. In the afternoon you waited on me, and found Bishop Soule at my room.

Bishop George appeared to be in a great hurry on account of the press of business. You were readily informed of the arrangement which had been made for the meeting in Baltimore, above alluded to, and that in consequence of its failure we had come on to see and consult with you on subjects of high interest to the Church. In consideration of the hurry of Bishop George, three points out of many were proposed, viz.: The appointment of a minister to the British Conference, the business of the Canada Conference in relation to that appointment, and a change of the effective Superintendents in order for each to visit all the Annual Conferences before the ensuing General Conference.

Bishop George gave it as his opinion that the resolution of the General Conference in reference to the appointment of a minister to England was only advisory, and left it discretionary with the Superintendents, and that the business was not of sufficient importance to justify the expense.

I did nominate William Capers as our representative to the British Conference, and you did object to him, alleging that he was a slave-holder. Bishop George did nominate Wilbur Fisk, and Ezekiel Cooper was named with expressions of strong doubt whether he could or would go in case he was appointed, in consequence of which I did not consider Brother Cooper as officially nominated. I think no objection was made to the character of either of these brethren.

The conversation then turned on the Canada business, and in about three-quarters of an hour from the time we met, Bishop George observed, in substance, that the pressure of business rendered it necessary for him to retire; that you would consider the subject; and both of you took leave of us.

I heard nothing more from you on this subject until the 17th, when a note was handed me by Bishop Hedding from Bishop George in the Conference-room, inquiring if you could have an interview with me in my room the next morning at six o'clock. My answer was, "Yes." The note was handed to Bishop Soule, approved, and returned, and we met accordingly at six o'clock on the morning of the 18th. After noting his want of time on account of the pressing business, Bishop George introduced the subject of the appointment of a delegate, by observing that he supposed that Bishop Soule and myself had not changed our minds, and that you were of the same opinion as before expressed. Bishop George then gave it as his judgment that it was best to send no representative, and that a letter to the British Conference would answer all the purposes, and save expense. Bishop Hedding was of opinion that the resolution of the General Conference required the appointment of a delegate, but thought it better to send none than to send one who was in possession of slaves.

To these decisions I believe no reply was made by either Bishop Soule or myself. Here I supposed the appointment of a delegate failed—a negative being fixed on it. After some conversation on the proposed change of the effective Superintendents, this interview, which continued about one hour, was closed, upon which Bishop Soule concluded to return to Baltimore.

On the 20th I received your note in answer to mine of the 19th, in which, contrary to my expectation, you introduced the subject of a delegate again, and say that you "should be glad to meet me and Bishop Soule as soon as your business would admit, and see if we could fix on some other man in whom we could all be agreed."

From this intimation, connected with the manner in which the way to our official interview was to be opened, in conformity to your convenience, it was reasonable for me to expect that I should have been informed when "your business would admit" of such a meeting; but the Conference closed on the morning of the 23d, and Bishop George left the city without speaking to me, and from neither of you did I receive the slightest information on the subject of the meeting.

As to writing to the British Conference to apologize for not sending a delegate, as you suggest, I do not see how this would remedy the evil; nor am I convinced that we are authorized to change the course directed. Our responsibility is not to the British Conference, but to our General Conference. To that body we must account, and they must answer to the British Conference as one of the contracting parties.

In conclusion, I still believe that the resolution of the General Conference rendered it obligatory upon the Superintendents to send a minister to England. I have labored to discharge this obligation to the best of my ability, but it has been defeated by the negative which has been fixed upon the appointment. Under these considerations, connected with the late period of time, I judge it most prudent for me to decline any farther agency in the case, not with a design to prevent the appointment, but for you to manage the business as you may think best.

Yours very respectfully, W. McKendree.

LETTER FROM BISHOP McKENDREE TO BISHOP ROBERTS.

THE reader will recollect that Bishop McKendree suffered a dangerous attack of vertigo—or, as he called it, apoplexy—while traveling on horseback from Tennessee to the Mississippi Conference, in the fall preceding the date of this letter, and that he was unable to leave that section of country until the following spring. In the meantime, the unfortunate condition of our Church in New Orleans attracted his attention, and deeply excited his Christian sympathies. We were without a Church, lot, or edifice, and it became doubtful whether the Legislature—composed largely of Roman Catholics and others not disposed to favor Methodism—would grant a legal charter of incorporation for our Church-property conformable to our usual deed.

The Brother Moore named in this letter we suppose to have been the Rev. Mark Moore, who, it seems, was then in the city as a missionary. He was a man of unusual talents and unimpeachable reputation; and although he is blamed for consenting to such a change in the deed, which he was trying to get recognized by the Legislature, as would secure its acceptance and passage, yet his motives are above suspicion. He erred, it is probable, but his design was good.

During many years Methodism labored under great discouragement in New Orleans, scarcely having "a local habitation or a name." Indeed, long subsequent to this date, notwithstanding many of our best and most gifted ministers in that region were stationed there, the cause languished, and was scarcely kept alive. This is the first year New Orleans appears upon the Minutes as a station —Mark Moore its *missionary*. The laborious and faithful ministers who have more recently labored there, have placed our Church, by the divine blessing, in higher position. May we not confidently trust that henceforth it is to wield an increasingly evangelical influence upon the destiny of the city?

Midway, Wilkinson county, Miss., Feb. 8, 1819.

DEAR BROTHER:—I wrote to you from this neighborhood about three weeks ago, which was my first attempt to write since I was taken ill. In that letter I gave a full account of myself, the Conferences, and the manuscript Minutes. It also contained suspicions of approaching difficulties at New Orleans, and was directed to the care of Brother Hoffman, Alexandria. My fears for our cause in New Orleans were but too well founded. I have lately received a letter from S. T. Anderson, of that place, from which the following extracts are made. With respect to the meeting-house, he says:

"When we shall attempt a subscription, as yet remains uncertain, and that uncertainty can give way only with the pressure for money, which is too heavy here to render such a measure expedient.

"We have handed in our petition to the Legislature for an act of incorporation. The bill to be presented does not please all of us. At a meeting at Brother Moore's, I was appointed to make the draft, the principal provisions of which were these:

"Vesting all the property of every kind, and the ministration thereof, in the hands of the trustees, and giving them power to choose their own officers out of their own body.

"Two absolute negatives by the eldest preacher stationed in the city by authority of the Superintendents over such elections, and a disqualification for six months after of any person so rejected.

"An acknowledgment of the authority of the Conference, or general Church, so long as Superintendents are at the head of it.

"At our counting-room this draft received the approbation of two or three members; but as it went the rounds, it appeared necessary to call a general meeting upon it, which Brother Moore did accordingly. I was not present at it. But then the two clauses recognizing the authority of the Church *as now governed*, and that of the *Superintendents in stationing the preachers*, were both stricken out at Brother Moore's instance, with some other trifling amendments. The bill thus amended was ordered to be copied and handed to our friends in the Legislature, together with our petition. These changes were not agreeable to some of us, but acquiesced in for the sake of peace, notwithstanding Brother Moore is apprehensive we shall not receive the moneys raised for us in the Mississippi Conference."

At the same time Brother Winans received the original draft, with the erasures and amendments inclosed in a letter from Brother Moore. From a former conversation with Brother Moore on the subject, and the face of the letter, Brother Winans thought this course was taken contrary to Brother Moore's judgment or desire. You may guess at the surprise consequent upon comparing Brother Anderson's letter with Brother Moore's.

The draft presented to the Legislature, which is in my possession, precludes every doubt from my mind of their intention to establish themselves upon congregational principles, independent of our form of government; and for this purpose, it would seem, they pushed forward subscriptions without our body to secure all they could from abroad before their intention was known.

Brother Moore has communicated nothing to me on this subject. I have written to Brother Anderson, and informed him that I will not assist them either directly or indirectly to build a house on that plan; that if they should carry their design into effect independent of us, I would neither receive it as a Methodist meeting-house, nor appoint preachers to it; that the object to which we invited the people's liberality, was a Methodist meeting-house in New Orleans, and that moneys thus obtained could not with propriety be applied to such a house as they intend to build. I hope you are of the same mind, and will pursue the same course.

This in substance Brother Winans communicated to Brother Moore three weeks ago by my direction. Since we received the above-mentioned letters, he has addressed him in opposition to their plan, in a very appropriate and conclusive manner.

Brother John Richardson has done the same.

Brother Moore wrote about the time of Conference, which letter I sent on to you. He has written one letter to me since, but said nothing of his design to serve the Connection, or of the state of New Orleans, except the prospect of his doing much good there. Hence this Conference could do but little on that subject—it stands as a station in the District without a preacher.

S. Parker and J. Lane (who have not come to their charges yet) are appointed to receive and appropriate the moneys collected for building in New Orleans. I would go to the place immediately and arrest their proceedings were I able, but do not believe I could support under the burden; therefore have to submit all to divine interference and your management. It remains for you to determine whether Brother Moore is to continue in that station, or another to be sent to take the charge. I should certainly commit it to another if I could, but have no man at my disposal.

You know how our kind friends in Baltimore and elsewhere have been imposed on to build such houses in other places. I hope you will not suffer it in this case.

My late affliction has effected me so seriously that I recover strength but slowly, and apprehend my return to effective service is not to be expected shortly, if it should ever come to pass; but this does not afflict me at all. I think I am perfectly resigned to my lot, and am willing to see the work in which I have been so long engaged, pass to my colleagues. May the Lord be with you, prepare you for usefulness, direct you through difficulties, and support you under sufferings!

I am now at Brother Winans's. They are well; so are the people in general through the neighborhood. He desires me to present his respects to you.

The preachers and people are happily united in this quarter, but our gratitude and religion do not seem to be in proportion to our abundant prosperity.

Yours affectionately, W. McKendree.

METHODIST TRACT SOCIETY.

In 1819, Joshua Soule and Thomas Mason were the Book Agents of the Methodist Episcopal Church, in New York, and the latter was the Corresponding Secretary of the Methodist Tract Society, recently organized. This note is the official notification of the Bishop's election as President of the Society. He was President also of the Missionary, the Bible, and Sunday-school Societies. He was the well-known, ardent friend of every Christian and benevolent enterprise.

New York, August 2, 1819.

Reverend and Dear Sir:—At the last annual meeting of the New York Methodist Tract Society, it was the pleasure of that Society to elect you for their President; (a brother having previously made you a member by the payment of the sum required by the constitution;) and at a subsequent meeting of the Board of Managers, it was made my duty to address you, and make you acquainted with the same.

We do not suppose, reverend sir, by electing you to the presidency of our Society, that we have added any thing to that distinguished honor which you already possess in the Church of God, but we desire your patronage in favor of our infant institution, and request your influence to promote the establishment of auxiliary societies in the different sections of our Church which you may pass through in your travels. I am also instructed by the Board to desire you to communicate any instruction which you may deem proper for us, and to forward any tract which you may be pleased yourself to write, or to select for publication; as also to suggest proper subjects for tracts.

In company with this letter, I send you a few copies of our Second Annual Report, by which you will be enabled to learn something of what we have been doing in this business.

That God may abundantly bless you, and spare you yet many years for the benefit of his Church, is the fervent prayer of your affectionate son in the gospel,

THOMAS MASON,
Cor. Sec. N. Y. M. T. S.

REV. BISHOP McKENDREE.

LETTER FROM ROBERT PAINE TO BISHOP McKENDREE.

In looking over the papers of the Bishop, the author found, to his surprise, the letter below, written by him in 1823, and carefully labeled and preserved; and but for the fact that it serves to illustrate the character of his venerable and beloved friend, it would not now be made public.

During several interviews with the Bishop, he had evinced great solicitude to obtain missionaries for the Indian tribes, especially for the Cherokees, the Chickasaws, and Choctaws. At last he asked me if I felt willing to place myself in his hands for that work. I replied that I would try to do any ministerial work to which he might assign me; but in view of the state of my health, which had not fully recovered from a long and dangerous attack during that Conference-year, he hesitated after mature reflection, and proposed that I should accompany him on his tour to the East, and possibly be transferred to some of the Atlantic Conferences. To this I made no objection, and we were to think of it, and determine when he should be about to start. My health failing to improve, physicians and friends urgently dissuaded me from the labor and exposure incident to the tour; and having just published a large and expensive pamphlet in vindication of our doctrines, and in reply to a very insidious attack by an eminent Hopkinsian minister, I found it necessary to see to it that the expense of its publication should be paid in advance, and consequently before I could be reïmbursed by its sale.

These facts were given to the Bishop as due to him and myself before he should decide, and then the result was with him. I did not add what I might have said truly, that my charge objected to my removal, and he finally yielded to their remonstrance and the above facts.

The next year I had the pleasure of accompanying him to Baltimore, as already narrated, where the General Conference of 1824 was held.

Franklin, January 27, 1823.

Dear Bishop:—Instead of going directly to my father's, as I intended to do when I parted from you, I have been detained here until now, partly by the badness of the roads and weather, partly with a desire to preach to my charge, but mainly by indisposition, caused by taking a severe cold; but if possible, I shall start on in a few days.

Since I saw and conversed with you, I have reflected maturely upon accompanying you immediately to the East; and from the delicate state of my health, my feebleness, and susceptibility of taking cold, together with the situation of my pecuniary affairs—of which I was not fully apprised when we conversed—I have concluded that it would be imprudent in me to leave this country immediately, at least without apprising you of these facts. I find, from the cold

I have taken, and from the fatigue and weakness which followed my attempt to preach on yesterday, that I am in a more delicate state of health than I was aware of, and not by any means so stout as I supposed. I also learn, from a conversation with Brother Hill, my pamphlet agent and steward, that my pecuniary matters demand immediate attention. In a letter to Brother Douglass, I have proposed that I will yet go with you, on condition that he will take my business into *his* hands and meet the demands against me; but I am aware of the propriety and force of his objections, and am convinced that my own attention and exertions are necessary. However, if you think that you will be better accommodated thereby, I shall feel it a privilege and a pleasure to accompany you. But if you can get along as well without me, Brother Wynns will certainly go with you as far as Knoxville, and even to Lynchburg, if you desire it; and by spring I will try to arrange my matters so as to be able to attend to my Red brethren, if Brothers Douglass and Dever adopt the contemplated plan. I shall glory in such an enterprise, and exert myself to the utmost of my little capacity toward the accomplishment of so laudable an end; but if Brother John Hersey can be procured, I should say he is the very man for it.

Be so good as to write to me at Murfreesboro, so that I may get the letter by the 1st of February. Brothers Wynns and Douglass will be there, and we will make our arrangements according to the information contained in your letter. May the great Head of the Church bless and preserve you unto eternal life! I am your son in the gospel,

ROBERT PAINE.

LETTERS FROM T. L. DOUGLASS TO BISHOP McKENDREE.

THE following letter from his intimate friend—his "Logan Douglass," whom he named to preach his funeral-sermon in his last hour—will show the condition and views of the Tennessee Conference. We omit the list of Appointments, as it can be found in the published Minutes, excepting the Cherokee Mission. From the number of men appointed to this work, it will be seen that the earnest and long-desired effort to Christianize the Indians was at last entered upon in earnest by the Tennessee Conference. The long-cherished wish of the good Bishop was now being fulfilled.

Mendenhall, December 7, 1827.

VERY DEAR BROTHER:—It has been several months since I received a line from you, and as I could not tell where a letter would find you, I have not written to you. The evening before I set off to Conference, I heard you had been in the neighborhood of Gallatin, and I was willing to indulge a hope that we should have your company, until I met with Bishop Soule, who informed me you would not be with us. He at the same time informed me you intended spending the winter among us. Several of our friends have asked me if you will not be at my house, and I take the privilege of telling them I expect you will. I should be glad you could drop me a few lines and say you will come, and the time when we may look for you. Our quarterly-meeting is to be in Franklin the 5th and 6th of January. We should be glad to see you then, and as much longer as you are willing to stay.

Our Conference was held in great peace, love, and harmony of sentiment. I think it was the happiest Conference I ever saw in the Western country, as to union and fellowship among the preachers. There were but few converts, but I think many good impressions were made among the people, and much good done in the establishment of Methodist doctrines. We admitted 12 preachers on trial, ordained 12 deacons and 7 elders, 7 located, 1 superannuated, (Richard Neeley,) and 76 appointed to the several stations.

The appointments to the Indian work are as follows:

CHEROKEE MISSION.

Wm. McMahon, Superintendent of Indian Missions.

Will's Valley, Greenberry Garrett.
Oostahnahla, Turtle Fields.
Echota, James J. Trott.
Oocthkellogee, Greenville T. Henderson.
Creek Path, John B. McFerrin.
Chatooga, Allen F. Scruggs.
Salakowa, Dickson C. McLeod.

The following brethren were elected delegates to the next General Conference: William McMahon, Thomas L. Douglass, Robert Paine, Joshua Boucher, John M. Holland, Finch P. Scruggs, John Page, James Gwin, and James McFerrin. Our next Conference is to be in Murfreesboro, December 4, 1828. There has been a little shaking among some of our preachers about the old Suspended Resolutions, but with one exception, perhaps, we are all nearly straight. We were determined to elect no man a delegate who was not an Old-hundred. We have seen and read the Address of members in Baltimore, and Dr. Bond's Appeal. I have been waiting and expecting that God would raise up some person to present things to public view in their proper light. Our Conference has taken a firm stand. Our delegation are sound, and the most of them *old men*, the fathers of the Church. The Holston Conference are also bringing in the old men, (Thomas Wilkerson.) I think if the Radicals boast of talent on their side—which I never thought was very graceful—they cannot lay claim to all the *age* and *experience.*

If you have A. McCaine's production, Emory's reply to him, or any other late work on our government, please to bring them with you when you come to see us.

I have been much afflicted since I saw you, but am in health at present, striving to serve my heavenly Master and get to heaven. Remember me in prayer. Frances wishes me to remember her to you, and joins me in wishing you a comfortable ride, and we shall both give you a cordial welcome under our roof.

As ever, very sincerely yours in Christ,

THO. L. DOUGLASS.

THIS letter marks an interesting epoch in our Church-history in the South-west. The fertile region west of the Tennessee River, extending to the Ohio and Mississippi Rivers, and including North Alabama and Mississippi, were about to be settled. An immense tide of immigrants were pouring into West Tennessee, and Mr. Douglass had been appointed to the charge of that work in connection with his proper District—the Nashville District. He made an exploring tour, and now urges the Bishop to send a Presiding Elder there. The suggestion was acted on, and our preachers soon occupied the whole region. The Methodists became the most numerous denomination in that whole country, and so continue to this day.

Mention is made in this letter of a young preacher who had recently died in Lebanon, Tennessee, in the full career of popular and useful ministerial labors. The name of Sterling Coleman Brown still carries a charm in the memory of the old Methodists in Tennessee. No young preacher among them had ever risen so rapidly to notoriety. He was the son of Lewis and Cassandra Brown, born in Brunswick county, Virginia, emigrated with his parents to Giles county, Tennessee, where he received a good English education, and some knowledge of the Latin and Greek classics. His parents were comparatively wealthy, and he had just begun the cultivation of his farm, when, at twenty-three years of age, he became converted under the ministry of Miles Harper. At once he began to exhort, hold prayer and class-meetings, and soon evinced a wonderful power to arouse and attract the multitude. In person he was tall, lithe, and finely formed, with sandy hair, large, bright blue eyes, a most expressive countenance, and a voice of peculiar pathos. His emotions were deep, his gestures emphatic, and he transfused his feelings into the hearts of his hearers. Crowds followed him, and converts by hundreds were the fruits of his labors. His career was as brief as it was brilliant. He fell in his third year. We had been schoolmates in boyhood; our families were intimately connected by marriage, his only sister being my step-mother, and his brother William being my brother-in-law; and, although he was several years my elder, yet we were much in each other's company, and our friendship was ardent. We were awakened to a sense of the necessity of religion about the same time—1817—confided our impressions to no one but to each other, and after a free and full confession of our feelings, amid the solitude and silence of the forest, where our Heavenly Father alone witnessed the scene, we deliberately shook hands to ratify our solemn pledge to each other and to our God, to begin at once to seek for pardon, and devote our lives to his service. On the next day—October 9th—we both professed conversion within five minutes of each other, I being by that much the elder Christian. *He kept his pledge.* We were licensed to preach, and joined the Tennessee Conference, at the same time. It was my mournful pleasure to wait upon him in his last illness, and witness the test of the dying hour in vindication of the genuineness of his piety. His parents were Methodists, and his mother was a lady of extraordinary intellect and piety. He was the elder brother of the Rev. H. H. Brown, and the cousin of Governor A. V. Brown, of Tennessee. By excessive labor and night exposure, he brought on a violent attack of illness, which, under the debility thus superinduced, soon ended his course of almost unparalleled usefulness and popularity. His last words to me were, "If I had a thousand lives, I would spend them all as an itinerant Methodist preacher. Farewell; I shall soon be past the portals of light."

Nashville District, Sept. 10, 1821.

DEAR BROTHER:—I wrote a few lines by Brother Maddin, who expects to attend the Kentucky Conference, informing you of his acceptable standing and usefulness the past year. I also wrote to you by Brother Corwine, in which I mentioned the subjects of the District Conference, and the situation of the Forked Deer country. I hope you will excuse me for troubling you again. The solicitude I feel for the prosperity of Zion is the only apology I have to offer. I have never communicated any intelligence to you, nor proposed any regulation for adoption, which I did not conscientiously believe to be for the benefit of the work of God; and with these feelings, I again wish to remind you of Forked Deer country. That section of our work calls for peculiar attention—the constant attention of a Presiding Elder. If there is a circuit formed on Sandy, as I expect there is, Beech River and Forked Deer Circuits will make three already formed. These ought at least to have one preacher on each of them, and two more ought to be sent as missionaries to form new circuits. The country is rapidly settling; numbers of our members are moving there from this District and from Carolina, and the Presbyterians who settled there apply to our preachers for preaching; and as they do not settle so as to form neighborhoods among themselves, we shall gather most of them who wish to enjoy religious privileges.

If Dover and Dickson Circuits can be attached to this Conference, then add Swan and Buffalo, and you will have seven circuits, which may be called Lower Tennessee District, or any other name you please to give it. Should there be any difficulty about any of the preachers from Kentucky Conference coming with Dover and Dickson, we shall be able in this Conference, I hope, to supply them. I hope to carry at least a dozen young preachers to Conference for admission into the traveling connection—some of our last year's converts.

Our beloved Sterling C. Brown has finished his work in this world—he fell a martyr to excessive labor. He died in Lebanon, at the house of Dr. Frazer, August 10th, with his confidence strong in God.

Our camp-meetings are going on—we have had about three hundred converts, and are looking for much greater times at the four remaining meetings.

I have had some sickness, the effect of fatigue. My leg remains very weak, particularly in the knee, which was considerably injured. I can walk tolerably well on level ground; when the ground is rough or broken, I get along with great difficulty; and riding much is very painful. My visit to Forked Deer was more than I ought to have attempted. I have not been able to visit either Caney Fork or Buffalo. I have had to serve them by proxy. Sometimes I think a little rest might be useful to me. Of this, however, I shall be able to judge better about the time of our Conference.

Praying that the Lord may abundantly bless and prosper his work under your care, I remain, as ever, yours in the Lord, THO. L. DOUGLASS.

LETTER FROM THE REV. IRA ELLIS TO BISHOP McKENDREE.

Ira Ellis was among our early and useful preachers in Virginia. In 1783 he was admitted on trial. In 1791 he had charge of a District, traveled many years, late in life located, and removed with his family to Kentucky some time after the date of this letter, and his remains repose there.

The following autographic letter was written in good style, and was neatly executed. It exhibits in its matter, its tone, and temper, a sensible mind, a loving and cheerful heart, and a strong attachment to his Church. The picture is morally beautiful—an aged and revered old preacher, surrounded by a pious and loving family, still at work for God, cheerfully and hopefully trusting his all to him!

Franklin Circuit, Pittsylvania C. H., Feb. 2, 1827.

Dear Brother:—For some time I have had thoughts of writing to you, but questioned whether the time you would spend in reading it would not be worth more than the letter; be that as it may, I have determined to say something, and should be glad it was in my power to inform you of any thing pleasing and profitable.

Through mercy I am generally able to keep up, but frequently subject to complaints and infirmities, to which most men are subject, especially in the decline of life. My memory fails me a good deal, especially about things of recent date, and all the powers of the mind are enfeebled. My strength also fails me—I can bear but little exercise without fatigue. I can scarcely sing at all; my voice is weak, and my teeth nearly all gone. My sphere of action is quite contracted, and I am very fond of home. My sight is still good, so that I can read the smallest print on a fair day without glasses. From these and such like things I try to learn a profitable lesson, and receive warning that my decaying tabernacle will shortly fall. O may I be found ready! In the midst of all, my dull heart is too backward, and I am too slow to believe and realize the precious promises. I still feel like trying to get safe out of the world, and would not exchange my hope and prospects for a world!

My wife keeps up, but is very feeble; her health, with her flesh and strength, appear to decline.

My children and their families are well as far as I know, and I have pleasure in them.

I still try to preach some, but prospects hereabouts are unpromising.

I have been begging (by subscription) money to build a Methodist meeting-house a few hundred yards from the court-house, but have at times been ready to give it up, but have at length determined to build. The house is let at $274—the hall, floor, doors, and window-shutters. This is a little more than the subscription. The house is to be twenty-four by thirty feet, framed, floors and weather-boarding dressed. Myself and son have undertaken it, and are bound to make good any deficiency. It is intended: 1. As a house for public worship. 2. A school-house. 3. To get a Sunday-school established there if we can. We hope the house will be fit for summer. I think if we had a Nolly, or some one like-minded, the ensuing year, who would make exertions for Sunday-schools, we might probably get one on foot.

I am sorry to learn that there are a number among both traveling and local preachers who wish to subvert parts of our Discipline, and introduce dangerous, and, I fear, destructive innovations in our Church. They ought at least to show us a better plan before we give up the present. If they cannot do this, would it not be best to advise all preachers and people who are dissatisfied with us, to go and do better—to let us alone, and only give us notice that they do not want us on our long-tried plan, and the traveling preachers will quietly withdraw, and go and serve those who want them. This was the mode pursued in 1793–4 between James River and Roanoke, and answered a very good purpose. They talk of "mutual rights," and if they would add, "mutual labors," it would do; but for local preachers to govern the traveling preachers, would be big with much evil. Who among them will go to Asia, to Africa, to the ends of the earth, and desire and seek nothing but God and souls, and unweariedly do and suffer among the heathens, and among the Indians, what many are now doing? This the traveling preachers are welcome to. I should be loth to be one that threw obstacles in their way; rather I would wish to be among those who would act as auxiliaries, and hold up rather than weaken their hands. I do not think, upon mature deliberation, that we have a great deal to fear. Their views, their motives, and their interests, will clash; and I have a better opinion of the judgment and piety of our members than to think they will barter the *traveling* for a *settled* ministry, especially when they will have to give *boot.* Let us trust God with his own cause, and he will take care of his people. If any traveling or local preacher is dissatisfied, there are the Baptists, the Presbyterians, the Episcopalians, etc., ready to receive them—let them go in peace; or if they can raise a Church of their own, be it so, only let them not rend the Church that has been their nursing mother from their infancy, and to which, under God, they are indebted for all they are or have as ministers.

Perhaps I have said enough—may be too much. I would hope the best.

I hope God will preside in the Conference, that harmony may prevail, and the stations be of divine appointment.

I see many good accounts in the Advocate. I want to see and feel a revival here before I die.

When you are at leisure, let me hear from you. Pray for your old friend and fellow-laborer in the gospel of Christ, IRA ELLIS.

BISHOP McKENDREE'S REPLY TO BISHOP GEORGE'S STRICTURES UPON HIS VIEWS OF THE SUSPENDED RESOLUTIONS.

THIS letter was in answer to the criticisms of Bishop George upon Bishop McKendree's objections to the Suspended Resolutions, as unconstitutional. We have already had occasion to advert several times to a difference of opinion between these equally good and true men upon this subject — a difference no doubt honestly entertained by both, and which involved neither mutual affection nor confidence in each other's piety and integrity. We insert it that our preachers and people may fully comprehend the question. It was the question of the day; and although that day seems to have passed away, and that question received its quietus, yet the same old issues may return to disturb the Church again.

DEAR BISHOP:—Yours of January 30th was duly received, and its contents particularly attended to. Your remarks on responsibility, the improvement of our system of government, and the constitution, will be the subject of my observations.

I consider the responsibility of a General Superintendent in our Church, (Presiding Elder, or any other preacher in charge, as an officer,) and his being "responsible" for the acts and deeds of all the preachers under his care, as ideas so clearly distinct as almost to exclude the necessity of showing the difference; and I assure you, when I speak of the former, I do not embrace the latter. I cannot think that when you thoroughly examine my letter you will find these ideas are so connected. If they are, I acknowledge it is an error, and was never by me designed to be conveyed.

The case respecting Bishop Roberts, which you introduced, shall illustrate my view of this subject. If our rules were properly administered, you would have no ground to say, "If sins were legitimately imputed to Bishop Roberts, then all the blunders of four years may be imputed to him and myself." In the trial of that case, the Bishop, or some member of the Annual Conference, should have charged Brother P. with neglect of his duty as pointed out in the 7th answer to the 2d question, 5th section, on the duty of Presiding Elders. Then if, upon examination, he was found guilty and condemned, he must have given satisfaction, or been punished. But suppose the Conference had acquitted him, in defiance of rule and discipline; then let the Superintendent, by virtue of his controlling authority, remove him from office as Presiding Elder, and put some one in his place who would enforce the rules of the General Conference. But if the Bishop should, by encouragement or by connivance, suffer the authority of the General Conference to be disregarded, and the discipline of the Church to become a perfect nullity, in this way, let him be tried by the General Conference, and suitably punished—not for "G. P.'s sins," nor "for the acts and deeds of others," but for the neglect of his duty. In this way, my brother, I think that the "Bishops, the preachers, and people would keep out of difficulties, and such mischievous Presiding Elders would be otherwise employed."

That the Presiding Elders, as well as other preachers in charge, are amenable to the Annual Conferences, sufficiently appears from the fact of the examination of their characters before that body. I recollect no expression in the Suspended Resolutions, which you seem to think will answer this important purpose, that is more clearly expressive of their accountability to the Annual Conference than the present form of our discipline makes them.

But if, instead of this, your system of an "identified responsibility attached to every officer, and an identified tribunal at which all those officers are to answer for their administration," were established, there the business would end, unless the condemned officer, whether Presiding Elder or other officer, should be allowed an appeal to the General Conference, as in other cases of Episcopal decision. If such appeal could not be made, of course the General Conference would lose their legal control of the administration. But this plan, as I understand it, would involve a pretty general revolution in our system.

I have no objection to the *improvement* of our system of government; only let it be done consistently with its fundamental principles, and then I submit. Nor do I consider it difficult to obtain improvements according to our system. On this sentiment, if the Lord permit, I may give as ample proof as the most vociferous among us have done; and I pray for grace to do it in a way more becoming the religion we profess, and the relation we bear to each other, than that which you and I have seen exhibited, to the grief of our souls.

In order, my dear brother, to compare ideas, if happily we might harmonize in our great work, I laid my views of our constitution and system of government before you, and waited in expectation of such corrections as might tend to compose existing difficulties. But while you tell me of the ruinous effects of "rigorous constructions, ambiguous premises, confusion in conclusions," etc., you neither point out error in my construction nor present me with one more favorable to our situation. Thus I have hitherto been left. Then by some I have been set up as a mark to be shot at—as loving unbounded power, dividing the Church, etc.—and all this for not seeing what none will show me, or for not submitting to their opinions without due consideration; yet the javelins and arrows of death, whether from seen or unseen agents, go on this side and that side, or may return from whence they came, for any thing they have to do with me. The Lord is Judge, and the righteous Judge will give righteous jugdment.

However, if you did not assist me in the expected constructions, you have favored me with an illustration which I presume you intended should answer all the purposes. In reference to my remarks on the Suspended Resolutions, which I think bear a close connection with the foregoing view of the system of government, you say, "I am really astonished at the idea of yourself and others, in saying the principle is ceded, and the constitution may be ruined. This to me is *mystery* all over. It appears to me there would be just as much propriety in saying that because a man had obtained liberty to take a twig or a graft from his neighbor's tree, he then, by virtue of that liberty or grant, had a right to cut down the tree and take the stock, roots, branches, and all away. Ambiguity in our principles leads to ambiguity in our conclusions; and if there is not mysterious ambiguity in saying a tree is ruined because it is pruned, and one or two superfluous limbs taken away, I am uncommonly bewildered," etc. I am prepared to submit my opinion, as it relates to the utility of the change, to the voice of the General Conference. Only show me that the delegated General Conference were as fully authorized to make the change as the man in your figure was to take a graft from his neighbor's tree, and my objections immediately cease. But, my brother, of whom was this liberty obtained? Of the preachers collectively? or of the Superintendents? or of the majority of their own body? It is presumed that liberty to make this change was neither "obtained" nor asked of their constituents; and I do not consider the Superintendents invested with authority to grant such "liberty." The liberty therefore must be granted by the delegated Conference. But this I must consider an assumption of power.*

You say, "The power ceded in the resolution as an abstract principle is, comparatively speaking, almost a nonentity." By considering the power abstractly, which you admit is ceded in the resolution, you seem to exclude every idea but that of its lessening the power of the Superintendents. But it is evident that the very same act equally respects that power and the form of discipline by which that power is conferred and supported — that it necessarily effects one of the restrictions on the powers of the delegated Conference; and this is what I emphatically call the *principle.* Therefore, it cannot be fairly reduced to your *abstract principle* of reasoning. In this way you reduce a subject of the utmost importance, in *my estimation,* to "almost a nonentity." Were I to disunite ideas so inseparably connected, and were you to say, "Mysterious ambiguity! mystery all over!" I really think I should stand corrected.

To me it still appears evident that the six restrictions on the powers of the delegated General Conference are equally binding on every class of restricted topics; that if the dele-

* This sentiment was confirmed by a considerable number who, from a disposition of accommodation, voted for the change, not so minutely examining its bearings, but who, upon more minute reflection, saw their error and voted for its suspension.

gated General Conference have a legitimate right to alter one, they may, in the exercise of that right, alter any or all of them, and so ruin the constitution *in toto*.

Were you, my brother, deliberately to reflect on the subject, as it respects the power of the General Conference, and how that power might affect our system of government, you might hesitate in saying, "I am really *astonished* at the idea of yourself and others, in saying the principle is ceded, and the constitution may be ruined: this to me is mystery all over"—and be able in some good degree to see "why it is that, after understanding each other so long, we should now sail abruptly to opposite points," and possibly admit that this tree ought not to be pruned until they have obtained liberty to do so.

I hope you will receive my assurance that if you should think any expression too hard, or of improper bearings, it is by no means designed; and that I intend no harm to the Church or to any individual—much less to *you*—on these subjects.

Yours affectionately, etc., W. McKendree.

Raleigh, February 27, 1821.

BISHOP McKENDREE'S PAPERS COMMITTED TO JOSHUA SOULE, DR. WILKINS, AND T. L. DOUGLASS.

It appears from the following letter, written—as we suppose—to the Rev. Thos. L. Douglass, that Bishop McKendree made provisional arrangement for such a use of his papers as may promote the cause of righteousness and truth, by leaving them to J. Soule, Dr. Wilkins, and T. L. Douglass, to be published at their discretion.

Dr. Wilkins's, May 5, 1823.

Dear Brother:—At my advanced age, accompanied with many infirmities, it becomes me to do all things with a more direct reference to the close of my pilgrimage than at a period when youth and strength afforded a prospect of a longer stay.

I am now ready to leave Baltimore to visit the Western frontiers, especially the Indian Mission. It may please the Lord to preserve me to visit the Atlantic States again, or to finish my course on the other side of the mountain. My business is *to be ready.*

In traveling through the United States, in that department of the work which has fallen to me, papers of various characters have accumulated upon my hands. I have found it impracticable to carry them with me, and have therefore deposited them in a trunk, which I leave with my old friend Dr. Wilkins. Considering it a possible case that events may transpire in my absence, in which access to those papers may be expedient, I think it improper for me to make them absolutely inaccessible. I therefore authorize you, jointly with my friends Dr. Wilkins and Joshua Soule, to examine those papers at your discretion, and to refer to them, if in your judgment it becomes necessary for the correction of error, or for the good of the Church; and in such a case, to make any use of them which you may think necessary. It is my desire that they may never be used, either before or after my death, for any other purpose than that of promoting the cause of truth and righteousness; and when and how this may be done, you will be most competent to judge.

Yours in love, W. McKendree.

LETTERS FROM JOSHUA SOULE TO BISHOP McKENDREE.

SUCH had been the state of Mr. Soule's health for some time that we have seen Bishop McKendree's anxiety for his transfer from New York to a more southern latitude. Asthma and rheumatism threatened his usefulness, if not his life. He came to Baltimore as a transfer in April, 1822, and at once entered earnestly upon his laborious duties, which were rather too onerous for his strength. Gradually, however, he recovered his health, and became a blessing to the city of Baltimore and to the Conference. He was at the time this letter was written a Bishop elect, having been elected in 1820, but had declined ordination in view of his opposition to the Suspended Resolutions. The "controversy" alluded to in this letter was about these resolutions. The Church in Baltimore and the Conference seemed to be resting on a volcano, which threatened the unity and safety of Methodism. Happily, Mr. Soule went there, and his influence was exerted with highly conservative effect. His old friend, Stephen George Roszel, had charge of the District.

Baltimore, Aug. 28, 1822.

DEAR BISHOP:—I have hitherto neglected to write to you, not knowing where to meet you; but assured that you would be at the Ohio Conference, I write to meet you there. Nothing very important has transpired in this city since you left here. It is believed that the state of the Society is somewhat improved, and many of the most substantial members are greatly encouraged in expectation of better days. But there is much to be done before the state of things can be considered really prosperous, and it requires *time* as well as *labor* to accomplish it.

Your letter, written to the Bishops while in New York, is in my possession. I found it, after you left the city, with other papers which you put into my hands for safe keeping—I shall preserve it, with all others, subject to your order.

I have heard very little relative to the subject of the controversy since I came hither. I have met many of the preachers in town and at two camp-meetings—have been received with great cordiality and apparent respect. Prudence seems to require that at *present* I should say but little. My sentiments are known, and I apprehend no man expects me to change them. I shall strive amid all circumstances to maintain that course of prudence, firmness, and dignity, on which I hope to *look back* with a consciousness of rectitude and satisfaction from every future period of my life. Having fixed *principles,* the intervention of casual circumstances cannot divert me from my course. Retraction must be the result of conviction, and that conviction must be that my *principles are wrong.*

Your friends here are generally in usual health. Old Father Wilkins has been very ill, and was not expected to survive; but he has so far recovered as to be able to visit his children and the house of God. In his sickness he appeared like an ancient patriarch, waiting with perfect resignation and triumph to see the salvation of God. Dear Sister Wilkins is still a patient, but great sufferer, under her old affliction. The rest of the family are well.

Dr. Baker has been very ill—life despaired of—but is now convalescent.

My health is a good deal as it has been for some years. I have been preaching three times a day on the Sabbath ever since you left us: this has for the two last Sabbaths affected my breast considerably. Many of my friends have remonstrated against this course, but I know not under present circumstances how to avoid it. If I preach but twice a day, I cannot satisfy the white congregations without neglecting the colored people more than I feel myself at liberty to do. I have entirely dispensed with ordinary visiting, attending particularly to the sick, the poor, and such as require official duties. What will be the result of my coming to Baltimore I cannot tell, but my fervent prayer to the Father of mercies is that it may not be in vain.

O my dear Bishop, I fear the glory has in a considerable degree departed from us! Men's minds have been so much engaged in forming schemes of revolution, that the weightier matters have been too much neglected. In many instances plans have been made by our ministers for a future livelihood, which have necessarily embraced studies foreign from the work of the Christian ministry. These studies have, in a greater or less degree, abated that holy and fervent zeal, without which, it is to be feared, our preaching will be as "sounding brass or a tinkling cymbal."

May the Lord revive us by the abundant outpouring of his Holy Spirit!

Yours most sincerely, JOSHUA SOULE.

SECESSION OF THE BETHELITES, OR AFRICAN METHODIST EPISCOPAL CHURCH.

THE following letter, although a long one, is interesting, and replete in some parts with historic interest. It shows how the dissatisfaction which had for some time existed between the colored people in the North and the white preachers finally culminated in the secession of the former from the Methodist Episcopal Church, and is of special interest to Southern Methodists at this time, when we, under very different circumstances, and in a very different manner from the case here referred to, are about to organize a separate colored Church. Whether the colored people in the South possess sufficient organizing and administrative ability to found and perpetuate a proper system of Church-government, including doctrines and discipline, without the coöperation of the white race, and to prevent subdivisions and disaffections among themselves, is a problem which, in the judgment of many, remains to be solved. But the Methodist Episcopal Church, South, has undertaken the task, and every friend to humanity must desire it may prove successful. Confidence in the ultimate success of this attempt will be greatly strengthened, if, in forming themselves into a separate organization, they shall be so impressed with a conviction of their need of advice and assistance as to induce them to continue so to seek the patronage and counsels of their white friends as to avail themselves of the aid they might thus find. In the meantime, education and the proper exercise of their rights as freedmen will gradually prepare them to take upon themselves full authority, and manage their affairs at their discretion. It is the decided opinion of the author, that their unity, safety, and prosperity would be greatly promoted by a temporary continuance of the supervision of their white friends; and so believing, and feeling a deep interest in their welfare, he can but look forward with high concern to their initial proceedings.

Dear Bishop: — The continual pressure of business since my return from the Conference at Troy, connected with my feeble state of health, has prevented my writing till now. I have much to say to you, but scarcely know where to begin. You were informed of the course pursued by the Philadelphia Conference in reference to a Memorial of the Africans in New York, Philadelphia, and other places, praying for the *patronage* of the Methodist Episcopal Church. These Africans had broken off from the Church, and formed themselves into an *independent body*, under a *distinct* and *different title*, having, at the same time, adopted and published a form of ecclesiastical government, in which they secure to themselves, independently of the General Conference and the Bishops of the Methodist Episcopal Church, the exclusive right to all *legislative* and *executive* power. But notwithstanding this *extraordinary position* of the colored people, the Philadelphia Conference passed sundry resolutions recommending it to the Bishops to recognize their Conference (about to be held in the city of New York) by presiding officially either in person or by proxy, and to ordain such as might be chosen by them to the office of deacon or elder. I confess I was not a little surprised when I read the communication containing the resolutions of the Philadelphia Conference, but that surprise was increased when I understood from unquestionable authority that Bishop George had called the Africans in this city together, and read to them the resolutions of the Philadelphia Conference, and at the same time encouraged them to expect patronage till this was done, *before* the sitting of the New York Conference; although a provision in the communication from the Philadelphia Conference had made the concurrence of the New York Conference necessary in order to carry the resolutions into effect. When the Memorial was presented to the New York Conference, it was committed, and in a report which was accepted by the Conference, it was conceded that the African Conference could not be constitutionally organized by any number of Annual Conferences; and although provision is made in special cases for the organization of a Conference in the interval of the General Conference, it was believed that the Africans could not be embraced in that provision. It was therefore thought to be inexpedient for one of our Bishops to preside in the Conference, or to ordain any deacon or elder elected by them. At the same time it was resolved that if the African brethren would agree to be subject in common with the white members to the order and discipline of the Methodist Episcopal Church, in such case, under the present existing circumstances, it would be advisable for such preachers of color as were regularly constituted, to be appointed to take charge of them until the next General Conference.

When the course of the New York Conference was communicated to them, their disappointment was very great, and they expressed much surprise that the Bishop and Philadelphia Conference should not know what was constitutional, and that they should recommend to them a course which could not be covered by the proper authority of the government. Under these considerations, they passed a resolution to abide by the instruction of the Philadelphia Conference. I verily believe they would unanimously have given up their discipline and returned to their former standing, had it not been for the resolutions of the Philadelphia Conference. They appear to tremble at every step they take, and fear lest they should pursue some course which would place them in such a situation as to forfeit the patronage of the white societies.

Our Conference, all things considered, was much more favorable than I had feared. The Doctor's* character passed without any arrest or unfriendly remarks, and although they considered him in common with other claimants, and made their appropriations accordingly, yet the Doctor received $50 from the moneys appropriated to missionary purposes, with which, however small it was, he appeared to be satisfied and pleased. Immediately after our return from Conference, I communicated to him your instructions relative to the $50 loaned him last year. He seemed to be almost overcome with a sense of gratitude and obligation. He requested and obtained a supernumerary relation.

With respect to Mr. Stillwell and his party, I think they have seen already the zenith of their prosperity and glory in this city; and if no unforeseen occurrence proves auxiliary to their success, I apprehend they will appear to great disadvantage before the close of the year. All my movements toward them tend to this—*Let them alone.* If they are left to navigate their own ship, steer by their own compass, and determine their latitude by their own quadrant, I have no doubt of the issue. The case of poor Crawford

---

*Dr. Phœbus.

was so far admitted to a rehearing at the Conference as to have a Committee appointed to hear and examine any evidence which might have transpired subsequent to the trial at the previous Conference: the evidence was heard, reported to the Conference, and all the documents read. The opinion of the Conference was in agreement with the report of the Committee, that the evidence furnished did not go in anywise to exonerate the accused. As the admittance of this case before the Conference may be considered as an extraordinary circumstance, I think it proper that you should understand the ground on which I favored such a course. I considered that Crawford had it in his power to involve us in very serious difficulties, if such a hearing of his evidence was denied. Crawford was able to prove, by the most unquestionable testimony, that the President of the Conference where his trial was had, subsequently to that trial, said, *that all the evidence on the trial was "ex parte" evidence; that it was a premature trial, and a hurried case.* I had heard the President make these remarks, and I knew that Crawford designed to make all the use of them that he could in case the Conference should refuse to hear him. It is easily perceived that it would be highly improper to introduce these considerations before the Conference. I therefore, in the first instance, stated them to the Bishop, in the most open and simple manner, with a view of the advantages which might be taken, and the uses which might be made of such observations from him. The Bishop felt the force of the remarks. Desiring to be out of sight as much as possible, and still to prevent mischief and reproach, I gave my view of the subject to two or three whom I knew to be the decided friends of the Bishop, and whose simple word without argument would probably decide the case, and thus it was.

Having, as far as my feeble state of health and the unceasing pressure of business would admit, taken into consideration the subject of your letter relative to a course with the Suspended Resolutions of the General Conference, I am inclined to favor your view of the subject. Bringing the subject before the Conferences in the way you proposed, will necessarily develop the principle involved in the controversy, and bring it before the *whole body* of the ministry for investigation. This, I think, is a desirable object, for as yet the merits of the question have been but very partially understood; and the more I become acquainted with the views of the preachers in this part of the work, the more fully am I persuaded that the change contemplated by the resolutions will not be as popular as many of its friends suppose. Indeed, it appears to me that I perceive an inclination on the part of some of its most decided advocates to let it fall asleep. This, however, has only determined my mind more fully as to the fitness of the course you propose to take. I find Bishop George very considerably alarmed (and I do not regret it) in his apprehensions of what may be the result. He has spoken and written to those who have appeared the most zealous supporters of the change, and the burden seems to be entreaty not to pursue measures which may terminate in the separation of the body. I conversed with the Bishop at the last Baltimore Conference, plainly, but respectfully. I assured him that whatever his views of the subject might be, it was not to be supposed that men who had *sentimentally* embraced our system of things, and who had *conscientiously* and *sincerely* supported that system for many years, would tamely give it up; and that it was not very grateful to the feelings of such men to have their opinions and their arguments treated with perfect indifference and contempt, yea, merely puffed at.

In bringing the subject before the Annual Conferences,

the real sentiments of those who have supported the resolution will probably be developed, and we shall more fully understand each other. As far as the Conferences act upon it in reference to the constitution, their *acts* will be an acknowledgment of the authority and obligation of the constitution, and will, so far, put that question to rest, both with the preachers and people.

This is a very desirable object; for while doubts exist with respect to the constitution itself, (I mean relative to its *validity*,) all must be in an unsettled state.

If the course should result in an acknowledgment of the unconstitutionality of the resolutions on the part of the Annual Conferences, two important objects will be accomplished: first, the validity of the constitution will be established; and secondly, a barrier will be raised against future encroachments on the Episcopal prerogatives, and consequently a point will be fixed where the minds of our preachers and people may rest in confidence and quietude. Nothing is more painful than uncertainty and doubt with reference to subjects of the deepest interest to us. I therefore conceive it to be of the utmost importance that we determine our landmarks, and that they never be removed, except under the existence of extraordinary and imperious circumstances.

Should a gracious Providence preserve you to visit the Conferences again, my ardent desire is that you may see a more happy state of things.

I was authorized by a late meeting of the Board of Managers of the Missionary Society to report to the Bishops that there was $3,000 in the treasury, for which they were at liberty to draw on the Treasurer. One hundred dollars has been since paid to the order of Bishop George, leaving the sum of $2,900 subject at present to Episcopal orders.

In consequence of my feeble state of health through the last winter, I was unable to be out evenings, and consequently could not attend the sales of books. I spoke to Brother Hyer concerning the apples for your friends in the Mississippi, and he and others assured me that it would be extremely dificult, not to say impossible, to get them to the persons in a sound state; and even if it could be done, the expense would be very considerable, so that it was thought very improper to attempt to forward them. I have therefore laid out no money for you. I received $20 as your dividend from the New York Conference, which I here inclose. I also inclose $100 from the Book Concern, awarded by the Committee for your extra expense. The Committee would be very glad to receive any information from you relative to your situation, and I think there is a disposition to meet the case of your affliction.

The documents on Indian affairs were committed, and after a very elaborate investigation, the Committee reported in favor of presenting a Memorial to the Congress, in conformity to the form of a petition which you forwarded. A draft of the Memorial was drawn up and laid before the Conference, but as the session was far advanced before this business was reported, it was thought proper to refer the draft of the Memorial to a special committee, with discretionary powers to alter or amend, as may be thought proper. Each Presiding Elder is to be furnished with a copy for the purpose of obtaining subscribers. It is not, however, contemplated to take a promiscuous multitude of signatures, but rather a selection of names which may command respect. It is to be lamented that there is a policy in existence which, if successful, will defeat the object of missions among the Indians in a very great degree. The toleration of a common and indiscriminate trade among them will bind them to a savage life, corrupt their morals, and produce private and national quarrels. By these means, the measures adopted for their instruction and improvement will be frustrated, all attempts to introduce and establish the arts of civilization and the habits of social life will be in vain, the hopes of the missionary will be blasted, and his life jeopardized.

If our National Government will so far interfere as to prohibit this ruinous traffic, and extend protection to those who may be disposed to exert themselves to bring the Indians to be civil and religious beings, a field will be opened into which the Christian minister should rejoice to enter. To talk of missions abroad while so many wandering tribes of untaught men people the vast forests of our own continent, is nugatory. Vast multitudes of these savage beings are within the geographical limits of the United States, and are on terms of amity and friendship with the government; but still they are strangers to God—they are destitute of the Scriptures—they know not the joyful sound of the gospel—they sit in darkness and in the shadow of death—they worship they know not what.

Whenever I reflect on the situation of these original proprietors of American soil, I am surprised that they have been neglected so long. We are deeply in debt to them, and it is high time we were exerting ourselves to discharge the debt. May the great Head of the Church smile on our feeble efforts, and succeed the labor of our hands!

Yours most sincerely, JOSHUA SOULE.

New York, July 5, 1821.

Baltimore, September 29, 1823.

DEAR BISHOP:—The particular object of this letter is to communicate to you the afflictive dispensation of Providence with which we have been visited in the loss of our Presiding Elder. Brother Fechtig departed this life last

Thursday, at three o'clock in the evening, in Georgetown, D. C., thus leaving the District destitute of a proper officer in the administration. The Church must feel the loss. He is called away in the morning of life, of usefulness, and of promise. But the ways of God, though mysterious, are *wise* and *just.*

A number of the preachers on the District have been much afflicted with sickness. McCann, Hamilton, Hinkle, and Steir have all been confined with fever, and some of them hung in doubtful suspense between time and eternity, but as far as I know, are at present convalescent. It will, I think, be necessary for you to supply the vacancy occasioned by the death of Brother Fechtig. You are probably better acquainted with the situation of the District than I am, as it relates to men and things. I shall not even pretend to *nominate.* We have been mercifully preserved in the city from severe affliction among the preachers, although Brother Davis has been but feeble, and in consequence of the dangerous illness of his father and family, and other causes, he has been considerably absent from the station. Brother Kennerly is now in Virginia. You have probably heard of the death of our old friend Wilkins, and Father Hagerty. They have both fallen asleep in a good old age, ripened, it is believed, for the glorious harvest.

Brother Emory was in town yesterday, and intends removing his family here next week: his health is considerably improved, but his family are very much afflicted. Dr. Watters, President of the College on the Eastern Shore, has established a seminary in the city, and will remove here with his family in October.

We have just received letters from J. Summerfield. The British Conference had closed its session in much peace and harmony. A melancholy occurrence is related. A coach in which were seven preachers on their way to Conference was upset, two of the preachers were killed, and all but one much injured.

Richard Reese comes over to America in the spring, as the delegate of the British Conference, accompanied by a junior preacher.

Brother Summerfield's health is considerably improved, but it is doubtful if he returns to the United States before spring.

I perceive by the Minutes that the New York Conference has *three* missionaries, two of whom are on *Long Island.* It is frequently inquired, "How are these missionaries supported? out of the mission fund?" I cannot answer these questions; but if it is so that these Conference missionaries are to be supplied from the general Missionary Treasury, I think it requires no extraordinary foresight to perceive that the operations of the Society will be paralyzed, and its grand object ultimately defeated. It is not to be expected that the auxiliary societies will pour their treasures into the general fund, to be drawn out and appropriated to local and insulated missions. It looks like taking the bread of life from the destitute and thinly-scattered frontier settlements, and from the poor, untutored Indians. If we must have Conference missionaries in this way, would it not be more noble to have them in those Conferences where there is an immense colored population, and to make the special object of their mission the instruction and salvation of these poor, uncultivated creatures?

I greatly desire to hear from you, and to know of your health.

Yours with much affection and esteem, J. SOULE.

LETTER FROM DR. SAMUEL BAKER TO BISHOP McKENDREE.

The following letter is characteristic of its author. It is full of domestic tenderness and of Christian sympathy. The writer can attest from experience as to these traits in his character; for after his long and wearisome tour with Bishop McKendree to the General Conference in Baltimore in 1824, he reached the city in poor health, and received the kindest medical attention from him; and again in 1832, he enjoyed the hospitalities of his refined and pious family. We long since heard regretfully he had passed away, leaving the memory of his professional talents, and his virtues as a Christian, a rich legacy to the surviving members of his family.

Dr. Baker loved and revered Bishop McKendree, and the Bishop held him as a physician and Christian in the highest estimation. They both loved Mr. Summerfield with a tender and strong affection; and the respect and love of such men are worth much. But doubtless they have long since met again; and the intercourse of such spirits in the realms of purity and peace, must constitute no inconsiderable source of enjoyment in that blissful world. How sublime is the Christian's hope!

Baltimore, Sept. 24, 1825.

My Dear Friend:—I avail myself of the good offices of our mutual friend, Bishop Soule, to inform you that through the gracious dealings of a kind Providence we are still preserved, and our health is rather improved. Mrs. Baker has been traveling to the North this season, and has received much benefit. Mrs. Dickins is still able to move about, although she is feeble, and is much harassed with her cough. Miss Eloise and our children are as well as usual.

Since you left this, we have met with a severe loss in the death of our dear Summerfield; but he is gone from a state of suffering to one of rejoicing! His memory is precious in our little circle. He was dear as a brother; and when we revert to his deportment as a Christian, his character as a minister of the gospel, and the suavity which marked his intercourse with the world, we may truly say that it was a privilege, rarely experienced, to enjoy such society. His like I ne'er expect to see again. His sun rose beautifully, shone brilliantly, is now beneath the horizon, but will be seen again with a glory far transcending the utmost conception of our imaginations!

Bishop Soule will be able to communicate good tidings in relation to the state of our people Heaven has visited us graciously. Many have been seriously impressed; a goodly number have been converted; and professors of religion seem to be contending for the higher degrees of faith. O that we might be "clothed with humility!" *This, this* is the saving virtue!

We should be much pleased to have your society. If infirmities should press upon you, while a kind Providence places it in our power, we shall be happy in offering you a resting-place, and no exertion shall be wanting to render your situation agreeable

If your time is not entirely occupied with your more important concerns, we should be pleased to hear from you.

All the family desire to be kindly remembered to you.

Yours affectionately, SAMUEL BAKER.

P. S. We have lately heard of the death of Mr. Summerfield's father. S. B.

LETTER FROM WM. McMAHON TO BISHOP McKENDREE.

THE REV. WILLIAM McMAHON, the writer of the following letter, was a native of Virginia, born in Dumfries, 1785, or 1786; admitted on trial in the Western Conference in 1812 — the same time at which Francis Landrum, Jonathan Stamper, Robert W. Finley, Thomas D. Porter, George Ekin, and John McMahon, his brother, were admitted—and traveled Silver Creek Circuit, under James Ward as Presiding Elder—having traveled Marietta Circuit the previous year, under the employment of the Presiding Elder. In 1813, he was under John Sale, Presiding Elder, upon Hinkstone Circuit. In 1814, he was ordained a Deacon, and appointed to Lexington, Kentucky, and, at the request of Bishop McKendree, traveled with him for some time. In 1815, he was on Shelby Circuit; in 1816, on Fleming Circuit, with Samuel Parker as his Presiding Elder. In 1817, he was appointed to the Nashville Circuit, where he married Mrs. Perkins: in the fall, they visited her father, the Hon. Seth Lewis, of Louisiana, traveling in company with Bishop McKendree; he returned in 1818, and was appointed to Fountain Head, with Wm. Stribling. He was Presiding Elder of Nashville District in 1819. His history since that time is too well known to require detail. As Presiding Elder, Superintendent of Indian Missions among the Creek and Cherokee Indians, and Agent for La Grange College, he labored with great industry and success. As a preacher, he has had few equals. He has borne the burden and heat of the day most heroically, and, amidst great privations and sufferings, has persevered to extreme old age, and yet lingers among us, respected for his integrity, talents, and usefulness. Few men have passed through so many trials and sufferings, or more deserved the respect and sympathies of the Church.

At the time of the writing of this letter, he had the oversight of the Indian Missions in the Tennessee Conference; and, finding that no appropriation had been made to pay for an interpreter, and knowing that without one the missionaries appointed to travel through the Indian Nation could accomplish but little good, he earnestly solicits advice and aid from Bishop McKendree for this purpose. Surely the good old Bishop was the soul and center of our missionary work.

Dear Bishop:—Shortly after I left you, I commenced a conversation with Brother Sullivan, on the most effectual method of serving the Cherokee Indians, and of subserving the design of the mission in that Nation during the present year, which led us to notice an obstacle to our usefulness which I presume had escaped your attention while we were together, which is this: our greatest wish and work in reference to the Cherokees is and will be, to preach the gospel among them as effectually and extensively as possible; but this cannot be done to purpose without an interpreter, and much depends upon the character of the man who may be thus chosen as the medium of delivering the word of life to the Indians. They must have confidence in him, or he can do no good. A man who is suitable and proper for this important business cannot be procured unless we can give him some compensation for his services, nor could we, indeed, reasonably request it of him, and especially when he knows that all the missionaries designated for this great work are allowed an equivalent for their services. This, I think, would be hurtful to the interests of the cause in the Nation. Now, sir, if you can authorize me to employ a man whom we shall approve for this work, I will use my best exertions, and, as early as possible, try to secure John Brown, if he has not yet left the Nation for the Arkansas, which I fear is the case—if he has not, I am sure I can get him, and of all others he is the man for this work. He is a good man, but, like most other good men, he is poor, and could not, perhaps, enter into our employment for a less sum than we give the others; nor would it, in my judgment, be advisable for us to make any distinction in this way between ourselves and the Indians. But I hope, sir, you will not misunderstand me. I do not wish to dictate to you: I only desire to apprise you of the serious difficulty which lies in the way of preaching the gospel to these people, beyond the neighborhood of the schools. If you find yourself authorized to cover the additional expenses of an interpreter, and think proper for me to engage one, please to write immediately, by mail, directing to Huntsville. If you do not incline to take up the subject officially, please to advise me as a friend what I had better do; for I do assure you that, situated as I am, I know not what to do in this case. Of one thing, however,

I am very certain—*i. e.*, itinerant preaching in the Nation will be a fruitless attempt, without some one to go with the preacher and interpret for him; and it will not do to trust to chance.

There is one more item which I will take the liberty to mention. Would it be proper for me, should I find, in the course of the year, that one of the missionaries is likely to do harm, and that the Indians have lost confidence in him, to remove him, and send some other preacher in his place, as I would change preachers on my District? I should like to have your advice on this subject, as I have some fears that this course may become necessary—I hope it will not; but should it be the case, I should be placed in a very painful situation, if I were compelled to witness an evil which might do much injury, and have no power to remedy it.

I hope you are well and happy. May the God whom you serve, and whose you are, go with you till you lay down your life and labors together, and find your reward in heaven! Yours very respectfully,

WM. McMAHON.

Pilgrim's Rest, near Huntsville, December, 1824.

LETTERS FROM REV. DR. CAPERS TO BISHOP McKENDREE.

CHEROKEE INDIAN MISSION.

AT the South Carolina Conference, held in Columbia, Jan. 11, 1821, Dr. Capers was appointed "missionary in South Carolina Conference and to the Indians."

Having entered in good faith upon this new and difficult work, he found many discouragements in organizing the mission. He had to erect houses, raise money, plan the work, and select the missionaries. It was a new thing—no such mission having been as yet fully carried into effect among us in the South. It was a step in the right direction, but a step in advance of the spirit of the time. Our Missionary Society had been but recently organized. No missionaries had been appointed to labor for the Indian tribes. The traveling preachers did not generally receive the small salaries allowed them in the Discipline; and if our people half starved their preachers at home, how much more likely were they to decline to give to the Indians! The missionary spirit was asleep in the majority of our members. Dr. Capers was an admirable selection as an agent to travel through the State and get funds to begin the enterprise; he was well known, gifted, popular, and active. He was adapted to arouse the torpid, and to give respectability and impetus to the cause. But being the first enterprise of the kind in the Church, and having had but little practical acquaintance with temporal affairs when he began to project plans for building houses and for agricultural operations to meet the expectations of the Indians and contributors, he soon found he had a very difficult task. Funds came in slowly in despite of his sermons and lectures. He was afraid to begin to build, lest he might not be able to finish according to his plans. Suitable men were wanting to take charge and teach. The friends of the cause were expecting great results from small means; and the Indians, always distrustful of the promises of white men, were likely to become impatient and still more suspicious. At the date of this letter, nothing had been done, except the collection of a trifling sum of money, while a feeling of desponding anxiety was beginning to come over the minds of the Indians and their friends, and an indefinite foreboding of future troubles to be encountered in the unknown path before them, made the good old Bishop who had projected the mission, and his gifted and pure-minded agent, a little restless and apprehensive. Hence letter after letter was dispatched to the Bishop. His judgment and energy were relied on, and before the end came, both were taxed to their utmost. The reader is aware that two missions were at last established—one of them was abandoned after several years of comparatively unsuccessful effort—the other, and principal one, lived on struggling with difficulties until the emigration of the tribe to the far West, and doubtless accomplished much good for the poor natives of the forest. But the results did not equal the efforts or hopes of the workmen.

It has taken a long time to impress our people with the fact that, to establish a first-class college upon a permanent basis, a foreign or an Indian mission, for extensive usefulness, is no light work, but requires much money and suitable men. These, with prudence, economy, and perseverance, may do a great work; but failing in any of these elements, the effort will be abortive, and the result disastrous.

Savannah, March 8, 1821.

Reverend and Dear Father:—Your favor of the 5th instant came duly to hand. I see a good reason why the Bishop should be cautious of an indiscreet haste in the establishment of missions among the Indians; and that although *a mission of the simplest form* might not cost more than the Conference Missionary may collect, (not to speak of other modes of obtaining moneys,) yet such an establishment as would embrace "agricultural arts" in the very outset, and which would have to employ mechanics, agriculturists, school-masters, and preachers, each separated to his appropriate department, would require more to support it than we can obtain by any means.

In what I suggested in my letter to yourself and Bishop George, nothing was contemplated beyond the simplest form of a mission, in which *the missionary* should himself be *preacher, teacher, and whatever else he can be,* only performing that under such regulations as may be given for the government of the mission. There should be two or more missionaries at each station, mutual in their labors, and distinguished from each other only as the preacher in charge from his junior colleagues. Such a mission, I presume, we can now support.

If Brother Hill might not answer for the charge of a mission, could he not for a *junior* missionary? Pardon me that I name him to you again: you name no *other* person.

Am I only to go among the Indians to inquire whether they will receive missionaries? This is known already. Am I to make engagements with them, to be fulfilled at some distant time to come? They are impatient of delay; and when that time shall have arrived, they will tell us, "Others have been more prompt, and are preferred." Besides, what warrant have I that my engagements will, *at any future time*, be fulfilled? It would seem from the objection now made against our acting, that a mission, *in no form of a mission*, ought to be entered upon until we are able to support the *most costly mission*—perhaps we should wait until we can give to a mission ten thousand dollars per annum. If so, farewell to our missions for ever!

But, my dear father, suppose we act with the means we have? If we cannot make a splendid establishment, in which the arts of civilized life shall all be embraced, and every thing be done that can better the *temporal* as well as the *spiritual* condition of the Indians, suppose we do what we are able? Let us preach to them, and teach their children to read the Bible and to pray. Let us teach twenty, if we cannot teach a hundred, children. If we do our *best*, God will help us to do still *better*.

I am glad to say that, from some conversations with Col. Richard A. Blount and Colonel Law, I am induced to hope we may, if we will, introduce the gospel among the

Creeks. Although their Council did, not long since, decline to receive missionaries, and the sense of the whole tribe may not now be accordant with our object, yet I understand that many of them wish for schools; and that among them the Indian General, McIntosh, has very decidedly declared for schools. Shall I visit them? Shall I improve any advantages that may be given me to institute a mission among them? How shall I do it? You will readily perceive that even in the simplest form of a mission, much preparation must precede it. Land must be opened, houses built, provisions procured, etc. Now, if Brother Hersey may hold our moneys and oversee the execution of the work among the Choctaws, who shall do it with the Creeks, or the Chickasaws, or the Cherokees? I can choose a spot for the mission, can say how much ground should be opened, and what houses built, in a given time, what provisions ought to be procured, etc., and can limit the amount to be expended in each of these particulars, and can, at the expiration of the time, see that all shall have been done and settled for; but in the interim, I must be differently occupied, and at a distance from the scene of operations. Now, if you would direct me to some person who might act in this behalf—remain on the spot and oversee the work preparatory to a mission—all might be easy; and without this, I cannot see that my visiting the Indians will be any better than a waste of time. The person thus employed would be in a situation favorable to improvement in many things that are of importance to a missionary, and, although upon the institution of the mission, he should be but the junior missionary, still he has gained an advantage that shall be secured to the mission. I repeat it, I would act with caution—I would not expend the amount of my collections—but I would do something, even although I might not be able to do every thing.

I notice with much feeling, reverend and dear father, what you say of your health. I would not burden you, but yet I was made a missionary by you; and when you did so, you gave me to understand that you would expect me to do the work of a missionary. If your health is not *worse* than it was, I must look to *you.* I have no hope that I will be able to do the work of a *missionary* unless you are able to do that of a *Bishop.* I have had a letter from Bishop George. I say again, I must look up to you. In the address of my letter I acted from courtesy—I now write to *you alone.*

I have traveled more than twelve hundred miles, collected one thousand dollars, and preached forty-eight sermons. You directed me, and I have pledged myself to the people. The moneys collected from them, for the exclusive purpose of Indian Missions, can be applied to no other use. As a candid man, I must see to it that the Indians have the benefit of the charities intended for them, however worthy *another object* may be. Am I to collect moneys that may never be appropriated at all, or appropriated to an object not contemplated by the people? Rather than this, I would myself go and carry the bounty of the people to the Indians in Ohio, or even in Canada. In this I seek no honor, no distinction—I only mean to be honest to you, to the Conference, to the people, to the Indians, and to God. I mean not to make myself any thing. I would not, knowingly, interfere with the work of the Bishops, even if I could. I will not act without your order; but pray order me, and let not the expectation of the many who contribute to this good work (and who, from the best feelings, will be anxious to know what disposition shall have been made of their bounty) be disappointed.

Your dutiful and most affectionate son in the gospel,

W. Capers.

DR. CAPERS IN TROUBLE.

Savannah, April 19, 1821.

Reverend and Dear Sir:—I have now gone over all that part of the Conference which lies south of a line drawn from Beaufort, by Black Swamp, Waynesboro, Louisville, Saundersville, to Scott's Ferry, on the Oconee. I am now about to remove my family into Sumter District, South Carolina. The extreme depression of the price of cotton, and consequent embarrassments of both town and country people, operate against the collections. The whole amount collected up to this date is $1,278.87½.

. . . .

My last to you (at Baltimore) was written under an impression that my letter to the Bishops (at Raleigh) had not given satisfaction, and that all it proposed relative to the engagements that might be entered into for the institution of a mission or missions among the Indians, was objected to; and this, lest we should overdo our means, or act incautiously in some of our engagements.

With regard to the means necessary for the support of a mission, I have given freely my views in my last. To me it would appear that a proper caution would respect the extent of any establishment that might be undertaken, no less than the undertaking one at all.

It was certainly a great misfortune to me (and I fear to the cause) that I entered upon this work without knowing what might be expected of me. I everywhere told the people that as soon as I could obtain means to make a beginning, I would visit the Indians, and that the amount of my collections would determine the extent of our establishment among them. I was even so sanguine as to say I expected to go out in April—immediately upon having gone over that section of my work, which I have now accomplished—

and I hoped that my having gone and undertaken among the Indians, would much increase my collections afterward. At present, I owe it to charity if I am not regarded more ready to promise than to perform. I would go, if it were only to save my credit; but could this justify the loss of two or three months from the collections? Surely if I go, it should be to accomplish something more than barely the seeing and conversing with the Indians, and something better than the postponement for a year of the work I might engage to do. But how can I ever visit them to purpose, unless there be some one to remain on the spot, and carry into effect our stipulations? Not indeed to open a school *immediately*, but first to have the house built, and the grounds cleared, when the school shall be established. This must require time, as well as the personal, constant oversight of some proper person. If there be an objection to my acting in the *pro tem.* employment of such person—as proposed in my letter to the Bishops—I can only say that the necessity of the case appeared to me to require it; but I regarded it as admissible only in an extreme case, and with the approbation of the Bishops; and even then, not to be extended to the traveling preachers. The Bishops alone can obviate the necessity for such a procedure. Will they do it? I named Brother Hill; he was objected to; but who may be employed rather than he? I can prefer no one—indeed, I know no one; and the Bishops neither appoint nor direct to one. In the meantime, my instructions are given me for the present year.

I have done what I could to meet the duties assigned me, and in this I have pledged myself to the people. They expect not merely that I will go the Indians, but that I will "use all proper means to facilitate the establishment of a mission or missions among them." After having obtained their money, how shall I tell the people that the work is postponed until after the next Conference? Had I not better go myself and remain among the Indians, if it were only to hide my mortification? Or in what would the cause be benefited were I to go, unable to do any thing; and upon my return, report long rides and talks held to no purpose?

My instructions directed me, I pledged myself to the people, and have I shrunk from so sacred an obligation? So it may seem perhaps—it *must* seem so, but I am not conscious that it is so; and I may add, I never could have consented to be placed in such a point of light.

I have received a communication from the Secretary of War, and a letter from Mr. McKinney. The former consists of two printed circulars, stating the conditions and extent of the Government's equal patronage and aid. The letter of Mr. McKinney would be a valuable introduction to the Indians or others. I doubt we could not shortly derive aid from Government, even if we begin a mission. They look directly to the things that are temporal.

With the sincerest and most dutiful regards, your son in the gospel, W. CAPERS.

DR. CAPERS RELIEVED.

Columbia, S. C,, July 2, 1821.

REVEREND AND DEAR BROTHER:—Your kind and encouraging letter of May 16 reached my brother's just after I had left there upon an excursion to Georgetown and Charleston. Upon my return, (quite lately,) I had the great pleasure to receive it, and a communication from Col. McKinney, and two letters of introduction from the Secretary of War—one to the Agent for the Creek Nation, and the other to Agents and Superintendents of Indian affairs.

I cannot tell you how exquisitely I felt upon reading your letter. I could have thanked you a thousand times for the tenderness with which you regard me, and consider those letters of March and April—which I had feared might betray too much my disappointment, and were written, perhaps, too strongly. But how shall I thank you for having appointed a Missionary Committee, and for instructing me to choose a man or two and dispose of them among the Indians? This was to define the words of my original instructions (*"to use all proper means"*) in the very fullest, best sense I could have desired. The money first, and then the men. And surely, for a mission, and *"to facilitate the establishment"* of one, both are *"proper means,"* and both should be used—but only at the instance of a Bishop.

At the date of my last letter, I had gone over that part of my work which lay conveniently to Savannah, and was about to leave that place, with my family, for Sumter District. My son's illness detained us a week, and then we were much delayed upon the road by rain and high waters. Over one creek I swam in my carriage, while my family and baggage were carried upon men's shoulders, on logs sunk a foot under water. At others, I was obliged to drive over floating, loose bridges, or lay bridges that were broken up, or have the carriage pulled by hands where the horses could not go with it, and these plunged through separately, or even to use a canoe, where we should have had a dry causeway. We were ten days upon the road, and at last arrived safely, and all well. We now had excessive rains for several weeks; and, as I greatly desired to take my daughter Anna to her grandmother, I waited ten days more, in hope of weather that might allow of my doing so. At last, and not before I had become very weary of my confinement, I set out, without her, for Georgetown and Charleston. By these delays my collections were interrupted from the 20th of April to as late a period in May.

Since that time, my collections have amounted to about $950, making the whole amount $2,200—a sum less than I had hoped to obtain, but not very inconsiderable, when the exceeding scarcity of money and the general embarrassments of the people are taken into account—besides, that I *dun* no man. I always remember that I may not obtain one dollar *to-day* in such a way as might hinder two dollars *to-morrow*. I must get money for the mission from men who are to be made the *friends* of the mission. To make friends, is the best way to get money.

After I had relinquished my purpose of visiting the Indians in the spring, I only stated to the congregations that the Bishops had advised me to employ a longer time within the limits of the Conference, that I might be fully prepared before I should introduce a mission among the Indians, and that probably I would not visit them before autumn. In Charleston, the advice of the brethren, Myers and W. M. Kennedy, approved this arrangement; and they recommended that if no explicit direction should be had from you in the meantime, I should in the fall of the year act upon the plan I had before proposed, and which you have now approved—construing your letter rather into an advisory caution than a refusal of what I had asked.

Perhaps I cannot now do better than to visit the Creeks some time late in August or early in September. If they treat with me, I may immediately return, and make arrangements for a mission among them, and, locating a missionary there, proceed to the Choctaws; or, if the Creeks *refuse* to receive us, I will go on to the Choctaws.

I cannot say that it is as easy a matter as I expected, to find persons willing to serve the Indians, and capable. Brother Christian G. Hill stands very decidedly preferable to any whom, as yet, I may have found; and, as for some time past nothing has been said to him on the subject—

thinking that either the preacher whom Bishop George so highly approved, or some other person or persons, would be directed into the work—this may be the principal cause of delay in future.

I have not had any communication from Bishop George since that which I mentioned to you. I do not know what preacher he preferred, nor even to what tribe the Indian he met with belongs.

With the most respectful and affectionate regard, your son in the gospel, WM. CAPERS.

LETTER FROM COLONEL McKINNEY TO DR. CAPERS.

The letter from Colonel McKinney, to which Dr. Capers refers with so much satisfaction in his last letter, is given below, and justifies some notice.

Mr. Monroe, in entering upon his second presidential term, in March, 1821, retained Mr. John C. Calhoun as Secretary of War, and Col. Thomas L. McKinney was placed in charge of the "Indian Trade Office" by Mr. Calhoun. It was fortunate for Bishop McKendree's plan of attempting to Christianize the Indian tribes, that at this juncture these gentlemen occupied positions in the civil government so closely connected with his benevolent purposes. We have already seen how promptly and efficiently Mr. Calhoun had interposed in behalf of missionary operations among the Indians, and we perceive now how faithfully his subordinate officer carried out the views of the President and his Secretary of War. Indeed, this letter not only evinces the fidelity of the office-holder, but the sympathies of a noble Christian heart toward the unfortunate Indians. We have understood the writer was a Christian, and the letter justifies the report. Has the day passed, never to return, when the high offices of our great country shall be held and administered, not for private and personal benefit, but for the public weal?

Mr. McKinney was intimately acquainted with Bishop McKendree, and entertained for him the greatest respect. Was it not fortunate for the Church, and especially for the cause of missions, that one held deservedly in such estimation for wisdom, energy, and purity of character, was the recognized leader of the cause of missions?

Rev. William Capers:

DEAR SIR:—I have received your letter of the 24th ultimo, containing an extract from Bishop McKendree's instructions to you, directing you to "travel extensively within the limits of South Carolina Conference, in order to do the work of a missionary; to make collections for missionary purposes, and especially for the support of such establishments among the Indians as may be formed under the superintendence of the Methodist Conference; to visit the Indians (Cherokees in particular) in order to ascertain the most eligible situation for a mission, or missions, among them; to facilitate by all proper means the establishment of such mission, or missions."

Such an undertaking cannot be otherwise than gratifying to every man who has thought upon the condition of our Indians, and the obligations which bind us to improve it. To see it countenanced by the Reverend Bishop, whose liberal and Christian virtues I so highly appreciate, and who has not given his sanction to the measures in which you are about to engage without the deepest and most thorough investigation of the subject, augurs favorably for the result of the undertaking. I proffer you my most earnest wishes for your success. I doubt not the entire practicability of a thorough change in the aboriginal character by the agency of missions. Facts are now common, going to demonstrate their readiness to exchange their habits; but especially to the rising generation does this matter belong. And who would not contribute a mite toward that happy change which embraces in the limits of a single generation a new race of men—a change from savagism to civilization, from paganism to Christianity? Who would not contribute a mite toward renewing the face of the desert, and introducing in the place of barbarism and deeds of blood the anthems of praise, kindness, and social and Christian blessings? This is the work which missionaries go to accomplish. The way is open. The Indians, feeling their necessity, are calling for help, and their arms are in many places wide open to receive the benevolent agencies which are going in from so many points for their relief.

Among the Cherokees a most valuable establishment is up and in operation. It is called Eliot, and is in charge of the Corresponding Secretary of the American Board of Commissioners for Foreign Missions, the Rev. Dr. S. Worcester. Its immediate and personal head is the Rev. Cyrus Kingsbury, a man peculiarly well fitted for the charge. In going amongst the Cherokees, it would be advisable to harmonize with the previous existing establishments, for many reasons: first, the work is the same; second, the parties to be benefited are the same; third, the motives of those who enter upon it are the same; and fourth, the Indians, respecting and even loving the Eliot establishment, would be more likely to recognize you as a laborer, having the good-will of their Elliott friends.

I do not mean that you do more than cultivate a good understanding with Mr. Kingsbury. Tell him from me, I know and approve of your mission, and believe it is in harmony with his own benevolent plans. Tell him, for my sake and the Indians, to take you by the hand as a brother. There is room enough for us all. All you will have to regard will be harmony in your operations; and surely there is no necessity for discord. I know you would be the last to promote any thing but peace and good-will.

If there is any thing in which you think I can be useful to you, pray command me. I may not live to hear that the face of the desert is changed, but like Abraham, I see the day, and rejoice in it.

Very respectfully and truly yours,

THO. L. MCKINNEY.

Indian Trade Office, Georgetown, Feb. 8, 1821.

LETTER FROM DR. JOHN EMORY TO BISHOP McKENDREE.

HIS REPLY TO BISHOP WHITE.

In its early days Methodism, both in England and America, was destined to struggle against opposition from every quarter. Although her Articles of Faith were but a concise, clear, and honest epitome of the teachings of the Bible, as were also her Rules and general Church-polity, yet Calvinists of every hue and order attacked her doctrines with a unanimity and fierceness which threatened her ruin. Fortunately, Mr. Wesley's life was long spared, and his pen most effectually defended the truth. God also raised up Mr. Fletcher, of Madeley, who, although a St. John in love and purity, had yet such logical acumen of mind, such loyalty to truth, and such classic beauty of style, that he wielded against the errors of his opponents an Ithuriel's spear, from which they shrank back discomfited. In the United States the contest was prolonged, but fierce attacks gradually became less frequent and less violent, until discretion has taught our doctrinal opposers to exercise more prudence.

In preparing the Sunday Service for the Methodist Episcopal Church in America, Mr. Wesley abridged the Liturgy and Thirty-nine Articles of the Church of England, to which, with the Homilies, he was accustomed to refer in defense of his views on doctrinal and experimental religion, as in harmony with the word of God. And yet, as in England so here, those who claim to be *par excellence* Episcopalians have not ceased to attack us upon the subject of the work of the Spirit. In 1817, the first Bishop of the Protestant Episcopal Church in this country published a sermon, or essay, upon "the assurance of the pardon of sin by the direct witness of the Holy Spirit," in which he held up our views as erroneous, and as peculiar to our Church. Dr. Emory became our champion, and defended our cause most triumphantly. This letter alludes to this controversy, as well as to his reply to another attack, from a different quarter. It is cause for gratitude to God, that whenever we have needed a champion, Heaven has furnished the right man at the right time.

The reference to "transfers," in this letter, relates, we suppose, to those who had become disaffected in the city and applied for letters transferring their membership, but really were thus withdrawing from the Church.

Philadelphia, August 21, 1817.

Reverend and Dear Sir:—I have not yet visited Maryland, and consequently have not had an interview with Dr. Jennings. I received a letter from him some time since, inviting me to see him in Baltimore, which I purpose to do soon—most probably next week, on my way to the Eastern Shore by that route.

I have finished my piece in answer to the Address of "the Charitable Society" of Connecticut, and have it ready for publication, should it be deemed proper by Dr. Jennings and those friends to whose impartial judgment it may be thought best to submit it. It has been considerably enlarged, and I have availed myself of some valuable extracts from Mr. Wesley and Dr. Rush—particularly the latter, who is fully in our favor on education in general, and especially that of the ministry; and being a disinterested character of such eminence, his authority is the more important.

I have been lately engaged in answering a piece on another subject of great moment to us and to the world. It was written by Bishop White, of this city, who signs himself "W. W.," and is in opposition to the assurance of the pardon of sin by the direct witness of the Spirit. He undertakes particularly to expose the Methodists for inconsistency on the subject, as he reproaches them (glorious reproach!) with being the principal and almost the only advocates of the doctrine. Although a Bishop of the Protestant Episcopal Church, he has committed some egregious blunders, and the goodness of my cause has enabled me, I trust, satisfactorily to refute him, and to vindicate the Methodists, and particularly Mr. Wesley, from his unjust charges and reflections. My answer contains fifty-two pages of letter-paper, in the sheet, not very closely written.

As we have no committee of Conference to authorize publications by preachers, it seems hard either to be lashed by our opponents without defense—having tied our own hands—or defend ourselves and the Church, and be lashed by the Conference for violation of rule. What is to be done in such a case?

Our editors have sent us a prospectus of a Magazine, They propose to commence the publication of it in January next. Were they ready to publish now, I would send them immediately the answer to "W. W."—especially as his piece appeared in a New York Register. But I think it ought to be published sooner. It might be *reprinted* in the Magazine, if approved of.

On Monday last, I received a letter of the 9th instant from Bishop George—then at Claremont, New Hampshire. He gives a very favorable account of revivals of religion in Canada, and the Northern department generally—says that he had seen the *instructions* of the British missionaries, and thinks the Conference in England entirely clear, and only needing correct information of the proceedings of their missionaries—so contrary to their instructions—which he proposes to give them by letter. He expects to be in New York on the 5th of October, and requested me to inform him of the tenor of your letter to England, which I shall do as well as I can recollect.

We are here in peace. I have given but four transfers since Brother J. R. went away, and one only of them was applied for *professedly* on the ground of his going away. A friend of his, who saw him at a camp-meeting in Delaware, informed me that he believed J. R. would have no objections to being stationed *at St. George's* next year, and thought it not very improbable, *if you should not be here.* Some think, if he can get an opportunity, he will join the Protestant Episcopal Church—and this he has intimated himself.

Should we have a publication soon, on either of the above subjects, in pamphlet form, a few copies may reach you by mail.

Requesting your prayers, with an affectionate remembrance of Bishop Roberts, as ever, yours, J. EMORY.

LETTER FROM DR. NATHAN BANGS TO BISHOP McKENDREE.

DR. BANGS has a national reputation as the earliest historian of the Methodist Episcopal Church, and the defender of her doctrines and polity. It is unnecessary to sketch his life. That he was "faithful in all his house," sincere, magnanimous, and a most devoted servant of God and his Church, none will question: even those who differed with him in Church-polity never doubted his purity of motive. He would have scorned to gain his ends by guile; and he extorted from his ingenuous opponents their respect and esteem. He was a voluminous writer and a great worker, having filled many responsible positions honorably to himself and usefully to the cause of Methodism. Honor to the noble and true man who devoted a long and useful life to the glory of God and the good of the Church! And honor to his equally pure and magnanimous brother, the Rev. Heman Bangs, who I believe still lives to bless the Church and adorn the ministry by his beautiful example of gentleness and love! Would to God the Church, North and South, were full of such men!

At the time this letter was written, Dr. Bangs was stationed in the city of New York, his helpers being Eben Smith, J. Robertson, Jas. M. Smith, and Peter P. Sandford; and this was his report of the condition of his charge, made, according to the custom of that time, to the Bishop.

New York, July 4, 1810.

DEAR SIR:—Through the mercy of God, I am now in a tolerable state of bodily health, though I have been recently afflicted, as have most of the stationed preachers in this place.

I have been here about four weeks, and we have had the happiness to see the Redeemer's cause advancing. Several have been converted, and the people of God appear in general persevering after holiness; but I also find some disagreeable business to attend to, in consequence of the backsliding of some. There has been a great ingathering in this place for a few years past, and I am apprehensive that there are some bad ones to be cast away. I find, however, that much caution is necessary, lest in plucking up the tares we pull up the wheat also. These things, with many others that might be mentioned, make my situation extremely delicate; but, blessed be God, that we (the preachers) are all of one heart and of one mind in the work, so far!

There has been much bustle and noise in the city to-day, but many of our people assembled at the hours of eleven o'clock in the morning and three in the evening for prayer, instead of mingling with the giddy throng to sport and laugh. I blame myself more than any of the rest for being in any measure attracted by the show.

I hope God is blessing you with an increase of health and vigor of mind. I doubt not but you enjoy the solace of a good conscience, though, perhaps, groaning under the burden of the charge which unavoidably devolves upon you. May God give you every needful aid to enable you to go forward in the glorious work in which you are engaged!

As to myself, I think I feel as much engaged as ever I did in the work of God, though I feel that I am an unprofitable servant, and often have to lament my littleness of faith and love; but God bears with my weakness and helps my infirmities, so that I am still enabled to say, God is mine, and I am his.

Please to give my love to Bishop Asbury.

I am yours, with love and esteem, N. BANGS.

SACRAMENTAL SERMON IN NASHVILLE, BY BISHOP McKENDREE.

THE WESTERN METHODIST (edited by Lewis Garrett and John N. Maffitt) for December 13, 1833, contains an editorial notice of the Bishop, prefixed to the discourse reported as preached by him, before the administration of the Lord's-supper, December 1, 1833, as follows:

The first Sabbath in December, although a damp and cloudy day, was signalized by circumstances of high interest to the Methodist Society in Nashville. On entering the splendid church, the first object to arrest the attention was the array of sacramental emblems in the altar, leading the mind back to scenes mournfully dear to every Christian heart. Above, in the pulpit, the form of the venerable Senior Bishop of the American Methodist Communion, McKendree, was seen in strong relief before the lofty curtains that fell between the desk and the recess. His countenance was pale, but serene; his locks were somewhat thinned by age, yet Time has but sparingly poured his silver over them; his dark, penetrating eyes have not been blanched by the frost of years; and his figure is still erect, and almost as unbending as a youth of twenty.

The recollections associated with the form of one who has been in the ministry half the lifetime of Methodism in the world, and who has devotedly filled the office of a bishop since the year 1808, were refreshing to the heart of every Methodist. Bishop McKendree will be seventy-seven years of age, if his life shall be spared to the 6th day of next July. Even under this weight of years, and having passed through hardships, in the early periods of his ministry, of which the velvet-cheeked clergy of the present generation can have no conception, still the Rev. Bishop sustains an easy, graceful carriage, and that dignity of manners so congenial to Virginia, the State of his nativity and education. One cannot see him and hear his voice in public without thinking of Patrick Henry, Thomas Jefferson, John Marshall, and a long list of illustrious names that have immortalized the "Old Dominion."

Bishop McKendree retains the acute and distinguishing faculties of his logical mind in full and unimpaired perfection. His memory may have failed in a degree, in regard to local and uninteresting things; yet in morals, in ethics—even in impassioned eloquence, and a lively perception of the sublime and beautiful—his intellectual faculties are in the green of their youth.

It can truly be said of the venerable Bishop, as Webster said to La Fayette, "Thrice fortunate man!" He remembers the time when the sainted Asbury announced in an emphatic voice, "The increase of members in the Methodist Church in America is this year *thirteen thousand:*" he has lived to the time when the journals of Methodism announce an annual increase of *seventy-one thousand.* The dangers of the howling wilderness are overpassed, and the Church has emerged from its shadows, and his eyes for half a century have been upon her paths, and his feet have been with her pioneers. The last days of such a man become inestimably precious. They are like the mystic leaves of the Roman sibyl—they increase in value as their number is diminished.

The following sermon was preached by the Bishop in a clear and distinct voice, accompanied by a weight of manner and character which cannot appear in print. The sketch which we give embraces the sentiments, and to a good extent the expressions, which were delivered on the occasion, although the hearers of the discourse may remember some beautiful touches that they may not find in it as we have printed it.

After the delivery of the sermon, the Rev. Bishop consecrated the elements of the Lord's-supper, and, assisted by the Rev. Presiding Elder of the Cumberland District, A. L. P. Green, and the Rev. F. E. Pitts, of the Nashville Station, administered the ordinance, first to the ministry and then to the membership. Four times the spacious altar was encircled by kneeling communicants, who

"Ate the white memorial bread,
And drank the sacramental cup."

The following is the Bishop's sermon:

"For the Jews require a sign, and the Greeks seek after wisdom; but we preach Christ crucified, unto the Jews a stumbling-block, and unto the Greeks foolishness; but unto them which are called, both Jews and Greeks, Christ the power of God, and the wisdom of God." 1 Cor. i. 22–24.

The text manifestly exhibits a diversity of sentiment, but from the beginning it was not so. When Jehovah informed Adam that the seed of the woman should bruise the serpent's head, all his posterity were then in his loins, and equally interested in the blessings contained in the promise. But that promise referred to the mediatorial government of Christ, and comprehended the salvation of the human family by virtue of the divine atonement. Therefore, all the sons of Adam were included in the provision made for fallen man.

From Adam to Abraham more light was given by the spirit of prophecy, and the design of the promise was better understood; but the promise on which the gracious plan of redemption rested remained the same, and the evidence for its support, though much enlarged, remained the same also. The contemplated blessings were equally accessible to all, and all had an equal claim to them. Hitherto there was no distinction, no preference of one above another, except what proceeds from faith and obedience on one hand, and unbelief and transgression on the other. But as men multiplied, sin abounded, and the world ripened for destruction. At length Infinite Wisdom selected Abraham and his posterity from the rest of mankind, and entered into covenant with them. According to this covenant, Jehovah graciously pledged himself to superintend the affairs of Abraham and his seed, to direct their course, to protect them against adverse power, and to supply their temporal and spiritual wants, on condition that they and their succeeding generations should faithfully obey him as their rightful sovereign, and walk before him in a perfect way.

By this means, Infinite Wisdom preserved the knowledge and worship of the true God in Abraham's family, which was eventually lost among the rest of men — ultimately to usher the true Messiah into the world, surrounded with such incontestable evidence as bids defiance to opposition and criticism.

But this covenant was with Abraham and his seed, to the exclusion of the rest of Adam's race—yes, and the rest of Abraham's father's children. But this exclusion does not affect the blessings contained in the promise made to Adam: these they continue to enjoy, as they did, in common with Abraham, prior to the covenant.

It only restricted the privileges peculiarly set forth in the covenant to the contracting parties, who in the first instance were Abraham and his seed. But the door was open to the Gentiles. It only remained for the Gentiles to believe and obey God as Abraham did prior to the establishment of the covenant, and submit to its conditions, in order to be adopted into Abraham's family, and enjoy all the blessings of his natural and spiritual children. But this dispensation of grace was not understood according to the design of its divine author. Nor did the parties treat each other with due respect. Hence the difference.

The Jews highly esteemed their distinguishing privileges. They considered themselves the children of God, the elect of God, the well-beloved and highly favored of the Lord, to the exclusion of all others; and as they rose in their own estimation, they depreciated the rest of men: they were esteemed as rejected reprobates and hated of God, until there was no dealing between the Jews and the Samaritans—yea, it was considered unlawful for a Jew to go into the house of one of another nation. And so fearful were they of being misled, that when the prophets—even Christ himself—taught different from their notions or traditions, they demanded a sign or signs—miracles—to prove their mission to be of God.

They expected the promised Messiah to come in pomp and great glory, to exercise regal authority, and reïnstate them in the power, authority, and honors they enjoyed under King David. But his appearance and conduct were entirely different. They demanded the signs of such a Messiah as they expected, and were disappointed; and therefore they rejected and crucified him.

In opposition to the Jews, the Greeks gloried in wisdom. The wisdom so highly prized by them, was the result of philosophic research. They possessed every advantage that human nature could have, independently of a divine revelation, and they had cultivated their minds to the utmost, and still remained ignorant of the true God; for the world by wisdom—philosophy—cannot find out God. The Greeks could not, consistently with their philosophy, believe that proclaiming supreme happiness through a man that was crucified in Judea as a malefactor, could ever comport with reason and common sense. They therefore rejected the plan of salvation as proposed in the gospel: by them it was esteemed foolishness.

In this state of things St. Paul appeared, and shone as a star of the first magnitude. Regardless of the conflicting views of the Jews and the Greeks, he said, "I am not ashamed of the gospel of Christ; for it is the power of God unto salvation to every one that believeth; to the Jew first, and also to the Greek." And therefore he constantly preached Christ crucified, as the only way to obtain pardon and peace, and get to heaven.

He affirmed that all had sinned—contracted guilt—and were left without ability to return to God, and extricate themselves from the painful effects of a guilty conscience. For this important purpose, by virtue of Christ crucified, fallen man is transferred from the Adamic law, which neither admitted pardon nor supplied ability, to the government of Christ, where all necessary blessings are supplied. Here pardon is granted to penitent sinners. Here grace is offered to repent, to believe, and moral ability given to obey the Redeemer's laws, and be happy in time and in eternity.

He proves that by sin man had lost the knowledge of the true God, and missed the way of happiness; that though by wisdom, or philosophy, he might become extensively acquainted with the things of this world, yet by wisdom the men of this world could not find out God, nor the way to enjoy him here or hereafter. To supply this deficiency, he preached Christ crucified, as the Creator of all things, who inhabits eternity, and graciously condescends to reveal himself to man so far as is necessary for his present and eternal happiness, and to point out the way to obtain and enjoy those blessings.

St. Paul shows that fallen man is not only guilty and ignorant, but that he is utterly unable to protect himself and manage his own affairs. But this deficiency is supplied by the crucified Redeemer, who graciously undertakes the management of our affairs, and as a King is amply provided with wisdom to direct all our affairs, power to protect in all cases, and funds to supply all our wants.

St. Paul constantly affirmed that the gospel, through Christ crucified, was the power of God to the salvation of the souls of both Jews and Greeks. His preaching was not in the wisdom of men, but in simplicity and power. Such was the energy that attended his eloquence, that he astonished and confounded the wise men on Mars' Hill, (Acts xvii. 22–34,) and, though a prisoner in chains, made his judge tremble on his seat. (Acts xxiv. 25; xxvi. 28.) He almost persuaded Agrippa to be a Christian, and through his instrumentality the gospel of the cross of Christ found its way into Cesar's household, his court, his army, and through the provinces of Rome; and, blessed be God! the work is still progressing, and will continue to progress, while the doctrines of the cross are preached in their primitive spirit and power.

Christ and his apostles did not apply the commands of God so as for one to supersede or lessen the influence of another; they were all enforced by the same authority. "Six days shalt thou labor and do all thy work; but the seventh day is the Sabbath of the Lord thy God: in it thou shalt not do any work," were enjoined by the same authority; therefore St. Paul said, "He that will not work shall not eat"—shall not live on the funds collected for the poor. Nor were those funds appropriated to tempt talented men with large salaries to lecture on any one grace, and collect moneys for particular purposes. But the preachers were equally enjoined, in the discharge of their ministerial duties, to exhort all Christians, by giving diligence, "to add to their faith virtue, knowledge, *temperance*, patience, godliness, brotherly kindness, charity," assuring them, "if these things be in you and abound," that they should be neither barren nor unfruitful in the knowledge of our Lord Jesus Christ.

We have attempted to give a specimen of the apostle's method of preaching Christ crucified, which, to the called—the genuine Christian, whether Jew or Greek—was found to be the power of God and the wisdom of God. By believing the gospel, they experienced pardon and the regenerating grace of God—were delivered from the guilt of past sins, and from the practice and love of sin. They were filled with joy and peace, and enabled to pass unhurt through the difficulties over which the Jews stumbled and fell—to suffer all things, and to go on their way rejoicing.

By viewing the system which the Greeks thought to be foolishness, in the light of revelation, it far surpassed the reach of human sagacity. That system was not a subject of rational investigation, but of pure revelation, in which the wisdom of God is astonishingly displayed in forming a plan by which fallen man may be saved, and God remain just when he justifies the ungodly. In Abraham and his posterity the knowledge of the true God and his worship was preserved, which was lost eventually among the rest of mankind; and a way was prepared for the introduction of the true Messiah, surrounded with such incontestable evidence as bids defiance to opposition and criticism. Having experienced the power and efficacy of the gospel, it only remains for him to continue steadfast in the faith—uniformly to obey the commands, and diligently seek and exercise the graces—to abide under the protection of the Almighty, and perfect holiness in the fear of God.

Therefore, let us examine ourselves; and if we have departed in any degree from the doctrine taught by the apostles, or from their zeal, spirit, and manner of enforcing them, or from genuine simplicity of manner or dress, let us return to the good old way with full purpose of heart, that the Lord may continue to bless and prosper us until the great work to which we are called is accomplished.

CHRISTMAS SERMON IN NASHVILLE, DEC. 25, 1833, BY BISHOP McKENDREE.

THE following discourse was delivered by Bishop McKendree in Nashville, Dec. 25, 1833. It was not so much a regular sermon as a Christmas talk of an aged preacher to his old friends and their children. He was near his end, and too feeble to bear the fatigue of much effort of body or mind. It is certainly not a fair specimen of the pulpit efforts of his palmy days, but was taken down by a hearer, and published in the Western Methodist. Who has not realized a sad disappointment in reading a discourse after having heard it from the lips of the speaker? How tame and commonplace it reads! We do not hear the accents of his mellifluous voice; we see not his graceful and impressive gestures; his eyes burning and bright with the inspiration of his theme; and his face expressing the thoughts of his mind and the emotions of his heart, are all wanting. The mysterious chord of sympathy, and the electric mental and emotional action and reaction which exist between the speaker and his audience, are absent. The contrast is often observed even under circumstances most favorable, insomuch that printed sermons are seldom read with much interest, but generally fall still-born from the press. Those only which develop great vital truths, and reveal the plan of salvation in clear, simple, and striking language, become permanently popular and useful among the masses.

We have to supplement the Bishop's Christmas effort with his venerable form, his lofty forehead—a few gray hairs resting upon it, the remainder falling back, and scarcely concealing the surface of his head—his wan and intellectual face, varying in expression with every new thought and feeling—now calm and quiet like a lake without wind or wave, then as if gently moved by a passing zephyr—anon thrown into a thousand ripples, reflecting the gleams of mental joy, and presently aroused to its highest efforts by sublime conceptions, which stir his soul to its inmost depths.

His text was a fit theme for the man and the occasion. The veteran of near fifty years' devotion to the task of developing the story of the cross, now, at the close of his life and labors, comes to join the wise men of the East and the simple shepherds of the vale, to behold and worship the wonderful Babe of Bethlehem, and unite with the angelic host in adoration and praise; and while in imagination we listen to the soft and silvery accents which proclaim, "Glory to God in the highest, and on earth peace, good-will toward men!" forgetting time and space, we seem to hear the heavenly choir, in the refrain of a human voice, responding in the celestial anthem.

It was an occasion of great interest to his audience. It occurred in a large and elegant church recently dedicated and bearing his name, and was addressed to a multitude whose parents and grandparents he had long known and served, and whose children now heard him as expecting to hear and see him no more.

"And there were in the same country shepherds abiding in the field, keeping watch over their flock by night. And lo, the angel of the Lord came upon them, and the glory of the Lord shone round about them; and they were sore afraid. And the angel said unto them, Fear not; for behold, I bring you good tidings of great joy, which shall be to all people. For unto you is born this day, in the city of David, a Saviour, which is Christ the Lord. And this shall be a sign unto you: Ye shall find the babe wrapped in swaddling clothes, lying in a manger. And suddenly there was with the angel a multitude of the heavenly host praising God, and saying, Glory to God in the highest, and on earth peace, good-will toward men." Luke ii. 8-14.

In this communication we have the most sublime, important, and interesting information ever made to fallen man. As it has respect to the perfections of God and heavenly things, it is sublime. And as it implies terms of peace, reconciliation with rebellious subjects, it is therefore of the utmost importance; and seeing that it embraces every individual of every nation, it is, of all subjects, the most interesting.

But men have no senses by which they can obtain correct ideas of God and heavenly things; nor can the human mind obtain ideas of any objects of which it is perfectly ignorant; therefore this is not a subject of rational investigation, but of pure revelation; and we may confidently rely on such information as the Lord may please to give—for our faith, instruction, and comfort. Evidence in support of the communication will appear by the persons through whom it is made, and the manner of instructing them. When a messenger is sent by any nation to transact business with another, he is supposed to possess natural and acquired abilities for the business assigned him. But among men, there were none found qualified for this business; therefore one was chosen from heaven to divulge the mysterious subject which prophets could not understand.

Therefore a messenger was sent from heaven to announce the birth of the Saviour. When this all-important fact was established among men, they were competent witnesses of that which they had seen, and heard, and felt. The angel had to address some of the lower order of men, yet he made his appearance in the glory and power of his heavenly character. To the poor shepherds this was a terrific appearance, and they were sore afraid. By this means the mind was sufficiently aroused to attend to their visitor; but the excitement was too great for them to attend deliberately to what they were to hear; therefore the angel said unto them, "Fear not, for behold I bring you good tidings of great joy, which shall be to all people." Evil is the object of fear; good tidings imply a desirable object. Thus the angel prepared the shepherds to receive his message, and then said: "For unto you is born this day, in the city of David, a Saviour, which is Christ the Lord. And this shall be a sign unto you: Ye shall find the babe wrapped in swaddling clothes, lying in a manger. And suddenly there was with the angel a multitude of the heavenly host praising God, and saying, Glory to God in the highest, and on earth peace, good-will toward men." As soon as the angel had delivered his message, a multitude of the heavenly host added their testimony to that of the angelic messenger, by giving glory to God in the highest for his wisdom and goodness in saving fallen man, and added their acknowledgments to the praises of the Redeemer for what God had done for them.

Truth never shuns, but frequently invites, investigation. The shepherds being instructed, hastened to Bethlehem for the purpose of examining into this matter. After they did so, and found the statements to be in perfect accordance with facts in every particular, they therefore, without delay, proclaimed the advent of the promised Messiah to the deeply-interested sons of fallen Adam. And the testimony of the shepherds is added to that of the heavenly host to support our faith and establish this glorious truth.

When atonement was made for sin, and the Saviour had entered fully into the government of his purchased possession, he chose twelve men as heralds to proclaim his reign, and publish the laws by which his subjects were to be governed. These, as well as the shepherds, were selected from among the common laboring class of men; they were fishermen by occupation, but by a miraculous supply of the spirit of wisdom, they were raised to the office of apostles, the most dignified station that man ever filled. By them the doctrines of truth were published and confirmed by the power of God working miracles through their instrumentality, confirming thereby their statements.

In selecting the unlearned from among shepherds and fishermen to fill high and responsible stations, the wisdom of God is manifested, and faith in the system of the Christian religion greatly increased. Had the learned, the rich, and powerful of the earth been chosen, the people would have gone after them, and religion would have rested on the wisdom of man (as it does in many cases) instead of the power of God, and there would have been some shade of plausibility to the charge of its being priestcraft. But this treasure was put into earthen vessels—illiterate men—

the case is therefore different; and to be followers of such men as God had chosen—men who direct us to look to and trust for salvation in a man who was crucified as a malefactor—was deemed unreasonable, unpopular, and disgraceful; and seeing that it exposed them to suffering and death, therefore there was nothing to influence men under such circumstances to become followers of such teachers but a clear conviction that they were taught of and supported by the Almighty God.

Had the glad tidings been restricted to the shepherds, it would have been a matter of great joy to them; but as the sensibility of a grateful heart is abundantly enlarged by a supply which he may enjoy in common with his needy fellow-creatures, so when all people—every individual of every nation—were included, the grateful heart must overflow with unutterable joy.

The subject-matter of the glad tidings of great joy is declared in these words—a Saviour which is Christ the Lord —Christ the anointed—the Lord—the Jehovah of the Jews. But our attention is more particularly directed to the Saviour. We have already seen that the advent of our Saviour was good tidings of great joy to all people. Then all people were interested in the Saviour, otherwise it would not be glad tidings to all; but this all-important truth does not depend on inferential reasonings—it is sufficiently supported by direct testimony. We are told in the Scripture that "God so loved the world that he gave his only begotten Son, that whosoever believeth in him should not perish, but have everlasting life. For God sent not his Son into the world to condem the world, but that the world through him might be saved." (John iii. 16, 17.) St. John says: "He is the propitiation for our sins, and not for ours only, but also for the sins of the whole world." (1 John ii. 2.) "And thou shalt call his name Jesus, for he shall save his people from their sins." (Matt. i. 21.) Again: "We trust in the living God, who is the Saviour of all men, especially of them that believe." (1 Tim. iv. 10.)

From these incontestable authorities it appears that all the sons of Adam are individually interested in and benefited by the divine atonement for sins: that Jesus is the Saviour of all, and that he wills the present and eternal happiness of all, we cannot doubt; but that man is an accountable agent—may accept or reject the gracious terms of peace and salvation—is equally true. Faith working by love is the condition on which God bestows the saving graces of the Holy Spirit; but sinful man is so taken up with the things of this world, that his eternal interest is put off for a more convenient season.

In this state of things St. Paul says: "We trust in the living God, who is the Saviour of all men, especially of them that believe." The apostle divides the human family into two classes—believers and unbelievers. Jesus is the Saviour of all men. He has sufficient means, and is willing to save all from their sins, and make them happy; but as the latter are accountable agents, he only saves as far as they will permit. Hear the language of Christ to an afflicted woman: "But Jesus turned him about, and when he saw her, he said, Daughter, be of good comfort; thy faith hath made thee whole." (Matt. ix. 22.) Again says Christ: "If ye abide in me, and my words abide in you, ye shall ask what ye will, and it shall be done unto you." (John xv. 7.) And again: "Ye will not come unto me that ye might have life;" and yet he is their Saviour. In the first instance, fallen man was rescued from the penalty of the law and restored to a state of accountability for voluntary actions, and grace is afforded to repent and turn to God; and frequent remonstrances of the Holy Spirit are given to correct and urge fallen man to his duty. In the second place, sinners are saved by Jesus Christ from the punishment due to their daily transgressions of the law of God. They are warned of their danger; they are graciously restrained by the Holy Ghost from committing sins, into which they would otherwise plunge; they are exhorted to put away the evil of their doings, and embrace the proffered terms of pardon and reconciliation; they are assured that, on condition of faith, Jesus is not only ready and willing to forgive what is past, but to save them from the nature and consequences of sin. But they reject proffered mercy, and by voluntarily persisting in their rebellions against God their Saviour, they compel him either to abdicate his kingdom or enforce his laws—the latter follows of necessity; therefore their ruin is altogether of themselves, contrary to the design of the gospel and the will of their rightful Lord and Saviour; for he does not save men *in* their sins, but *from* their sins. Therefore none are saved but those who forsake their sins and believe in him. He that cometh to God must believe that he is, and that he is a rewarder of them that diligently seek him. This is the state of sincere seekers of religion. The Lord acknowledges such as disciples, saves them from the practice of sin, and enables them to apprehend the design of the gospel, and ardently desire to know Christ as their Saviour. This desire moves men to seek the knowledge of Christ in the use of the means; they are conscious of their unhappy situation, and are making feeble efforts to come to the Lord, weary and heavy laden, hoping for and looking to Christ for the much-needed and graciously-promised blessing; their prayer is heard, their sins are pardoned, and by the operations of the Holy Ghost the soul is regenerated and born again. The Spirit not only performs the work, but gives the subject knowledge of what is done, and the knowledge of sins forgiven, frees the conscience of what is past, and fixes it as a sentinel to examine and decide on the propriety or impropriety of what we think of doing.

By these means we are guarded from doing wrong, and excited to do that which is right; but conscience acts in conformity with the judgment; therefore, in order to preserve a proper conscience, the judgment must be correctly informed; then in communicating and receiving instruction, great attention should be paid to the revealed will of God. Conformably to the designs of the gospel, Jesus graciously saves the penitent sinner from the practice of sin; but the believer—the regenerate soul—is saved not only from the practice, but also from the guilt and love of sin, In the language of St. Paul, "He is a new creature: old things are passed away; behold, all things are become new." (2 Cor. v. 17.) His spiritual senses are waked up; he now views things in the light of revelation. Sin and folly, which he formerly loved, now are objects of aversion and hateful unto him. But his aversion to God and revelation is now changed into love and admiration. Though regenerated and born again, he is not free from the remains of the carnal mind, for when he is tempted by the world, the lusts of the flesh, or the pride of life, he perceives something within which would join with the temptation and involve him in sin; but that indwelling grace by which he perceives the snare, prompts him to resist the temptation, and pray for deliverance; and he is thereby preserved from contracting guilt, and overcomes the temptation; but he is left to mourn on account of the remaining propensity to evil and sin.

"'T is worse than death my God to love,
And not my God alone."

He rejoices in the victory obtained over the temptation, but the apprehension of falling some day or other, as by the hand of Saul, causes much solicitude. He feels temptation to sin, and finds there is something within which would unite with the temptation; hence he concludes that this something within, which would unite with the temptation, is of itself sinful. To such, the doctrine of perfect love which casteth out all fear, is of the deepest interest. He therefore makes known all his wants — this in particular—unto Jesus, and prays in faith for deliverance from this troublesome inmate. He now perceives the difference between the passions and the quality of the passions. The passions of the soul remain unchanged in their nature, but the superadded propensities to sin are destroyed, and the passions are inflamed with love to God, who hath done so great things for him; and now being made free from sin, in a sense far exceeding his former experience, he has his fruit unto holiness in a more refined and extended degree than before. As the soul, when converted and born again, undergoes no change in its physical nature, but in its dispositions relative to sin or holiness, the passions, when purified by the power of grace, undergo no change as passions of the soul—as such, they are the gift of God, and are given for wise purposes; but the passions are cleansed from sinful propensities, and prepared to enjoy God more perfectly.

For this purpose St. Paul says: "Warning every man, and teaching every man in all wisdom; that we may present every man perfect in Christ Jesus." (Col. i. 28.) And speaking of the Church, St. Paul says: "Christ gave himself for it, that he might sanctify and cleanse it with the washing of water by the word, that he might present it to himself a glorious Church, not having spot or wrinkle, or any such thing, but that it should be holy and without blemish." By setting the doctrine of sanctification too high or too low, its influence may be prevented. It is neither more nor less than perfect love—loving God with all the heart, and our neighbor as ourselves.

If an American eagle was tried by the French or Spanish standard, it would be found to be deficient; but when tried by the American standard, though it is not virgin gold, yet it is found to be perfect by the standard of American coin; so if Christian perfection is tried by the perfection of Deity or of angelic perfection, it must be found wanting; but when infinite wisdom examines fallen man by the gospel, he finds many perfect Christians. To such we would say, As ye have received Christ Jesus the Lord, so walk ye in him. By grace ye are saved through faith. This will apply to the sanctified as well as the justified; therefore, in order to obtain this blessing, the subject must believe the doctrine, honestly abstain from all appearance of evil, which is the condition upon which the blessing is bestowed, (1 Thess. v. 22, 23,) and humbly and confidently look to Jesus in the use of the means, until you obtain the desired blessing. *Faithful is he that calleth you, who also will do it.*

THE END.

www.ingramcontent.com/pod-product-compliance
Lightning Source LLC
LaVergne TN
LVHW020923110826
845150LV00004B/751

* 9 7 8 1 4 2 5 5 5 4 6 3 7 *